INDIA AND FRANCE IN A MULTIPOLAR WORLD

Centre d'Etudes et de Recherches Internationales: Founded in 1952, the CERI is France's foremost centre for research on the international political system. It has forty full-time fellows drawn from different disciplines, conducting research on comparative political analysis, international relations, regionalism, transnational flows, political sociology, political economy and on individual states.

[Centre d'Etudes et de Recherches Internationales, 56, rue Jacob, 75006 Paris, France - Tel.: (33) 1 58 71 70 00 - Fax: (33) 1 58 71 70 90 - Email: info@ceri-sciences-po.org - Website: http://www.ceri-sciencespo.com]

India International Centre: Inaugurated in 1962, the India International Centre was set up to provide a forum for the exchange of ideas. To meet this objective, the Centre arranges talks, discussions, seminars and conferences. It also organizes cultural presentations of the performing visual arts, screens films and holds expositions. The Centre maintains an excellent library and brings out a journal, the *Quarterly Journal*. It has a membership of over 4600 drawn from India and abroad.

[India International Centre, 40, Max Mueller Marg, New Delhi 110 003 - Tel.: (91 11) 461 94 31 - Fax: (91 11) 462 77 51 - Email: iic@delnet.ren.nic.in]

Centre de Sciences Humaines (Centre for Social Sciences and Humanities): Created in New Delhi in 1989, the CSH is part of a network of research centres of the French Ministry of Foreign Affairs. The Centre's research work is primarily oriented towards the study of issues concerning the contemporary dynamics of development in India and South Asia. The activities of the Centre are focused on four main themes, namely: Economic growth and sustainable development, International and regional relations, Institutional structures and political constructions of identity and Urban dynamics.

[Centre de Sciences Humaines, 2, Aurangzeb Road, New Delhi 110 011 - Tel.: (91 11) 301 62 59/301 41 73 - Fax: (91 11) 301 84 80 - Email: public@csh-delhi.com - Website: http://www.csh-delhi.com]

Centre d'Etudes et de Recherches Internationales
Centre de Sciences Humaines
India International Centre

India and France in a Multipolar World

Proceedings of a Seminar

16–17 February 2000

MANOHAR

CENTRE DE SCIENCES HUMAINES
2001

First published 2001

ISBN 81-7304-383-3

Published by

Ajay Kumar Jain for
Manohar Publishers & Distributors
4753/23 Ansari Road, Daryaganj
New Delhi 110 002

Typeset at

Digigrafics
D-69, Gulmohar Park
New Delhi 110 049

Printed at

Rajkamal Electric Press
B-35/9 G.T. Karnal Road Indl. Area
Delhi 110 033

Contents

MULTIPOLARITY AND INTERNATIONAL SECURITY

ECONOMIC MULTIPOLARITY AND GLOBALIZATION

CONCLUDING SESSION

Foreword

On the initiative of the Indo-French Forum, a seminar on 'India and France in a Multipolar World' was organized on 16-17 February 2000, by the Centre d'Etudes et de Recherches Internationales (CERI), Paris, the Centre de Sciences Humaines (CSH), New Delhi and the India International Centre, New Delhi, with the support of the Robert Schumann Foundation, Paris and the French and Indian Ministries of External Affairs.

Shri Ramakrishna Hegde, Co-Chairman of the Indo-French Forum, in his opening remarks, observed that the essence of multipolarity was sharing of power, responsibilities and opportunities by all, and not one single nation. Drawing attention to the influential role played in the past by the Non-Aligned Movement in preserving the autonomy of decision-making in a bipolar world, he stated that to ensure multipolarity, the need of the hour is to reform the UN system, with adequate representation of all regions of the world in the UNSC. To achieve multipolarity in economic terms, genuine multilateralism has to be ensured and, to prevent economic imperialism in the garb of free trade, it is essential to restructure the WTO's mandate.

In his inaugural address, Mr François-Poncet, Co-Chairman of the Indo-French Forum, emphasized the importance of a multipolar structure for a strong, peaceful and balanced international order. Referring to the near unanimous consensus in France in favour of a multipolar world, he stressed that Europe would be a strong pole in such a world and marked EMU and the emergence of a common foreign and defence identity as steps in this direction. Calling for the enlargement of the permanent membership of the UNSC with India and Japan as permanent members and the possible inclusion also of Brazil and Mexico, he suggested a close examination of the veto power in order to make UNSC an effective decision-making body.

Mr Jean-Marie Guehenno, Board Chairman, French National Defence College, analysed the conditions prerequisite for the functioning of a multipolar order. He averred on the need for some commonly agreed upon principles on the line of the preamble of the UN charter and that the principle of sovereignty has to be diluted on the lines of the European integration experiment. International institutions need to be strengthened and, to improve their perceived legitimacy, they must be restructured to reflect the interests of all and not just a few privileged nations.

American attitudes towards global multipolarity were outlined by Mr David P. Calleo, John Hopkins University, Washington, who said that these are influenced by three deeply-rooted traditions of American foreign policy: isolationism, global hegemony and realism (an attempt to find a balance between the former two). Isolationism has now evolved into unilateralism. In order to usher multipolarity within the Western world, an understanding is necessary for a collaborative structure between the US and western Europe.

The conditions for the creation and subsequent survival of a multipolar world were delineated by Dr Raja Ramanna, Member of Parliament and former Chairman Atomic Energy Commission of India. These included strengthening of the UN to provide security and the decision-making processes, combating terrorism and religious extremism, and limiting both conventional weapons and weapons of mass destruction.

Ms Thérèse Delpech, Research Associate at CERI, stressed the need for democracy in a multipolar world in order to ensure compliance with international law and pointed out that almost all of the hot spots in the world are results of confrontations between democratic and despotic regimes. She emphasized that India is a centre of stability in the region, a fact which was not adequately recognized by the US.

Dr Najma Heptulla, Deputy Chairperson, Rajya Sabha, advocated a strong parliamentarian dimension to state policies in the conduct of international affairs. She said that this was necessary as parliaments are the ultimate repositories of legitimacy and it is their responsibility to ultimately ratify international commitments and enact legislations in pursuance thereof.

Expounding the Chinese perspective on the nuclear security, Mr Lanxin Xiang, Professor, Graduate Institute of International Studies, Geneva, pointed towards the ambiguity of the Chinese reaction to the Indian nuclear tests. While underlining the enhanced importance of Sino-Pakistani relationship, he was of the view that the prospects of a Sino-Indian conflict on the border issue had subsided and the nuclearization of South Asia has made the idea of regional security arrangement more probable. It is also not likely to hinder economic development in the region. Thus, an alarmist view of the West about a nuclear conflagration in South Asia may not be well founded.

Air Commdr. Jasjit Singh, Director, Institute of Defence Studies and Analyses, analysed the emerging patterns of a new world order and dwelt upon the hypothesis of engagement of Russia, China and India as independent poles with the US-led alliance of EU and Japan in a conflicting or cooperative mode. Elaborating the norms for future UN interventions and principles of Cooperative Security, he stressed that UNGA endorsement should be mandatory for future military interventions.

Mr Zaki Laïdi, Special Advisor to the Commissioner for Trade in the European Commission for Trade, and Sh. Montek Singh Ahluwalia, Member, Planning Commission, focussed on globalization and its impact on an emergent multipolar world. In analysing the links between multipolarity and multilateralism, the question of linking trade with labour and environment standards was also commented upon. Mr Laïdi, while cautioning against disguising non-tariff barriers as labour/environment standards, favoured such linkages. Sh. Ahluwalia opposed them and, in this context, cited the failure of the Seattle talks.

Mr Peter Weilemann, Konrad Adenauer Foundation, Berlin, focussed on the new characteristics of globalization, its impact on traditional nation states and the inter-relationship it is likely to generate between the world of trade and international politics. Globalization is driven by the technological and information revolutions. It presents a threat to the territorial state as boundaries become increasingly meaningless. It has also led to the emergence of economic blocs, which are soon likely to acquire political roles as well. To ensure participation of all countries in this framework, a strong international financial structure is required, with institutions like the WTO playing a regulatory role.

The concluding session of the seminar was addressed by Mr Hubert Védrine, the French Foreign Minister, and Sh. Jaswant Singh, the External Affairs Minister of India. Mr Védrine observed, with satisfaction, the consolidation of Indo-French ties as the result of a number of high level bilateral visits, including the visit by President Chirac to India in 1998 and the projected visit of the President of India to France, in April 2000. While pointing to the all pervasive dominance of a single 'hyper-power' and the perils of the resultant unilateralism, he outlined the conditions for structuring a multipolar world. An important factor for the stability of such a structure would be a strong European pole with France as an influential power within. The poles that emerge must engage in cooperation and not confrontation. India, being the world's greatest democracy, must be fully involved into this restructuring process. Stressing upon the need for a restructured and reinvigorated UN, he was of the view that India has a rightful place in an expanded UNSC. Only a strong UN would be able to deal effectively with such emerging sovereignties as the mafia and organized crime networks. Though the values of democracy and respect for human rights are becoming universal, there is a need to reconcile the issues of state sovereignty *vis-à-vis* interventions to prevent gross human rights violations. Mr Védrine reiterated the French commitment to work for a stable, secure and truly multipolar world.

Sh. Jaswant Singh observed that multipolarity, perhaps, best reflects the diversity of human nature and values and polycentricism offers the best alternative for the world in flux, in the post-cold war environment. Only a collective security order, based not on hegemonic but legitimate power, can ensure peace. He warned that this security order will have to face new asymmetric threat perceptions, which would demand a coalition of interests. India and France, being inheritors of a rich civilizational past, were uniquely placed to ensure and facilitate the new multipolar framework. He proposed an Indo-France initiative to organize a global 'Congress of Cultures'.

The presentations and subsequent discussions in the seminar considered the related concepts of poles, multipolarity and unipolarity. There was significant unanimity that the end of the cold war and the bipolar world has been marked by a period of instability and transition and a multipolar world offers the best hope for stability and security. It was also generally agreed upon that rather than an inexorable clash of civilizations, growing cooperations would be the more predictable scenario in future international relations. There was convergence in the belief that a democratic order makes for a safer world, even though this perception was tinged with a recognition of the fact that what is desirable is not always achievable.

The relevance of the concept of sovereignty in a multipolar world was discussed at great length. There was limited convergence of views on the continuing importance of the nation state to organize political communities, to mediate between various interests groups and to manage the often conflicting demands between growth and equity.

There were detailed discussions on the role of the US at the apex of a unipolar structure and its far-ranging economic, military, technological powers and cultural influences. The participants tended to approach the issue of dealing with the American pre-eminence through dialogue and understanding and not in confrontationist terms.

The discussions at the seminar reflected a vagueness about the conceptual content and the institutional framework for a multipolar world. In this context, the construction of the European pole through the EMU, and the formulation of a common European defence identity, attracted close examination.

There was a near unanimity for recognizing the UN as the cardinal institution to ensure a cooperative security order. Reforms were advocated as essential in order to rejuvenate the UN. The UNSC expansion was considered imperative for better representation and democratization of the Council in order to truly represent the existing realities.

True multilateralism was advocated as the economic dimension of multipolarity. However, the Indian side expressed concern about the protectionist tendencies, garbed as social and environmental safeguards, and acting as barriers in heralding true multilateralism.

It was generally agreed upon that international terrorism, religious extremism, narcotic trade, etc., can be construed as 'poles' which, in turn, constitute a grave threat to the stability of a multipolar structure; the Indian side expressed more serious concern about such threats than the French side. On the nuclear issue, some difference of perception was apparent; the French side thought that international non-proliferation regimes in their present form were helpful in reducing the nuclear risk, and the Indian side pointed at their inadequacies and consequent non-acceptability.

The seminar was an attempt to secure a better understanding of the Indian and French perceptions of the concept of multipolarity. The differences in the views expressed helped to generate a better understanding of thc diverse approaches to the concept. At the end, there emerged a convergence of thought on some of the issues which marked the first step towards the meeting of minds on the issue.

This volume contains the papers presented and the discussions held at the seminar, as well as the addresses delivered by the French Minister of Foreign Affairs along with the Indian Minister of External Affairs. It is hoped that this publication shall provide a useful resource for readers interested in contributing to the establishment of a multipolar world order.

Director
India International Centre

N.N. VOHRA

Acknowledgements

This book contains the proceedings of a seminar entitled 'India and France in a Multipolar World', held in New Delhi on 16-17 February 2000. It was jointly organized by the Centre de Sciences Humaines, New Delhi, the Centre d'Etudes et de Recherches Internationales, Paris and the India International Centre, New Delhi.

The organizers would first like to thank the Robert Schumann Foundation as well as the French and Indian Ministries of External Affairs, whose support has enabled the seminar to take place. They are grateful to Mr Dileep Padgaonkar, a member of the Indo-French Forum and Executive Editor, *Times of India*, and Mr Michel Foucher, Technical Advisor to the French Foreign Minister and Director, Centre for Analysis & Forecasting, Paris, for agreeing to serve as the rapporteurs from the Indian and the French side, respectively. They would also like to express their gratitude to His Excellency Mr Claude Blanchemaison, Former Ambassador of France to India, for his constant support and encouragement.

Finally, a special word of thanks to all the participants, who, though they have not all been identified by name in the course of the discussions, contributed enormously to enriching the debates following each session of the seminar.

Contributors

MONTEK SINGH AHLUWALIA is Member of the Planning Commission. He has served with the World Bank and was Commerce Secretary and Finance Secretary, Government of India.

DAVID P. CALLEO is Professor of International Relations (Dean Acheson Chair) and Director of European Studies at John Hopkins University's Paul H. Nitze School of Advanced International Studies. He has taught at Brown, Yale and Columbia Universities, the University of Bonn and Munich, Institut d'Etudes Politiques in Paris and the Graduate Institute of International Studies in Geneva. He also served as a consultant for the US Under-Secretary of State for Political Affairs, Eugene Rostow.

THÉRÈSE DELPECH is Director of Prospective in the French Commission of Atomic Energy. She is also member of the Special Advisory Committee on Disarmament of the United Nations, member of the Scientific Board of the Monterey Institute (American Think Tank) and Associate Fellow at the Centre d'Etudes et de Recherches Internationales. She was previously Special Advisor for Political-Military Affairs in the French Prime Minister's Office (1995-7).

JEAN FRANÇOIS-PONCET: is currently Senator and Co-Chairman of the Indo-French Forum. Earlier he was State Secretary and General Secretary of the Republic Presidency before becoming Minister of Foreign Affairs (1978-81). He has also been a Professor at the Institut d'Etudes Politiques, Paris.

JEAN-MARIE GUEHENNO is currently Assistant UN Secretary General for Peace Keeping Operations. He is also member of the Advisory Committee of Disarmament of the United Nations and Chairman of the Board of the Institut des Hautes Etudes de Défense Nationale. He was previously Senior Audit Manager of the French 'Cour des Comptes', Ambassador, Permanent Representative of France to the West European Union (WU) and Director of the Policy Planning Division in the French Ministry of Foreign Affairs.

RAMAKRISHNA HEGDE is Co-Chairman of the Indo-French Forum and was Chief Minister of Karnataka, Deputy Chairman of the Planning Commission and Union Minister of Commerce.

NAJMA HEPTULLA is Deputy Chairperson of the Rajya Sabha. She has been a Rajya Sabha MP of the Congress party since 1980.

ZAKI LAÏDI is Special Advisor to the Commissioner for Trade in the European Commission and also a Research Fellow at the Centre d'Etudes et de Recherches Internationales (CERI). He is also Professor at the Institut d'Etudes Politiques in Paris. He was Visiting Professor at the European Centre of the John Hopkins University in Bologna.

RAJA RAMANNA (MP), Atomic Scientist, was Chairman Atomic Energy Commission, Secretary, Department of Atomic Energy and Minister of State for Defence.

Air Commodore JASJIT SINGH, AVSM, VrC, VM, IAF (retd.), former Director of Operations of the Indian Air Force, is currently Director of the Institute for Defence Studies and Analyses, New Delhi, since 1987. He is also Consultant to the Standing Committee of Defence of the Parliament and Member of the National Security Advisory Board. He was earlier a member of the International Commission for a new Asia.

PETER WEILEMANN is Deputy Director of Political Research and Head of the Division on International Politics and Economics at the Konrad Adenauer Foundation, Germany. He was previously an Assistant Professor at the Research Institute of Political Science and European Questions at the Universities of Cologne, Mainz, Hamburg, Georgetown, Washington, D.C.

LANXIN XIANG is Associate Professor at the Graduate Institute of International Studies, Geneva, where he teaches 'International Relations of the Far-East'.

Indian and French Approaches to Multipolarity

Introductory Speech

JEAN FRANÇOIS-PONCET

Mr Chairman

May I first thank you and the India International Centre of New Delhi for receiving us today. We are very grateful for this welcome as well as this unique opportunity to meet the most distinguished members of India's International Community.

I also want to thank the International Studies and Research Centre of Paris, the CERI, the Centre de Sciences Humaines, New Delhi and the Robert Schumann Foundation for the intellectual material and financial help in organizing this seminar.

Ladies and Gentlemen

Why has the Indo-French Forum taken the initiative to suggest that a seminar on the multipolar world be held? The purpose of the Indo-French Forum, as you have very aptly stated, Mr Chairman, is to promote the relations between our two countries, to suggest to our governments initiatives likely to promote cooperation between both countries in areas where it is lacking but a potential exists. We have done so for the past two years with, we believe, some success. Now, how does multipolarity fit into this framework? It so happens that both countries, regardless of the majorities in power, believe that a stable, peaceful, balanced international order requires a multipolar structure. This is what we, by and large, believe. This is what our governments say. But, what do we really believe? What do our governments exactly mean? What stands behind the words we use? Do we, on the Indian and on the French side, really mean the same thing? Obviously, the future of Indo-French cooperation would rest on a very solid basis. Actually, on a very promising basis, if, beyond the words, we can ensure that a genuine meeting of the mind exists regarding our view concerning the political, economic and cultural future of our planet. This is the purpose of our seminar and, of course, it fits perfectly in the purpose of the Indo-French Forum. It is an ambitious goal. We are lucky. I would say, we are blessed, Mr Chairman, to have both our Foreign Ministers who will come and conclude our seminar and will tell us what they officially understand by multipolarity. As far as we are concerned, we, who belong in one way or another to the foreign policy communities of our countries, have to approach that subject unofficially, as frankly and as candidly as possible, which does not mean that our foreign ministers don't speak frankly and candidly, but we have a greater freedom of speech and I do hope that we will make use of that freedom.

Having said that, Mr Chairman, let me briefly ask my dear co-chairman, Minister Hegde, to help me try and set the stage on the French side. As I just mentioned, there is a very large, I would say, an almost unanimous consensus in France in favour of a multipolar world, which of course, does not mean that we believe that such a world exists today or that it will necessarily emerge any time soon. The consensus I am referring to concerns the direction in which we believe we should be moving.

Ladies and Gentlemen, how does the world of today look?

I think we would probably agree that the world of today is global or is in the process of becoming globalized. And that whether we like it or not, it is unipolar. The US, after the USSR's demise, is the only power left with a truly global military reach. Our Foreign Minister, whom we shall listen to tomorrow, describes the United States as a 'Hyper Power'. He likes to distinguish the great powers as they were called in the time of the Vienna Treaty in 1850, as the European great powers, the super powers of the cold war, the US and the Soviet Union, and America being the hyper power of today. He emphasizes that when he uses that word, he doesn't have a critical connotation but a purely descriptive one. It points to the fact that the supremacy of the United States extends not only to the military field but to practically every sector, economy, currency, technology, mass-produced cultural goods. Now, globalization and unipolarity, the present-day realities are concepts and realities that France is inclined to challenge. Globalization, of course, is not a policy. It is a fact. It is the child of technology. And what we oppose is what I would call runaway globalization. What we object to is sort of a sense of helplessness that sometimes permeates the debate of globalization. The feeling that nothing can influence it and that, in particular, we have to accept its propensity to produce uniformity. We strongly believe that diversity, especially in the cultural field, is a factor of enrichment for our planet. We believe that uniformity would be a huge step backwards. Cultural diversity is, as far as we understand it, the basis of our national identities. What France stands for is managed globalization. Concerning multipolarity, we must, of course, ask ourselves, ladies and gentlemen, when we look at the world of today, whether multipolarity is not a dream, a French and Indian dream contradicted by reality. In other words, in what future direction is the world actually moving?

Now, in my opinion, we sense and we believe that the world is moving, and will continue to move away from its present unipolar structure towards a multipolar reality that will breed a more balanced and thus, a more stable international order. This belief is based on the likelihood of three developments concerning Europe, Asia and the United States itself. Let me briefly turn to these three points:

Europe

The Economic and Monetary union, which we have already achieved, has always been considered a necessary detour towards political union. The way to political union is, of course, proving to be long and bumpy. But, steady progress is being made on that road. A European foreign and defence identity is slowly but, we believe, surely emerging. The appointment of NATO's former Secretary General, Mr Solana, as something of a European foreign minister is a significant step in that direction. From the outside, it sometimes seems as if Europe was a foot-soldier of a US-dominated NATO. This is the way the intervention in Kosovo has been perceived not only abroad, but also within Europe. None of this may be close to the truth in terms of military hardware. It does not accurately account for the political dimensions of that operation and we can possibly discuss that during our session. In short, what we believe is that the Atlantic allies, while being maintained, will gradually develop into a two-pillar structure in which the European pillar will increasingly act autonomously and the military side of the Trans-Atlantic relation is but one of its dimensions. The economic and financial side of the picture is, especially in times of peace, as important if not more so, and in that respect, the birth of the Euro has an enormous potential which is gradually becoming apparent. We believe that it is going to fundamentally change the Trans-

Atlantic balance in the economic and financial field. The Euro, we believe, is more than likely going to free not only Europe but the rest of the world from its unilateral dependence on the Dollar. So, so much for Europe!

The rise of new world powers in Asia, China, India and Japan is the second factor that will impact the world's unipolar structure. China's economy will overtake America's in terms of GDP size, not necessarily quality, sometime between now and the middle of this century. India's economy, if it maintains its present course of reform, will catch up with China. It may already have overtaken China in such crucial sectors as the Information Technology and the Internet. Both India and China are nuclear powers which, in time, will acquire a global reach. As we know from our European experience, that means that in order to maintain a strategic balance, nuclear weapons don't suffice.

A strategy of flexible response has to be put into place. It requires large conventional forces and that is terribly costly. This is what the United States had to do in order to check the Soviet Union during the cold war in Europe, and it only managed that during more than thirty years with the help of large European, especially German contingents. There is only one alternative to this conventional requirement—an effective anti-missile defence and that is exactly what the United States is trying to do. Is it technically possible? It remains doubtful. What is not doubtful is that it has a very destabilizing effect. It requires the United States to discard the ABM—the Anti Ballistic Missile treaty concluded with the Soviet Union—which is an integral part of the nuclear balance between both countries. In other words, doing that is playing with fire. And this brings me to the United States.

Concerning the US, there is one crucial question—will the US want to cling to its present hegemonic structure? Will it durably accept the constraints and the responsibilities such a status carries with it? The responsibility to maintain peace and security the world over, to be nolens volens the policeman of the planet. Professor Calleo will answer that question during our session. I personally doubt that the United States will durably want to shoulder such responsibilities. I doubt it for three reasons:

First, because the isolationist sentiment in the US has not totally disappeared, it is not likely to disappear.

Second, because imposing on the rest of the world decisions that are often taken under the pressure of domestic lobbies and are not always in the better interest of the United States itself, will not make the United States popular in the world. I happen to believe that the American public wants the United States to be popular, and doesn't and will not durably accept its unpopularity.

And thirdly, because it is less than obvious that the United States will durably muster the economic and financial means to sustain its present global hegemony. The international status of the United States is at the origin of its huge external commercial deficit, a deficit that is offset, as you know, by equally huge influxes of private external capital. These capital in flow happen to a large extent because the rest of the world has no alternative but to hold Dollars. But the willingness to hold Dollars would diminish quite dramatically as the Euro becomes a widely-accepted alternative reserve currency. When this happens, and I believe it has started to happen, the US will have to raise its interest rates, which will slow down its economy and diminish its economic capability of shouldering the international responsibilities which are today its own.

Ladies and Gentlemen, what all this means is that the world is moving, whether some like it or not, towards a more plural distribution of wealth and power. This leaves us with one vital question to which I won't have time to give an elaborate answer, Mr Chairman, because looking at the watch, I see I should be concluding pretty soon. And that question is the following: is the multipolar world to which we are inexorably heading, going to be a better and more stable and more peaceful world, as India and France believe? The question is going to be at the heart of our debate. Let me try and devote just a few short concluding remarks to that question.

Two global and antagonistic views of the future have been put forward since the end of the cold war. We all are familiar, with those views: One is Fukuyama's optimistic view of a world in which democracy and the market economy, having become universal, peace prevails and history ends. The other view is Huntington's, the other professor's view, which is a pessimistic view. He announces that the clash of civilizations will replace the clash between nations leading to confrontations which could be merciless. Most observers in my country reject these two extreme views. Most believe that in order to make the multipolar world, a liveable, peaceful and prosperous place, one must considerably reinforce and reform the existing multilateral institutions, the most important of which is the UN and its Security Councils. This implies two important changes. First, we must enlarge the circle of permanent members of the Security Council so as to adequately distribute wealth and power in the world. And this means, of course, that India and Japan must become permanent members and probably one day, Brazil and possibly Mexico.

Secondly, the Security Council must become a decision-making organ. If it is paralysed, it inevitably causes nations or groupings of nations to take the law in their own hands. Can the Security Council be effective with the veto? Can the veto be done away with? These are the questions, ladies and gentlemen, that we have been struggling with in the European Union. We don't call it the veto. We call it unanimity voting. And unanimity breeds inaction and stalemate. Everyone agrees that doing away with it has so far proven impossible. Multilateralism, however organized, is the obvious answer to multipolarity and it requires significant difficult structural changes.

I believe it also requires a change in mentalities, especially on the part of the West. The relationship between the West and the rest, to quote an expression I don't particularly like, is probably at the heart of the changes in mentalities which have to happen. And changing that relation, making each side understand and accept the point of view of the others is, I believe, Mr Chairman, the very subject of our seminar. And it is also, may I add, the essence of the dialogue between India and France. Thank you very much.

Introductory Speech

RAMAKRISHNA HEGDE

'I see no poverty in the world of tomorrow, no wars, no revolutions, no bloodshed; and in that world, there will be faith in God greater and deeper than ever in the past.' These are the words of Mahatma Gandhi, the Father of the Indian nation.

Multipolarity essentially implies that in the world that we live, an international order is established where power, responsibility and opportunities are shared by all nations and there is no scope for any single nation to establish its dominance on others, which is a pre-requisite for achieving world peace.

The end of the cold war a decade ago led to a period of transition which, however, did not result, as widely expected in Europe and India, in the emergence of a multipolar order. Instead, there has been a tendency towards unipolarity with the United States of America as the only pole. It is self-evident that although the USA is undoubtedly a great power, it cannot resolve major international issues, whether in the area of security or politics or economics by itself. History is replete with instances where arrogance of power has led to disastrous wars. If the world is to be made free from strife, the USA has to build a coalition and it has often demonstrated its capability to do so. The challenge before us, India and France, is to ensure that a coalition of poles emerges, which can ensure that unipolar hegemony is not imposed upon the international community. This would help to reverse the recent trends in imposition of unipolar values and standards on a wide variety of issues: human rights, nuclear and missile proliferation, multilateral trade and intellectual property rights, etc. This exercise would mean influencing the USA, with whom France and India have excellent bilateral relations, to accept the concept of plurality and multipolarity in the interest of economic and social justice and world peace.

It may be recalled that after its independence and during the cold war, India always maintained its distance from any power bloc, rejecting the idea of a bipolar world. In the cold war era, Indian political leaders opposed the matter of international relations being driven by antagonism between two rival power centres. Accordingly, India played a leading role in founding the Non-Aligned Movement in 1961. This movement gathered strength over the years as the colonized nations of Asia and Africa acquired independence and chose the path of non-alignment to safeguard a degree of independence in decision-making in political, economic and military terms. This movement subsequently played an influential role within the United Nations and other international groupings on critical issues such as apartheid, disarmament and world peace, so that economic development of the underdeveloped nations could take place without any hindrance from armed conflict.

Today, in this period of transition, like-minded nations such as India and France must join hands to bring a new world order in which all countries have equal opportunities and all nations have a role to play in international affairs. Two issues acquire importance in this connection: firstly, the urgent need to reform the United Nations, with a view to ensuring greater democratization, and secondly, the creation of a pluralistic security order based on a cooperative approach to security.

What is the structure of the United Nations today? It is an anachronism, representing the world as it existed half a century ago at the end of World War II. Today, the United Nations has 185 members, a quantum leap from the 50 that it had at the time of its inception, a time when much of the world was still under colonial rule. Many of these countries under colonial rule have taken their place as independent members of the international community. Look at the UN Security Council, the most powerful body within the United Nations. It still represents the balance of power as it existed at the end of World War II. Can you say it represents the whole world? Each of the five permanent members was given a veto on the assumption that balancing their interests and areas of influence would ensure a stable world. Today, this council is not qualified to represent the will of the international community. Of the five permanent members, three are European nations while the fourth is the USA. Where is Asia, the largest and most populous continent in the world in this Council? China alone cannot be considered as an adequate representation. Asia accounts for the world's greatest energy as well as other resources on which depends the future prosperity of the world. Asia accounts for some of the largest countries, the largest standing armies, three declared (and one undeclared) nuclear powers and a large number of missile producing and exporting countries. Where are Africa and Latin America in this system? They are also regions of rich culture, history and natural resources. There is an urgent need to reform this body. The reformed Council must represent all these regions adequately. Only then can the United Nations truly represent the will of the international community and only then will its decisions have credibility.

Coming to the second aspect, i.e. the need for creating a pluralistic security order, which would be accommodative of diversity and the growing strength and confidence of the emergent economic and security players. In a world of growing interdependence, the concept of security cannot be visualized in narrow military terms. A crisis in one part of the world will affect the rest of the world. We have witnessed this interdependence during the recent South-East Asian crisis when Western financial markets were also hard hit. In this situation, a pluralistic security order, working through a network of cooperative structures, would be capable of dealing with the challenges of the changing situations.

India is, through its constructive and cooperative policies with Asia, contributing to the building of greater confidence and stability in the region. The development of India's nuclear capability is part of its resolve to build a multipolar world wherein Indians will have strategic space and autonomy in decision-making. The Indian view of regional security goes beyond the passive absence of conflict to the active building of trust and confidence with its neighbours. India, in its long history, has never committed aggression on any country. Nor has it tried to prove its superiority of military power. Actually India has been a victim of aggression in its pursuit of peace. This approach characterized India's responsible and restrained handling of the Kargil crisis. It is also in keeping with this philosophy that Indians have engaged in rich and productive interaction in the political, economic, security and cultural field with its neighbours.

Economic multipolarity is also a critical element in this stable security environment. The failure of the Seattle round of negotiations of the WTO must be traced to the attempt of a few developed countries to impose a one-sided agenda on the rest of the world. The WTO itself must be restructured in keeping with the principle of multipolarity. If WTO is true to its mandate it must not allow economic imperialism to rule under the garb of free trade. Least developed countries, developing countries and developed countries should have just and equitable share in the world market.

Sharing democratic values is an essential part of the multipolar world. It has to be seen in the context of a more enlightened environment where unbridled pursuit of national interests has been overtaken by an acceptance of a shared commitment to democracy, rule of law, pluralism and promotion and protection of human rights and fundamental freedom. It is this approach that brings France and India together in a common determination to ensure that those tendencies that manifested themselves in the tragic and inexorable train of events leading to World War II are not repeated in the twenty-first century.

We, in India, unhesitatingly support the idea expressed by the French Foreign Minister that we must work together to reject a politically, economically and culturally unipolar world and the unilateralism of a sole 'hyper-power' (*hyper-puissance*). We believe that in the decades to come, the European Union will emerge as an important pole of the new world and I am sure, so will India. Unions and groupings of other developing countries should also emerge as countervailing forces to face the emerging menace of a unipolar world. Unilateralism must be countered by multilateralism and antagonism by amity and cooperation. Our call for multipolarity, in the context of the enlightened world order of today, does not mean a return to the belligerent system of balance of power. It is a world in which the old politics of domination, uninhibited pursuit of national interests and rivalry for exclusive control of markets and resources and weapons of mass destruction will be renounced. It is a sharing of power and responsibilities in the international system just as these are shared within individual democratic nations.

France and India are uniquely placed to develop, with a common vision and approach, the values essential for the evolution of a multipolar world. Let us strive together to achieve this goal. If we succeed, and I hope we will, Mahatma Gandhi's ideal quoted above will be realized and the world be worth living for everybody.

Working Towards Multipolarity: A New International Order in the Twenty-first Century

Multipolarity and Multilateralism

J.M. GUEHENNO

Multipolarity has become a very fashionable word. On 23 April 1997, China and Russia issued a joint statement in which they agreed that they would, 'in the spirit of partnership, strive to promote the multipolarization of the world'. A month later, on 16 May 1997, China and France, in another joint statement, took note that the world was 'moving toward a multipolar structure that is replacing the bipolar structure inherited from the past', and also agreed 'to strengthen multipolarity'.

It is indeed easy to contrast this relative lack of US interest for the concept of multipolarity with the apparent convergence of such different countries as Russia, China, and France. It is tempting to interpret current international politics as a struggle between the United States, which would like to maintain their present pre-eminence in a unipolar world, and all other countries, who would have a joint interest in working together to limit US power so as to create the basis for a multipolar world.

The reality is more complex, and multipolarity is not a code word for anti-Americanism. We should not mix analysis and judgement. Multipolarity is first a concept that describes a particular type of international system; it can also become a policy goal, if multipolarity is considered as the international counterpart of democracy: the recognition that each country has a sovereign right to determine its future. During the cold war, this was not the case, and we could all be critics of the bipolar world, because it was both immoral and dangerous. It was immoral because it limited the freedom of choice of the people of many countries whose political choice were made dependent on strategic considerations that had nothing to do with their aspirations. France, as a member of NATO, was firmly in the Western camp, because its strategic situation required it, but it never accepted the legitimacy and sustainability of a bipolar world, and always spoke in support of a multipolar world in which the artificial division between East and West would have been overcome.

The world was a dangerous place then, because the apparent

stability created by nuclear deterrence and the balance of power between the two superpowers was the result of an unprecedented arms race in human history. It was precarious. The opening of any new archive makes us actually more aware of the immense dangers of the bipolar confrontation. Moreover, the cold peace at the centre transferred to the periphery the East-West rivalry, and peripheral wars were fought, which cost many lives: Korea, Vietnam, Afghanistan, Angola were vicious wars, whose wounds, in some cases, have not healed yet. The regrets that are sometimes expressed on the stability of the cold war are politically unacceptable and strategically unwarranted.

The post-cold war world that is emerging—and that negative definition is a good illustration of our difficulty to understand the new situation—is more ambiguous, and requires a more methodic approach. We have to answer three questions:

- First, what is the meaning and extent of multipolarity in a globalized world?
- Second, is multipolarity desirable?
- Thirdly, what policies should we follow to promote a multipolarity that is conducive to peace, progress, and democracy?

Images are misleading, because we have for decades visualized the bipolar world as a sort of architectural structure with two pillars, the demise of one pillar seems to suggest that there is now one remaining pillar towering above the rest of the world. The word unipolar has been coined to describe this new situation in which the United States would have become 'the only superpower'.

It is indeed true that rarely has a country combined so many facets of power. The United States is not only the most powerful military power, far ahead of any other country, but it is also an economic, a technological as well as a 'cultural' superpower. It is not only at the forefront of the techno-industrial revolution that is changing the world economy, it also dominates the content of the new channels of communication that are being opened, and these 'intangible' assets seem to be a key element of its power. From high culture to mass media, the US seems to have acquired a powerful grip on the minds of the people, throughout the world. Its universities attract some of the best students, its TV news programmes are watched by its enemies as well as its friends, its mass market entertainment products give flesh to the dreams of millions of people.

It is, therefore, tempting to identify globalization with Americanization, and to compare the present situation with the Roman Empire, when a common culture, supported by the power of Roman legions and the authority of Roman law, dominated the Mediterranean world, extending its influence all the way to the confines of India.

If that was the right assessment, the concept of multipolarity would be forgotten in a few years, and the 'page currently under development' on the State department web site would not have to be completed. However, it is much more likely that the page will have to be developed and amplified: today's world is anything but unipolar.

It is indeed an illusion to believe that a pole of the bipolar world can collapse without having an impact on the other pole of the international system. Actually, the end of the bipolar world should lead us to re-evaluate the very idea of 'poles'. The cold war not only unified the world strategic scene, it also unified the foreign policies of the major countries. There was a dominant idea, and in the case of the United States, the dialectic opposition between East and West provided a focus that not only helped build a domestic consensus on foreign policy, but gave a strategic orientation to the various and otherwise often conflicting facets of American foreign policy.

This is no more the case, and the foreign policy elite not only has to take into account the constraints of a democratic state much more than the British imperial elite did at the time of the British Empire, but has to adapt to a new form of democracy. In today's America of fragmented communities, relatively small but committed groups defined by a single issue can wield influence beyond what sheer numbers might suggest. The search for a foreign policy, which is the expression of a national interest transcending the narrower perspectives of various interest groups, is more and more elusive. It often seems that any attempt at a sustained 'grand strategy' has become over-ambitious. The Bush Administration was the last one to try, but 'the new world order' now has an empty ring. A successful American foreign policy looks more and more like a policy which accommodates various interest groups while manoeuvering around crises and managing the daily pressure of domestic and international media. This does not mean that the United States will no longer have an activist foreign policy, but that their successive endeavours are less and less linked by an orchestrated strategy. The shift in the NATO strategy of enlargement at the end of 1994, the twists and turns of American-Chinese policy, to mention but two examples, illustrate this evolution. The United States may be an imperial power, but it is not an empire by design. For the first time in history, an empire is born unwittingly. This extraordinary event begs a question: is it still possible to analyse American power in the traditional terms of power politics, and does the very notion of a 'pole' of power, still make sense if that power is no longer consistent expression of a political will?

This does not mean that America has become isolationist. The end of the cold war has not made the Americans indifferent to foreign affairs, and it would be quite excessive to compare present attitudes with the isolationism of the 1920s, since the American economy is now fully integrated in the world economy, to a point where many Americans have been exposed, through their business contacts, to the foreign world, in Asia as well as in Europe. Actually, business people are now often more internationalist than politicians—who sometimes boast of their absence of foreign exposure. Indeed, opinion polls consistently show that a majority of Americans support the United Nations and an international involvement of the US. The views of Senator Jessie Helms are definitely a minority view, but that support to internationalism is shallow. In the absence of a political threat to the American idea of democracy, the traditional suspicion that Americans entertain *vis-a-vis* government is no more compensated by the patriotic urge to give political support to the American government. While the American people continue to support a strong military, they are very doubtful of the usefulness of foreign spending, the magnitude of which they massively overestimate (believing that the US government spends 10 per cent on foreign aid when it actually spends much less than 1 per cent . . .). Most Americans, in the tradition of American exceptionalism, believe that the best contribution that America can make to the world is by setting an example to be followed, and they are wary of the compromises which are part of any multilateral negotiation. They also believe that example is best promoted not by the American Government but by the many actors who together represent the American experience—which for the rest of the world is perceived as the American power. The American foreign policy appears to be but a small part of it.

American multinationals have existed for several decades, and they had a political impact which was supportive of American foreign policy when they massively invested in Western Europe in the 1950s and 1960s, thus strengthening the Atlantic Alliance. But, as their weight and power have radically increased, quantitatively and qualitatively, with the opening and globalization of capital markets, which followed the globalization of trade, their relationship with the US government is anything but harmonious. Microsoft is at the same time a powerful symbol of American global power and an illustration of its complexity, as it faces a major legal challenge from the US government. Likewise, IBM, General Electric or Goldman Sachs cannot be linked to the US government in the same way as United Fruits has been; actually, in the latter case, it seems that the relationship has been reversed. It was once alleged that the company was used as a front for CIA operations in central America; it now appears that its influence weighs on the US position on the banana international trade issue. Big American multinational companies generally get the support of the US government, especially when government to government relations are involved—as in arms sales or public procurement—but it would be wrong to suggest that their global reach is based on that support, and that they contribute to a broader strategy, to a master plan aimed at furthering American power as such. On the contrary, the pressure of capital markets and shareholders forces management to give priority to business, over political considerations. Conversely, while the US government naturally follows policies broadly supportive of US business, it has recently shown less determination in its traditional policy of opening up markets and promoting free trade. While this may partly be attributed to the degradation of relations between the Presidency and Congress, which has not granted the 'fast track' power that would have enabled the president to go beyond NAFTA, it also reflects the growing difficulty of reconciling conflicting interests, in economics as well as in politics. US policy is not driven by business, because there is a very wide range of business interests that conflict with each other, and business pays little attention to politics.

A similar analysis can be applied to another facet of American 'soft' power, the Internet, news and entertainment industry, of which the new giant AOL Time Warner is the most powerful symbol. The Internet is actually a good example of the ambivalence of American power. American companies for the moment play a dominant role in the Internet Revolution; they control key parts of the infrastructure (the so-called 'backbones'), and the early development of the Internet in America has given them a temporary comparative advantage. The American economy, at this stage, derives more benefits, in terms of productivity in established businesses, and jobs in the 'new economy', than any other country in the world.

However, the very logic of the Internet, which makes it possible to streamline businesses, to cut intermediation costs, and to circumvent the constraints of geography, opens new opportunities worldwide to the competitors of American corporations. Meanwhile, the new 'virtual communities', based on a shared single interest, transcend national borders, thus further contributing to the already noticed process of fragmentation as well as dilution of the American polity. As the 'American experience' is shared by a still small but fast growing and influential international elite, it is unclear whether that elite becomes a willing promoter of an American national interest, or dilutes that national interest in an extended 'private sphere', where the 'pursuit of happiness'—i.e. in today's world, the accumulation of private wealth—overrides all other more traditional 'political' considerations.

The first assumption of a unipolar world—that there actually exists an identifiable American 'pole' is, therefore, at best doubtful. It ignores the rapid decentralization of so-called 'international' relations, which not only has deprived diplomats and defence professionals of their monopoly, but also changed the nature of political entities, including the United States. As the currency of power changes, new actors and new forms of power emerge, which cannot be automatically associated with the political communities in which they first appeared.

The second assumption of a unipolar world—that the other 'poles' have been overwhelmed by the dominant power—is also questionable: an increasingly heterogeneous world makes it difficult to apply a traditional 'balance of power' analysis to the interaction between a decentralized, loosely knit, increasingly problematic 'American pole' and the rest of the world: while some of the other 'poles' may wield much less power, they are often more coherent because they remain centralized and strictly limit the role of non-governmental actors. It is easier for, let's say, Iraq or Korea to play the traditional games of power politics than for the US government. In other cases, it is the actual weakness of the state and the difficulty to link a non-governmental actor to a state that can become very frustrating. The obsession of the US with Osama Bin Laden is revealing in that respect. Lastly, there are intermediate situations, such as Russia or China, in which the heterogeneity of the country itself, democratic but authoritarian in the case of Russia, authoritarian but challenged by new powerful economic interests in the case of China, makes it impossible to have a dimensional view of power. The world is definitely not unipolar, but multipolarity has to be better understood and defined.

Multipolarity has been the normal state of the world for most of modem human history, and since the art of diplomacy was to find the right balance of power between various poles of power, professional diplomats have often been tempted to consider multipolarity not only as the normal state of affairs but as the ideal model in which they can exhibit the full range of their talents. Indeed, after the Napoleonic wars, which were a revolutionary attempt by one state to replace that balance by the domination of a single pole of power, the nineteenth century gave the impression that the European continent had eventually found a lasting balance, in which a concert of nation-states could be achieved. The bonds of blood and shared conservative values seemed to have created a lasting harmony in a Europe of kings and princes. That order was slowly to unravel. As Prussian power grew, France reasserted itself, and the dynamic forces of nationalism and democracy put an end to the subtle calculations of professional diplomats. In an age of collective passions, moderation and self-restraint were in short supply, and the concert of nations ended in two disastrous world wars.

The tragic experience of the two world wars was the inspiration behind the project of European integration. The Europeans understood that they had to go beyond the system of balance of power to manage intra-European relations, if they were to avoid the return of war. However, this rationale could not be extended to the relations of Europe with the rest of the world, which explains why European integration is often interpreted as a mere change of scale in a linear view of history. After the city-state came the nation-state and, according to that interpretation, we are now entering the age of continent-states. The aim of diplomacy should then be to organize the concert of continent-states more lastingly than we organized the concert of nation-states.

There is, however, no guarantee of success and multipolarity, considering the particular characteristics of our age, could prove even more unstable and dangerous than the concert of nations, if we do not manage it properly. A smaller number of active participants in the global power game does not necessarily imply smooth relations between them. Actually, as the stakes increase, any disagreement may become more bitter and difficult to resolve. And any shift of alliance will have major consequences on the overall balance of power.

Moreover, bigger political entities will inevitably be more diverse, and the domestic process—democratic or non-democratic—through which their various and often conflicting interests are reconciled, becomes ever more complex and slow. The risk of global gridlock—the impossibility to adjust and reconcile the interests of the major actors—is thus compounded by the risk of domestic gridlock. The failure to agree on an agenda for a new trade round at Seattle was a good example of this risk of global paralysis. There is no 'global community' which has a shared interest in compromise. The already noticed heterogeneity of our world not only is a major obstacle to the consolidation of a 'common ground' without which an agreement is unlikely, but creates asymmetries in perceptions as well as interests. These asymmetries could, in principle, facilitate trade-offs, but that would require that each major player have the capability to manage its own domestic trade-offs and be in full control of all the facets of its 'foreign policy'. As has already been noticed, this is not always the case. Strategically, this evolution can be very dangerous. On the one hand, the world is fragmenting strategically, so that there are several, apparently independent, strategic theatres, which have their own dynamics: the Balkans, the Caucasus, the Middle East, South Asia, East Asia, the Congo Basin and so on. On the other hand, the world is becoming ever more interdependent, as the international flows of capital, goods, and information keep increasing. We are in such a situation where the links that bind us together may prevent a crisis from remaining local, and should be a reason for caution, as was the case in the cold war, but where differences and local strategic characteristics are powerful enough to give a local crisis its own momentum.

The contrast with the period of the cold war is in that respect striking, especially when one considers the role of nuclear deterrence and nuclear weapons. During the cold war, all strategic theatres were linked to the central confrontation between East and West, and the radical nature of that confrontation was emphasized by the nuclear arms race between the two superpowers. The other nuclear forces, even when they were independent forces, as the French deterrent, were perceived and analysed in that bipolar context, and they actually helped further unify the global strategic theatre. Nuclear deterrence was always understood in the perspective of the global confrontation. This situation is now changing, and in some cases, it can be argued that nuclear weapons may fragment the global strategic theatre, rather than unify it. Their presence, or hypothetical presence—as in the case of North Korea—reduces the options of the external players, and gives added emphasis to the regional balance of forces, thus increasing the risk of initially local crises acquiring their own momentum. And yet, local bilateral confrontations, through the nuclear dimension, cease to be bilateral, and involve third countries. Whether these new triangular relationships increase stability or, on the contrary, increase unpredictability, will depend on the circumstances and the willingness of all players to collectively manage this new multipolarity.

The implications of this particular strategic conundrum lead to a broader point: multipolarity, just as democracy can turn into chaos and war if there are no strong institutions to accommodate differences, and guarantee their compatibility. That does not mean that multipolarity, as an illustration of the diversity of the world, is not desirable. It has always been a fundamental tenet of democracy that differences are part and parcel of a vibrant society, while homogeneity is stifling. There is no reason not to extend that view to the world, and nobody wants a homogenized world in which differences will be suppressed. As it was noted at the beginning of this paper, multipolarity should reflect the right of human communities to assert their sovereignty and organize their polity as they wish. But multipolarity needs to be managed if it is to lead to stability and peace.

Multipolarity is already a fact, and the real issue is not whether we want to move the world toward a multipolar system, but how we can make sure that a multipolar world remains desirable and legitimate. We have to define the conditions under which multipolarity can function effectively, so that it can become a policy goal.

The first and most fundamental condition is that all the major participants, who give meaning to the word, agree on some common principles, without which there can be no common ground. If a multipolar system is governed only by raw power, and if the principles embodied in the preamble of the UN charter are perceived to be but empty words, there is little doubt that it will be very precarious, and that it will eventually lead to war. The concert of nations were endured only so long as there was a common culture that moderated national ambitions.

The search for a common ground means that the principle of sovereignty cannot as such be the cornerstone of a stable multipolar system. The principles that the Europeans have accepted in their mutual relations should be slowly and cautiously extended. In an interdependent world, all nations must accept that, to be legitimate, a national decision should not only express the sovereign will of the people, but that it must also take into consideration the interests of its neighbours. The idea that the ultimate aim of a nation, or of a group of nations, is to be able to manage its own destiny without having to pay attention to the rest of the world is unsustainable and dangerous.

However, if that attitude is to become a reality, international institutions need to become much stronger than they are now. Nations will accept limiting their sovereignty only if they are convinced that their voice can be heard, and if they can negotiate concessions in a mutually advantageous manner. The strength of international institutions directly depends on their legitimacy. If international institutions are perceived to reflect the interests of a few privileged nations, if the majority of nations do not feel they 'own' the international institutions, there is little hope that strong enforcement procedures to settle conflicts, whether they be in the economic or political area, will be accepted.

In practical terms, it is indeed obvious that progress toward that aim will be slow, and will be effective only if a step-by-step approach is taken. Two suggestions can be made in that respect. First, issues should be 'unbundled', and a functional approach to the complex issues that we have to manage globally is probably the best. If we try to create too much linkage between issues of a different nature, we are likely to be overwhelmed by the complexity of the negotiations that we will have engaged into, and we will fail. The second suggestion is that we should try to combine regional and global approaches. As was noted earlier, one of the dangers of our global age, which combines a weak 'international community' with a growing need to assert one's national or local roots, is that local or regional crises have their own momentum, which eventually impacts on the global system. In such a context, the risks of misunderstanding in conflict situations are high, and the only way to reduce them may be to have parallel tracks, combining regional and global dialogue, so as to manage the risks of conflict in all their dimensions.

Multipolarity can then become multilateralism, and the interdependence of our world, instead of being perceived as an illegitimate limitation of our respective national sovereignties, could open the way to a more collegial and more effective management of our joint futures.

Multipolarity and the United States

DAVID P. CALLEO

Three American Traditions

American attitudes toward global 'multipolarity' are mixed and ambivalent. The mixture comes in large part from contrasting traditions in the ways Americans look at relations with the rest of the world. While America may be a relatively young civilization, the United States is one of the world's oldest states, with deeply-rooted traditions of foreign policy. To simplify hugely, these may be described as 'isolationism', 'global hegemony' and 'realism'.

Throughout its first century as a state, isolationism was a major, indeed, predominant strand of American statecraft. It prescribed careful non-involvement in Europe's quarrels. As a reward, isolationists taught, the US would be able to avoid the powerful governmental apparatus and heavy military expenditure typical of Europe's states.

Americans would be left free to enjoy the rich bounty of their continent and to develop a political system and culture that emphasized individual freedom and enterprise, as opposed to state-loyalty and mass mobilization for warfare.

This isolationist view was, however, challenged from the start by a 'Hamiltonian' tradition that tended to see the US as a state like others, but with particularly brilliant prospects for continental and global power. Hamilton admired the British, and hoped the US would ultimately emulate Britain as a global power. Throughout most of the nineteenth century, however, America's expansionist drive was fully occupied with expansion on the North American continent, achieved at the expense of the aboriginal inhabitants and the neighbouring state of Mexico. By the end of the century, the US began to expand outward. In 1898, the US went to war with Spain and established its primacy in the Caribbean and, shortly thereafter, began building the Panama Canal. The war with Spain also led to US occupation on the Philippines, and thus made it officially an

Asian power. This globalist transformation was accompanied by a corresponding rejuvenation of the old Hamiltonian tradition. By late nineteenth century, a powerful group of American intellectuals and politicians began to see the United States not only as a great power among other world powers, but as the successor to Britain as the global system's hegemonic power. This view grew in tandem with enthusiasm for a liberal global political economy, one characterized by free trade and national self-determination for all peoples. The US began sensing the competitive power of its giant economy. Like Britain at its apogee, it began to see free trade and national self-determination as the logical strategy for a global hegemon, whose commercial and naval power far outdistances all rivals.

This globalist hegemonic view briefly predominated in American policy at the end of World War I, with Woodrow Wilson's grand plans for a new American-led international political-economic system. Behind Wilson's schemes was a broad theory about the nature of a liberal global system, a theory that continued to develop despite Wilson's own failure. According to this theory, in order to function properly a liberal global system required a hegemonic leader. This liberal hegemon needed to take the lead in preserving peace and a 'world rule of law'. It should discourage colonialism and the imperialism of others. The hegemon also had vital global economic functions. The hegemon was needed to manage the world's financial system, to protect the rights of investors and to provide abundant liquidity during the crashes and panics to which the world money markets were otherwise susceptible. A hegemon was also needed to grease the wheels of trade. The hegemon should be the buyer of last resort in the world economy. In other words, provide a distress market for commodities in times of glut. During shortages, it should open its reserves to relieve the dearth. In short, it should use its power to smooth out the gluts and shortages that disturbed orderly world trade.

As everyone knows, nationalist isolationism and globalist Wilsonianism clashed in the great domestic struggle over whether the US should join the League of Nations. America's hegemonic globalists lost that struggle and 'normalcy' returned. The US continued to eschew Wilson's global political and strategic ambitions throughout the interwar period. Having intervened in World War I to prevent German victory, the US then refused to guarantee the peace that it had created. But the US did, on occasion, exert leadership in the economic sphere, as, for example, in the Dawes and Young Plans—efforts to solve the debt and reparations questions that bedeviled the world economy in the 1920s. It was difficult for the US to avoid a commanding role in the global economy. The war transformed the US into the world's leading creditor nation. In the 1920s, American capital financed the fiscal deficits of Weimar Germany, along with much of the global investment of the city of London. In short, the US was a very powerful global actor in the interwar years, but refused to accept the leadership in providing security that global hegemonists believed was the obligation of such power.

World War II brought Wilsonian globalism back into favour. After the wartime consolidation of a powerful presidency under Franklin D. Roosevelt, the US was much better prepared constitutionally to take on the role of world leader. World War II also saw the creation of vast US military and intelligence establishments, a greatly expanded diplomatic corps and a large 'industrial-military complex'. In other words, World War II gave the US an impressive governmental structure with which to manage a world position. After World War II, the cold war intervened to perpetuate these institutions. They began to seem a permanent fixture of a new American constitutional system, one that boosted the power both of the presidency and of the bureaucracy, thus transforming the political system for a global role.

The isolationist-globalist dichotomy does not fully describe traditional American perspectives on foreign policy. It is possible to speak of a third tradition, what might be called American realism. Throughout our history, this tradition has served to blend and balance isolationism and globalism. Its votaries have regularly tended to reject either the isolationism of the first tradition or the interventionist globalism of the second. They do accept that the United States is inevitably a world power and must play a leading role, but also emphasize that the US needs to define its external interests carefully and husband its national resources. Realists have also tended to stress that America's external world role can distort and destroy its domestic democracy. Followers of this tradition are generally not averse to cooperating with others to maintain order and prosperity in the world. But their multilateralism, if less enthusiastic than that of the Wilsonian globalists, is perhaps also more genuine. They do not yearn to see the US as a new global Rome or a new British Empire. While they may share many perspectives in common with the Wilsonians, realists are followers of the balance of power. They are disciples of Talleyrand rather than Napoleon.

These three American traditions have co-existed throughout the twentieth century and are very much present in the nation's political consciousness today. In periods of stress or rapid change, the three struggle to provide the most convincing explanation for what is going on and also the most convincing rationale for what must be done. During the cold war, the globalist tradition was pre-eminent, but the realist tradition also had a powerful role in refining globalism and checking its excesses. The resistance among writers like Morgenthau and Kennan to the escalating war in Vietnam provides an obvious example. A more subtle illustration is the accommodation that evolved in the late 1940s between the US and the states of Western Europe. The years immediately following the war saw very considerable friction between American globalist plans and the aspirations of European states, who wanted national recovery and transformation, together with regional integration. By 1947, the US had come up with the Marshall Plan, which not only generously supported European national aspirations but also encouraged European States to develop a strong confederacy of their own and, in principle, to become far more self-sufficient through collaboration among themselves. At the base of this generous policy was the belief that American national interest would be better served by a strong integrated Europe that would be able to keep order internally and protect itself against the Soviets, rather than a disunited and quarrelsome Europe that would remain a costly and dangerous dependency.

Throughout the post-war era, isolationist sentiment was itself never far beneath the surface. The American political system was unused to the constraints of having to work closely with allies or the heavy expenses of leading them. American criticism of 'free-riding' was constant, as was the American anxiety over the risks of extended nuclear defense. Americans were also not compatible with the Imperial Presidency that world leadership seemed to require. Among the other branches of the Federal system, a revolt against that presidency slowly gathered strength. The populist outburst against the war in Vietnam gave warning of future trends. So long as the cold war lasted, however, the confrontation with the Soviets remained sufficiently vivid to subdue isolationist impulses and sustain multilateral and Presidential discipline.

TRADITIONAL VIEWS AFTER THE COLD WAR

The end of the cold war obviously meant a changing world system and recent years have seen a struggle among the three American traditions to explain and react to it. The globalist impulse has been the most obvious. American 'triumphalism' has been a natural reaction following the Soviet collapse. The American political imagination is strongly tempted by the vision of a unipolar world with the US as the only superpower. The vision has had ample practical reinforcement. The United States now possesses an immensely formidable military capacity, unmatched by any combination of other powers. In addition, the US in recent years has enjoyed an extraordinary prosperity. Triumphalism thus has a strong economic dimension. Liberal globalism has been in fashion among businessmen, economists, journalists and many academics—not only in the US, but around the world as well. This fashion reflects technological and political changes that have encouraged the integration of the world economy.

In its current American version, globalism is often accompanied by a hegemonic, neo-Wilsonian view of world order. By now, there are elaborate historical and geopolitical theories to support this view. Any liberal world system is seen to require a leading power to manage it. The British, it is said, performed this vital hegemonic role in the heyday of the Pax Britannica, but grew progressively unable to continue it as the nineteenth century came to an end. The result was World War I. The subsequent failure of the US to assume Britain's role led to the continuing breakdown of the international system, exemplified in the depression and the World War II. Thereafter, thanks to the urgent challenge of the cold war, the US did accept its hegemonic bites. These included not merely creating and accepting responses and participating in the United Nations, but also organizing collective defense to deter Soviet aggression in Europe and Asia. The US also grew highly conscious of its responsibility for promoting and managing the global economy, and sought to carry out its economic functions through multilateral systems like the GATT, or, latterly, the WTO. The Dollar became the world economy's reserve and transaction currency, and the US thereby was the manager of the world's money supply. The US also became the world's 'consumer of last resort', a development of particular finance to Asia. The US opened its markets to Asian producers, first to the Japanese and the various 'little tigers', finally to China and, to some extent, India. Large-scale American importing has often provided the opportunity for rapid export-led growth in Asia. In effect, US policy called into being a sizeable part of the export industry in many Asian countries.

Hegemonic geopolitical theory, it must be noted, does not necessarily offer an optimistic prognosis for America's future. One of the most distinguished American scholars with a hegemonic bent has been the economist and historian, Charles Kindelberger, who is also notable for his pessimism about the ultimate consequences of playing a hegemonic role. For Kindelberger, it seems only natural that a world power will have its 'climacteric', followed by a melancholy decline. The exercise of hegemony hastens decline, Kindelberger explains. The hegemonic power provides the public goods of order and economic crisis management to the rest of the system. Other powers benefit, disproportionately from these public goods, insofar as they do not make a comparable contribution to them. The result is that in due course, other powers grow more prove rapidly than the hegemonic power, burdened by its global duties. The historian Paul Kennedy talks of 'overstretch'.

As the hegemonic power weakens from over-extension, there is a strong tendency for it to become a 'hegemon in decline'. This means that it begins to use its hegemonic position to shore up its own faltering economy. Whereas, the healthy liberal hegemon is defined as a great net contributor to the international system, the hegemon in decline becomes an exploiter of that system. These 'declinist' views reached a certain apogee during the period of renewed globalism under the Reagan Administration that resulted in a serious American financial crisis in the late 1980s. Thanks, however, to the Providential collapse of the Soviet Union, America's overstretch was greatly relaxed in the 1990s. Since the US had, by far, the largest comparative defense expenditures among the major Western states, it enjoyed the greatest peace dividend. As a result, the US during the Clinton Administration, was gradually able to reverse its heavy fiscal deficit. American prosperity of recent years has been heavily dependent upon the consequently improved fiscal situation. Somewhat ironically, it is the sharp drop in defense spending that has given American globalism its strong second wind.

Globalist triumphalism naturally appeals to the surviving cold war governing classes in the United States, in particular, to the various foreign policy elites that have found their own personal fulfilment through conducting or analysing the American global role. These cold war survivors are institutionally well entrenched in the various huge bureaucracies—the Pentagon, CIA and State Department, as well as NATO, along with the large number of think-tanks, consulting firms and academic institutes concerned with America's global position. These groups, along with numerous business firms and their dependent regional interests, form a natural constituency for globalism that emphasizes America's own leading role.

Despite its upsurge in the 1990s, American globalist triumphalism is not as confident as it may seem. There is an uneasy sense that America is becoming increasingly unpopular in the world, and that other powers are inexorably rising. Some see the European Union as bent on extending both its scope and its membership in a fashion that points to an ultimate challenge to the US. The European Monetary Union creates, in the Euro, a serious rival to the Dollar as the world's leading reserve and transaction currency. The EU's Common Foreign and Security Policy and common defense policies point to a Europe much less dependent on its American military protectorate. With European proposals for ESDI, NATO itself is being pressed to evolve away from American hegemony toward a more balanced trans-atlantic alliance, one that permits independent European action. Meanwhile, the EU is supposedly ready to extend its membership so that it becomes the principal organizer of the pan-European space. Together, these initiatives point to a lessened American role in Europe and perhaps beyond.

Asia, of course, offers a still more formidable set of challenges to America's vision of global hegemony. Japan has long been a particular concern for American alarmists, but others see China, and perhaps India, as much more important in the long run. China already has a well developed nuclear deterrent and India has been strengthening its own nuclear capabilities. The Chinese economy is expected to become the world's largest in the course of the next quarter of a century. Some Americans see an ominous parallel with the 1880s, when the US overtook Britain as the world's largest economy. In short, behind triumphalism are considerable apprehensions about the future.

Thus, while globalism seems the predominant tradition on the present American political scene, the other traditions are, in fact, alive and well. Isolationism continues, even in our self-consciously interdependent world. To begin with, isolationism remains much more feasible for the US than for most other advanced states. All countries may be interdependent, but most are a good deal more so than the US. While the US does have possible antagonists who are great powers, or great powers in the making, it has no immediate neighbours that threaten it militarily. Elsewhere, the US is less exposed than its allies. It is in a very different military relationship to China, for example, than Japan, Korea, Taiwan, Russia, or even India. Similarly, the US is not nearly as exposed to the consequences of disorder in the Balkans as Italy, Germany or France. And while the American economy is much more internationalized than formerly, it remains notably more autarkic than European national economies. This autarkic character, together with the global role of the Dollar, continues to insulate the US from many of the international pressures that trouble other advanced economies, let alone the more vulnerable developing economies that depend heavily on global markets.

Nevertheless, not even the most fervent isolationist can ignore that the US has grown deeply involved with the rest of the world. No one who suggests drastically curtailing the manifold linkages can be taken seriously. Thus constrained, isolationist feelings often take the form of resentment of other states. Resentment, combined with a heightened sense of national power and invulnerability encourage 'unilateralism'—today's updated version of isolationism. These reconstituted isolationists believe the US can largely do what it wants. If other countries wish to trade with US, it is up to them to accommodate to American rules. Any kind of attempted constraint on American policy, particularly from international organizations, like the UN Security Council or the WTO, arouses great impatience. Militarily, there is a strong tendency to take unilateral action against 'terrorists' and 'rogue states', whether the UN sanctions such actions or not. These isolationist-unilateralist attitudes are strongly represented in the Congress, where the prevailing view is that many of our allies are 'free-riders' and that America pays an outsized proportion of the costs of maintaining world organizations. Many see international organizations as a racket managed by ambitious cosmopolitan technocrats, often privileged refugees from developing countries whose own domestic arrangements remain a scandal. Another common attitude is contempt for the incapacity of other states to manage their own affairs. This is noticeable in American reactions to recent European efforts at more autonomy. Whenever Europeans are left to their own devices, it is said, sooner or later, catastrophe follows and the US has to step in to clean up the consequences.

Lingering isolationist sentiment is responsible for many of the contradictory characteristics of current American foreign policy. On the one hand, isolationists are diffident towards world involvement. They generally oppose putting American troops in physical danger for international purposes. Such a position significantly limits what the US can do to develop effective collective security in the world. But isolationists also are inclined toward erratic unilateral interventions. Hegemony and unilateralism are, at heart, incompatible. A truly hegemonic policy requires steady public support for coherent long-term goals. Effective leadership of multilateral alliance is not easily compatible with alternating moods of indifference and anger. The erratic juxtaposition of hegemonic and isolationist tendencies in the American system, thus, produces a volatile situation of some danger for both the US and its allies, particularly for those allies who count on the United States to preserve the status quo in Europe or Asia.

The volatility of American policy is exacerbated by institutional changes within the US, in particular, the decline of the American Presidency. The recent problems of the Clinton Administration, however idiosyncratic, are also part of a larger pattern since Nixon's time. Many parts of the American political system have united to cut the Presidency down to size, to get rid of the imperial prerogatives acquired since Franklin Delano Roosevelt's tenure. The Congress, the courts and the states have all collaborated to erode presidential power. At the same time, the huge bureaucratic, academic and industrial structures that grew up together with the Imperial Presidency, mostly remain. Without strong Presidential power, these institutions grow increasingly headstrong. National policy is more and more vulnerable to hijacking by special domestic interests. Again, institutional indiscipline that reinforces the lateralist tendencies in American policy is not easily compatible with an untruly hegemonic policy, which requires steady, long term and steady direction, together with an adequate and reliable allocation of resources. Needless to say, America's erratic imperiousness dismays other states and reinforces pluralist tendencies in the world system in general. Both Europeans and Asians wonder whether the US is a reliable world leader, and begin to make other arrangements to insure against American decline.

Fortunately for the United States and the world, American globalist and isolationist traditions are often brought in to some form of disciplined reconciliation through our third current in American foreign policy—the realist tradition. This is an intellectual and cultural tradition with roots in academia and the press, churches, unions, business and professional communities and in civil society. As a tradition, its tendency is to see the US more as a great power not unlike other great powers, with characteristic vices as well as virtues, rather than a providentially blessed historical exception. Realists can hardly deny that the US has a leading role to play in the world, but they tend to be sensitive to the dangers of physical and moral overextension. Realists, therefore, reject isolationism but are sensitive to the isolationists' fears that domestic welfare and balance are being sacrificed to excessive external ambitions. Realists grow nervous at the hubristic implications of complacent triumphalism and runaway globalism. Realists also tend to be more critical about extending national commitments, or pursuing military superiority. This sense of national limitation encourages a respect for multilateral institutions and discipline. Ideally, realist balance and skepticism provide a basis for reconciling globalist enthusiasm for world responsibility with isolationist devotion to domestic balance and interests.

A balanced US policy depends not only on the inner equilibrium of American politics, but on objective conditions in the rest of the world. Pluralist trends in the world suggest that the present period of American pre-eminence is limited. Other powers are already rising: Europe, China, India, Indonesia, Iran, perhaps Russia too. The primary strategic problem for American policy is how to use this transitory period of facile pre-eminence. Should the US oppose the rise of others and try to hang on to pre-eminence as long as possible? This, of course, is the natural tendency and there are many signs of it. The alternative is to build cooperative structures whose aim is not to institutionalize American hegemony everywhere, but to promote stable regional balances, based on practices of multilateral cooperation. That is what the states of Western Europe have created among themselves since World War II, generally led by strong American encouragement. Such an evolution seems not only in the world's interest, but in that of the US itself. American appreciation for it, however, is likely to grow insofar as the costs of hanging on to hegemony grow more and more obvious. In other words, the future of American policy will depend not only on American self-determination on the accidents of political leadership—but also on the evolving military and economic situation around the world. There is some reason to suppose that the world's evolution will not encourage American global hegemonism.

The Real World: Prospects for Military Hegemony

In Europe, the US appears to be hanging on to its cold war military leadership by enlarging the membership and scope of NATO. Creating new tasks in Eastern Europe, Central Asia, the Middle East and North Africa should continue to justify America's commanding role and heavy military presence. This strategy has led to sharp conflict with Russia, as NATO pushes into the former Soviet Empire in Eastern Europe and threatens to extend its military reach into Central Asia. This American policy also produces growing frictions with the Europeans, whose interests do not lie in quarrelling with Russia, or indeed, with the powers of the Middle East, who want a more balanced alliance internally. Short of provoking fresh quarrels with Russia, Europe's security problems are more and more domestic in character—crime, drugs, ethnic neighbourhood conflicts, mass movements of terrorized populations, etc. These sorts of security problems are not particularly amenable to American management. Americans are not eager to engage their own forces in such messy situations. Nor are Americans particularly well endowed with the necessary political and economic resources. In short, the changing nature of Europe's security problems seems likely to work towards a new division of labour, in effect, an American devolution of power within the Atlantic Alliance.

In Asia, where the US confronts rising nuclear superpowers, China is thought to be the principal threat. The difficulties are greatly exacerbated by the American position on Taiwan. Some Americans even fear China as a potential global rival. Its economy certainly will overtake America's in due course, at least in sheer size of GDP. Since there is a strong educational and scientific dimension to the Chinese economy, it should ultimately be formidable technologically as well. Militarily, China already has the makings of a serious intercontinental nuclear deterrent. Unless the US can develop effective missile-defenses against a major opposing system, something that few believe possible, deterring China in the future will increasingly require a policy of 'flexible response'. In Asia, as in Europe, during the cold war, the threat to defend the territory of others by starting a nuclear war will grow less and less credible against an antagonist with a capacity to retaliate massively against the US itself. Flexible response means having a reasonable range of conventional options between surrender and nuclear war. This requires enough conventional force to defeat aggression with non-nuclear means. As cold war Europe demonstrated, such a strategy is extremely expensive. To sustain it in Europe, the US required NATO with its particularly heavy contribution of conventional forces from Germany. Despite the heavy German input, there were bitter debates over burden sharing, as well as over the strategic issues of keeping American 'extended' nuclear deterrence credible.

If a similar strategic evolution eventually leads to flexible response for Asia, who will be America's allies in sustaining the heavy requirements for conventional forces? Japan, we often suppose, is the obvious candidate. But it seems less than certain that the Japanese will take readily to the role of an Asian Germany, the local provider of conventional forces who, nevertheless, abstains from having its own nuclear deterrent. Will Japan embrace a policy likely to alienate it permanently from China? Arguably, India is sufficiently well protected by its geography, and sufficiently vulnerable to disruptions from Pakistan, so that it will not be eager to enlist itself in the anti-Chinese alliance. Ironically, Russia, with its huge, thinly populated territory, already invaded demographically by the Chinese, seems America's only natural ally. At the moment, however, America's NATO policy in Europe alienates Russia also in Asia. America's hegemonic policy in Europe is at war with its hegemonic interests in Asia. The result of this geo-strategic 'dissidence' is an otherwise highly unlikely Russo-Chinese alliance. Rationally, America's preoccupations with Asia should encourage its interest in a self-sufficient Europe able to maintain order in its own space and also strong enough to build a collaborative relationship with Russia. In other words, America's Asian interests ought to encourage a 'tripolar' Europe that permits American-Russian collaboration in Asia.

The likely diffidence of Asia's own powers to join in an anti-Chinese alliance perhaps suggests a different regional solution than the recreation of Europe's old bipolarity in Asia. The model showed not to be a bipolar standoff with two rival hegemonies confronting each other and dividing the continent into two camps. Rather, the US should hope to build some kind of more cooperative security system, preferably including China as well. Arguably, China should be convinced that it is in its own interest to be 'contained', in a relatively fluid system of several great regional powers, with no one—the US included—pretending to be hegemon. Needless to say, this is a task that will require major changes in the American political imagination as well as that of the Chinese and their neighbours. At best, it will take long time. Meanwhile, the US seems likely to grow increasingly preoccupied with Asian security. This is not because Asia is more important to the United States than Europe, but because Europe has its own structure in place to stabilize the continent. It calls for a cooperative pan-European system that needs American participation but not overweening American hegemony. Asia is unlikely to have such an indigenous structure for a long time. The US is thus likely to see its own role in Asia as more critical than its role in Europe. Given the probably heavy demands of such a role, American globalism will have to limit its ambitions. American realists, at least, should favour a self-sufficient Europe that becomes a real ally rather than a costly dependency. Arguably, American realism should also do its best to avoid altogether an Asian policy so hegemonic that it polarizes the region into American and Chinese camps.

Economic Constraints on Hegemony

America's leading role in Asia has been at least as much economic as military. In effect, the US has been Asia's hegemonic consumer of last resort. The open American market has been a prime incentive for much of Asia's extraordinary growth, a good deal of which has been export-led. One consequence is that the US itself has very large trade and current account deficits, much of which can be ascribed to its unbalanced trade with Asia. In macroeconomic terms, of course, the high external deficits reflect the country's habitually low savings rate currently negative—the obverse of its heavy consumption and investment. This situation has developed over a long time. As a result, the problem of financing large external deficits is, by now, thoroughly familiar.

A number of distinct formulas have succeeded over the years. At the moment, financing depends heavily upon a large influx of private foreign capital for investment in the booming stock market. Such a situation seems unlikely to endure indefinitely and another formula will eventually have to be found. During the Reagan Administration, America's external deficit was balanced by large inflows of private or public foreign capital to finance the American domestic deficit. This formula was closely related to the macroeconomic policy in the Reagan years, which combined very large fiscal deficits with tight money. Foreign capital was attracted by the high interest rates and rising Dollar. The result, of course, was a huge growth of America's government debt during the Reagan era, a phenomenon that led to an upsurge of concern over America's 'decline'. Since Reagan's fiscal deficits were closely related to his much-increased defense spending, the US began to fit the model of an overstretched hegemon in decline.

The end of the cold war provided US fiscal policy with a large 'peace dividend'. Sharp cuts in defense spending, plus adroit handling of debt financing put the US fiscal policy in surplus by the end of the 1990s. The government's new interest in saving, however, has been more than offset by the rest of the economy's high level of consumption and investment. As a result, the external deficit has grown rather than diminished. Despite the high level of domestic demand, inflation has so far been prevented by the strong Dollar.

Nearly all of America's solutions to its external deficit have depended heavily on its role as provider of the world's principal international currency. Since the Dollar has been uniquely available and acceptable, foreign governments and big multinational firms have been constrained to hold it. The world's great supply of Dollars has needed to find a resting place somewhere. As a result, the US has always been able to count on selling its debt or its domestic assets with relative ease. This ease is expected to diminish, however, as the Euro becomes a principal rival to the Dollar as the reserve and transactions currency. In the future, multinationals and governments will have an alternative to holding their reserves in Dollars. Logically, this will make it more expensive to finance future American deficits. For the US to attract the habitual inflows of foreign capital needed, interest rates will have to rise more than formerly. Higher interest rates should, all else being equal, serve to depress the economy. A powerful impulse for policies to reduce the external deficit seems the likely result.

Such an evolution is a serious threat to Asia, where any rapid reduction of the American trade deficit is likely to result in a major crisis. It is the US that has, in a sense, called into being the export industries of Asia. The sudden loss of the American market will be a severe and disruptive blow. Perhaps an orderly transition away from Asia's dependence upon the American trade deficit will occur, possibly through a compensating growth of regional trade. But the transition is unlikely to be smooth. It seems unlikely, for example, that the EU will become Asia's buyer of last resort. Presumably, the relatively autarkic Asian economies will suffer much less than those smaller countries where exports form a very large proportion of GDP.

In summary, US economic pre-eminence in Asia has been based heavily on its role as the region's consumer of last resort. But that role has been tied to a hegemonic global monetary role that has grown increasingly uncertain over past decades and which seems likely to be further restricted with the advent of the Euro.

In many respects, the military and economic problems that confront the United States reflect a more plural distribution of power and wealth in the world. The problem for the US is how to adjust to such a trend. Ideally, it should use its remaining period of leadership to encourage orderly structures commensurate with a more pluralist distribution of world power. Still a great autarkic giant, the US is not really dependent on continuing its global hegemony. To be sure, isolationism is obviously not a practical policy. Indeed, in its unilateralist version isolationism is increasingly dangerous. To avoid the excesses either of hubristic globalism or imperious isolationism, the US needs to redesign its internationalism according to a less hegemonic model. To do so, the US needs to draw more heavily on its realist tradition. Fortunately, that tradition does exist and may be expected to reassert its influence as the current triumphalist euphoria lessens. An optimist, looking at the current Presidential primaries in the US, may perhaps convince himself that the signs are not unpromising. In due course, there may be a certain reconfiguration of American foreign policy traditions. Globalism and isolationism may somehow be brought into a Realist synthesis. The US may accept to exercise its leadership in a more genuinely multilateral context. One, frameworks is certainly appropriate to a more plural world. To create such a noble task for American state-craft is a worthy and natural evolution from the great accomplish-ments of the twentieth century.

There remains, of course, the possibility that the US will fail to adapt to a multipolar world, as the British and Germans failed to accommodate each other before World War I. In that case, the prospects for the twenty-first century are not very cheerful. Much will depend on whether the United States and Western Europe are themselves able to reach an accommodation over the coming years. A revision and renewal of transatlantic collaboration based on a new division of labour and balance of leadership will consolidate what has been achieved in the West. It will incline the US as well as Europe towards a useful world strategy and perhaps also suggest a regional model useful to others. If the West can cope with its own multipolarity, perhaps there will be hope for Asia as well.

Working towards Multipolarity: India and France

NAJMA HEPTULLA

Shri Ramkrishna Hegdeji
Mr Jean-François Poncet
Members of the Indo French Forum
Distinguished Diplomats and Invitees

I express my gratitude to Shri Hegde for inviting me to express my views today on the occasion of this two-day seminar on India and France in a Multipolar World. I was initially required to speak in the first session yesterday, but due to my unavoidable presence at the tenth UNCTAD at Bangkok as the President of the IPU, I had to request Hegdeji to allow me to speak today.

I have been told that in the last two days, you have held intensive discussions on various aspects of multipolarity, including its definition and evolution, its regional dimensions and economic multipolarity.

The concept of multipolarity signifies an international order that is different from the bipolar world of the cold war era and the single power domination after the end of the cold war. The present situation is one where the United States of America, the unchallenged victor of the cold war has emerged as the supreme power in the world. A phenomenon, which has been described by analysts like Samuel Huntington as one in which a single state acting unilaterally with little cooperation from others can effectively resolve major international issues. However, this structure leaves no scope for other states or combination of states to prevent it from doing so. Thus, all those who, naturally, oppose this idea, must come together to create a counterweight.

Multipolarity is, in other words, a concept of a world where legitimate interests of all major and significant powers are respected and where they can continue influencing international developments. It is the sharing of the power and the influence, the acceptance of autonomy in decision-making by various countries, respect for diversity in idea, concepts and ways of life.

India has never accepted the vision of a bipolar world. This was the principle underlying India's advocacy of the Non-Aligned Movement. This movement was the response of the three significant countries of Asia, Africa and Europe to a bipolar vision. This movement acquired a lot of advocates as various countries of Asia and Africa became independent. These newly independent countries, which were weak economically and inexperienced politically, could not remain entirely aloof from superpower rivalry. However, in the bid to retain some margin for manoeuvre, almost all the countries chose the path of non-alignment. India, as a founder member of the movement, was expressing its vision of a world which went beyond superpower rivalry. This was the first expression of the Indian conception of a multipolar world, in which different countries would have the ability to take steps in pursuit of the national interests.

Traditionally, India's involvement in Asian affairs has been a civilizational engagement. Ideas and faiths originating in India have spread across the region. We have never engaged in colonization or attempts to exercise our hegemony. In recent years, our efforts to embark on the process of economic reforms are to re-establish India's benign and cooperative engagement with the rest of Asia. It must be emphasized that India's nuclear tests do not constitute a threat to any of the nations in the region. In fact, the tests have held to remove potentially dangerous ambiguities in the region and underline the urgent need for a rational approach to bilateral relations. In the immediate neighbourhood India continues its approach of offering greater economic and political space to its neighbours. Maintaining regional stability is a key security objective for us since it enables us to devote our resources to meet the urgent needs of development.

We believe that the rise of new global players from Asia provides a window of opportunity for creating a cooperative security framework, as opposed to the hegemonic domination of one or the shifting balance of power arrangements.

We also believe that the basis of the Indian nuclear policy is the pursuit of a world free of nuclear weapons, which could enhance not only India's security but that of all nations. We took a decision at the dawn of the cold war era, to reject its basic premise and chose the path of non-alignment. India's foreign policy was, therefore, based on its desire to attain a global balance of power that is based on universal and non-discriminatory disarmament.

In 1999, we took the decision to conduct nuclear tests in order to update and validate a capability demonstrated almost 25 years ago. We did not, in these tests, violate any international treaty obligation. We cannot accept a regime, which arbitrarily divides the nuclear haves from nuclear have-nots, and differentiate between the right of nations to safeguard their security.

In the post-cold war period, an Asian balance of power is emerging with new alignment and forces. India has, in order to safeguard our sovereign and oral interests, opted to correct an imbalance and thus, contribute to a stable balance of power in Asia. The need in today's world to balance rights and obligations of all nations and end unequal division must be recognized.

We consider the process of European unity, which has been evolving in an extremely significant manner. We are aware that with the launch of the Euro and the steps towards a new common foreign and security policy, Europe has taken major strides towards becoming a power to reckon in the world.

The challenge to a unipolar world is both political and cultural and countries such as ours must work together in this context. The European Union will be an important pole of such a world and it is necessary for all the poles to cooperate. Multipolarity must be seen in the context of an enlightened world order where nations work together to uphold common values. In short, multipolarity must be seen as sharing of power, responsibilities and opportunities within the global system in such a way that this occurs without prejudice to sovereign rights of democratic nations. We must work together to counter the tendency of powerful countries to conduct crusades. We must ensure that the tendency to intervene without the authorization of legitimate international organizations like the United Nations is checked.

France has been the founder member of the Inter-Parliamentary Union. IPU, as a world body of the democratically elected national parliaments, has always endeavoured to provide a parliamentary dimension to State policies. Whether it is international peace or world trade, IPU feels that all state interventions should involve parliamentarians.

It has been felt that in a parliamentary democracy, parameters are the repository of legitimacy. They are the supreme fora to enact a law and hold the governments accountable. So far, parliaments have not been actively involved in diplomacy or multilateral negotiations. International relations and diplomacy have been the exclusive domain of foreign ministries. However, parliaments need to enact the laws in accordance with international treaty commitments, whether it is a multilateral agreement on security or economy or on financial architecture. Hence, it is necessary that as an institution, parliaments must be involved in the treaty negotiations.

Inter-Parliamentary Union, during its long history of 112 years, has been involved in developing a parliamentary dimension of diplomacy. We too have witnessed the bipolar or multipolar and now unipolar diplomacy. However, we have continued to debate upon specific issues as also the general economic, political and social conditions in the interest of global society.

Our experience has been that democratic parliamentary institutions must be involved in any debate over multipolarity. But here also, I shall qualify my observation by saying that there are democracies and democracies. For example, in our neighbourhood, Pakistan has never been a true democracy. Most of the time it has been ruled directly or indirectly by powerful military leadership. In such a set-up parliamentary diplomacy has not been given a fair chance to develop.

Further, I observe that debate over multipolarity is usually held in the context of a nuclear arms race. There is a need to expand it in view of new forms and modes of rivalries. Not many citizens have died of a nuclear disaster after the world wars. However transaction, terrorism and sub-conventional warfare has taken a massive toll on lives and the human rights of innocent citizens. It has demoralized the civic society and has left set practices of a civilized international behaviour redundant.

Such tendencies must be addressed to and contained by the community of nations. They ought to rise above the bloc considerations and polarity set up.

I have worked very closely with the French Parliament on several bodies of the IPU for more than a decade. My association with the President of the French Senate, Mr Christian Poncelet and the Senator Mr Michele Vauzelle, who is also a member of the Preparatory Committee for the Presiding Officers Conference, has been a source of great inspiration for me.

During my last visit to Paris, I had the opportunity to discuss various issues of international concern with the Speaker of the National Assembly of France, Mr Laurent Fabius. I explained to him during this meeting and I again reiterate that India looks at France as a country, which, while part of the Western alliance, is capable of taking an independent position on issues of vital interest. The key to resolving security issues lies in a closer understanding and dialogue with friendly nations like France, with which we share a common vision.

With these words I once again thank you for giving me this opportunity to share my views today.

Reshaping the International Order

AIR COMMODORE JASJIT SINGH

There are different interpretations of the nature of the international order as it has existed in recent years, leave alone what shape it is evolving into. The only perception that seems to be widely accepted is that the world is in a state of transition. At one end of the spectrum there is a view that the world, after the end of cold war, was rapidly fixated into a unipolar system around the United States. This perception undoubtedly served to expand the images and perceptions of influence of the United States. But, in reality, the strength of the United States was not merely because of its own capabilities across the board being greater than that of any other state, and nor was it because there was no visible power of any consequence in opposition or countervailing position. Like during the cold war, this strength has been immensely enhanced by the military, political and economic alliance of the United States with advanced industrialized countries, mostly members of the OECD, wherein US leadership was willingly accepted and maximized through reinforcement by these countries. It is important to remember that this alliance has been perceived to be mutually beneficial in spite of occasional differences on specific issues. Within this framework, it is also clear that various countries, especially major powers, are pushing for a relationship among major and middle powers that would serve their own national interests best. Under these circumstances we need to ask: Are there real incentives among the developed countries to seek any fundamental change in the nature of equations among major powers?

On the face of it, the answer to that question is no. But this itself requires us to look deeper into the nature of the international order and the factors that are changing it. To start with, there is a need to recognize the fact that the assumption that a 'bipolar' international order existed during the cold war needs scrutiny. The cold war and consequent confrontation was certainly bipolar in nature with the United States and the Soviet Union respectively trying to attract countries to their sides to expand their leverages, especially against each other in what became an apparently ideological conflict. But this does not inevitably lead to a conclusion that the international order itself was bipolar. The power and dominance of the two superpowers did give such an impression. But even if we accept the inference that the international order was bipolar during the cold war, we must qualify it by affirming that this was significantly moderated by the non-OECD countries seeking a less polarized environment. The bipolarity of the cold war was somewhat diffused by the emergence of new sovereign states that refused to be part of one block or the other and sought, like India did, policies that gave true meaning to independence that they had acquired after decades of struggle against the imperial powers. These countries pursued non-alignment to maximize their choices and options in pursuit of their own national interests. The backing of a superpower would strengthen those options even though such support mostly came from the Soviet block countries who needed greater legitimacy by supporting the developing countries on international, political, economic and even security issues.

The concept and policy of non-alignment, however, should not be confused with the Non-Aligned Movement (NAM), which itself experienced significant pulls and pressures arising out of divergent national interests. The principle and strategy of non-alignment was adopted by India as a means of non-involvement in military alliances and staying out of conflicts that were not of direct concern to it. Although grossly misunderstood in the West (and also by Stalin's Soviet Union), it sought to pursue India's own national interests, liberally interpreted as part of the larger human needs. At the broader level, the philosophy of non-alignment sought a degree of reconciliation between the two confrontational blocks on one side and the developed and underdeveloped worlds on the other, where India became a bridge of sorts. The enthusiasm for the UN among the developing countries in general and India in particular also resulted from the expectation that the UN was the logical and representative instrumentality for a more equitable world order where free states could freely cooperate for mutual welfare and prosperity.

Contrary to conventional wisdom, cold war was neither the sole nor the most critical reference point of non-alignment which emanated and grew in a wider complex of national and international factors in the post-World War II period. The roots of the policy of non-alignment can be traced back in India to at least 1939, when the leading Indian National Congress Party (at its session at Haripur) passed a resolution that: 'India was resolved to maintain friendly and cooperative relations with all nations and avoid entanglements in military and similar alliances which tend to divide up the world into rival groups and thus endanger world peace.'[1] In the context of alliance systems and the risk of conflict implicit in them, writing in *The Discovery of India,* Jawaharlal Nehru had already argued for non-alignment.[2]

The formal birth of the concept of non-alignment can be traced to the broadcast made by Jawaharlal Nehru (at that time the Vice-Chairman of the Viceroy's Executive Council in India) on 7 September 1946, indicating the response of a major nation about to emerge as an independent sovereign nation-state, when he stated that:

> We propose, as far as possible, to keep away from the power politics of groups, aligned against one another, which have led in the past to world wars and which may again lead to disasters on an even vaster scale. We believe that peace and freedom are indivisible and the denial of freedom anywhere must endanger freedom elsewhere and lead to conflict and war.[3]

Nehru also declared that, 'We shall take part in international conferences as a nation with our own policy and not as a satellite of another nation.'[4] These words were also in response to the great power relations that had, not yet, but were about to break out into a cold war. The confrontation had not reached the stage when the Great Powers would start making definite demands on weaker states. The stance, therefore, provided a breathing space for India to consolidate itself for the future when the demands did start to come. For India itself, the concerns about the erosion of freedom as a result of the expansion of the cold war were related to the meaning of freedom. Nehru had declared in 1949 that 'It (freedom) consists fundamentally and basically of foreign relations. That is the test of independence. All else is local autonomy. Once foreign relations go out of our hands into the charge of somebody else, to that extent and in that measure you are not independent.'[5]

Non-alignment, thus, was chosen to be an instrument of foreign policy by India in order that it might give fuller meaning and content to its newly achieved political independence. Formal transfer of political power was, by itself, not adequate as future framework of policy which would allow autonomous choices in policy that would protect and promote national interests, which essentially revolved around acceleration of the socio-economic development of the weak deindustrialized societies. Peace, therefore, was seen as a prerequisite to the achievement of this objective; and the cold war and its politics as intruding, if not restricting the choices that were needed if necessary flexibility and autonomy was to be maintained.

The principle and concept of non-alignment, taken to its logical conclusion, would encourage the transition of the international order toward a less confrontationist, more cooperative and non-polarized non-hegemonic international order. While it was not possible to achieve such an order, the necessity or potential for such a framework has not gone away. On the other hand, the present transitional states of the international order only reinforces the expectation that the international order is far more polycentric than what is generally recognized. It offers opportunities to reshape the international order and environment. Some of the main elements that need to be addressed in reshaping the international order would include:

(*a*) Objective assessment of the existing international order including the dominant trends affecting it and the nature of the international order that would serve the interests of the vast majority of sovereign states in the world.
(*b*) Existing international (inter-state) security paradigm and the necessity to evolve a new paradigm. This would naturally include issues of sovereignty, intervention and international peace and security.
(*c*) International institutions and actions to support the evolution of a new international order.

The Evolving International Order

The rapid changes in the political architecture of the world with the end of cold war have generated a strong sense of uncertainty and even vulnerability in the world. It is obvious that the world order is in a state of transition, and generally believed to be multipolar. But, by definition, mutlipolarity would imply more than two powers, with each of them (as a pole) having a set of states under its control and influence. Except for the US, which with its 'political-milieu' and economic alliance system represents a strong pole, no other power is operating as a 'pole' in the real sense, even though increasing cooperation (as in the OIC or CIS) may convey an impression of such a phenomenon. It can be argued that with the passage of time, polarization is likely to develop among states. One such scenario can be the polarization between the industrialized developed states of the north and the developing countries of the south. Another scenario is bipolarity centred on the USA-China at the core.

The reality is that new centres of power (with some old ones regaining their position) have been emerging in the past two decades or so. This defines the true contours of the international order. The nature of this evolution is such that the world order can best be described as polycentric. There are certain characteristics of this polycentric order that also define the nature of the international geopolitical architecture. These may be summed up as follows:

- Substantive asymmetry of power, capability, and willingness to exercise that capability already exists among the leading centres of power in today's world. This imposes concurrent pressures for competition and cooperation among states, especially the leading centres of power.
- Cooperation and competition is increasingly issue based and driven by national interests. States may cooperate in economic matters and yet differ strongly on strategic goals.
- Uncertainty and fluidity in international affairs is accentuated by the information revolution which no longer allows governments the luxury of long reaction time, or the predictability available in earlier times.
- As we advance into the twenty-first century, the following half-a-dozen primary centres of power and capability are likely to influence politico-military and economic dimensions of the new international order:

(1) The United States of America is the most complete power and has maximized its influence through military, political and economic alliances/partnerships. However, the power of some other states has been rising in comparative terms.
(2) Japan has established itself as a techno-economic superpower. But it hesitates to convert this into political influence and is very shy about exercising its military power.
(3) China is growing rapidly across the board and will soon represent the second most powerful centre of power in the world. Its political system is likely to continue along the

current vector, making China the most powerful corporate authoritarian state in human history.

(4) The European Union (with France and Germany at its core), coming together in increasing ways and coordinating its policies, is emerging as a major centre of power. However, while individual countries are likely to coordinate their policies with alliance policies and interests, significant autonomy in national policy choices is likely to continue in the coming decades.

(5) India as the world's largest democracy is now on the move in economic and technological terms. It has successfully progressed in what can only be described as the human history's most ambitious experiment—of transforming a traditional society into a modern one, of transforming an agrarian-based economy into a mixed industry-service sector-agricultural economy, rapidly increasing social mobility transforming the country into a classless society, and so on, all through processes of consultative politics. The World Bank estimates that India will possess the fourth largest economy in the world by 2020. It has a resilient democratic system which has, if anything, gained in strength during the past half century. The country has overcome the fundamental deficiencies in agriculture (where it remained dependent on import of food grains for two decades after independence) although nearly 87 per cent people lived on agriculture in 1950. India emerged into independence in 1947 after 200-years of de-industrialization (see Figure 1). India had accounted for over 24 per cent of the world's manufacturing output in mid-eighteenth century. But during the British rule, it came down to a shade above 1 per cent by the mid-twentieth century. These were the decades when today's developed countries were progressing rapidly on the basis of the technical-industrial advances. Incidentally, control over a superior technology also resulted in the ability of metropolitan powers to establish extensive empires, thereby acquiring control over huge material and manpower resources which added to their capability to dominate. But, since independence, India has made rapid strides and now has the world's second largest pool of highly competent scientific and technological expertise while its software and I.T. strength is likely to play a major role in the coming years.

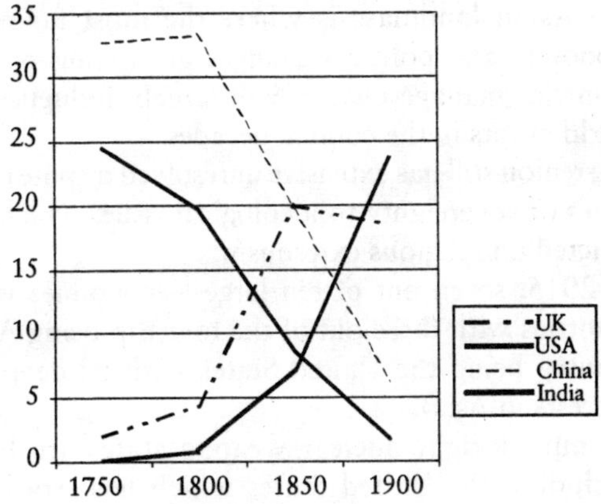

FIG. 1: WORLD MANUFACTURING OUTPUT (in %)

India's economic growth, not as dramatic as that of China or the East Asia 'Tigers', has nevertheless shown an increasing rate of growth in recent decades, as indicated in Table 1.

(6) Russia has been seriously weakened by the collapse and break up of the Soviet Union and the continuing economic vulnerability and political-social crisis. The Red Army is struggling to retain its basic capabilities. But it still possesses a huge nuclear arsenal and the basics around which it could rebuild a powerful state.

The centre of gravity of the emerging international order and strategic affairs is increasingly shifting to the Asian landmass (and contiguous island territories). The twenty-first century is likely to be Asia-centred due to some of the reasons outlined below:

TABLE 1: INDIA'S GDP GROWTH RATE
(Average growth rate for the decade in per cent)

Year	*GDP Real Growth*
1951-60	3.92
1961-70	3.7
1971-80	3.31
1981-90	5.46
1991-2000	5.95*

*GDP real growth for the past nine years has averaged 6.59 per cent.

(i) The Asian landmass is where the most far-reaching social, economic and political changes are taking place. How these countries manage change will largely influence the course of world events in the coming decades.

(ii) The region still has extensive unresolved disputes extending from issues of sovereignty to ideological issues which are often constructed on religious extremism.

(iii) By 2015, seven out of ten largest economies would be Asian countries with three out of the four top being Asian (the other country being the United States with its deep and extensive interests in Asia).

(iv) Six out of eight nuclear weapon states are located in Asia (including the United States which has strategically shifted forward into the Asian contiguous oceans and will remain an 'Asian' power); and the seventh (France) has legitimate interests in the Indian Ocean.

(v) World's energy 'demand heartland' composed of Japan, China and India is in Asia, and so is the energy 'resource periphery' extending from Siberia, Central Asia, Persian Gulf, north Indian Ocean, South China Sea, and East China Sea. Future needs and availability of energy resources are likely to further emphasize the Asia-centred world order while enhancing the role of major centres of power.

What conclusions can be drawn from the above analysis?

The central conclusion is that while multipolarity within the Western alliance system exists (which makes this construct unipolar in the global context), the international order is inexorably moving toward greater democratization and plurality. The more prominent characteristics of the emerging international order are listed in Table 2.

TABLE 2: INTERNATIONAL ORDER: COMPARATIVE CHARACTERISTICS

Bipolar	*Polycentric*
Predictable, rigid	Unpredictable, flexible
Confrontation or cooperation related to cold war	Concurrent cooperation and confrontation based on national interests
Ideology-based foreign and security policy	Functional policies
Hegemonic	Non-hegemonic?
Eurocentric	Asia-centred

A far more plural international order as compared to the cold war period already exists. The challenge ahead of the international community is how to vector and expedite the environment toward a non-polarized non-hegemonic plural system with a degree of assurance that a reversal (including to a bilateral cold war) does not take place. A large number of measures and issues will need to be considered in assessing the direction and progress toward such a goal. But, in essence, we need to ensure that polycentricity, which is already taking strong roots, should be encouraged and the future international order should be built towards strengthening polycentricity rather than allow it to drift toward any form of polarity.

International Security Paradigm

A competitive paradigm of international security has been in existence for more than three centuries. This is essentially due to the international system now being composed of sovereign states. The shift from dynastic kingdoms to nation-states since the seventeenth century has also led to the emergence of a competitive paradigm of inter-state security. The concept of sovereign state, with the inevitable ego-centred state system at its base, implies building up state security to the maximum possible limits. This has actually tended to push nations to seek security at absolute levels. In turn, this inevitably generates threat perceptions in other countries, who, being sovereign states themselves, then seek national security at ever higher levels. An implicit and explicit competition for achieving a higher level and assurance of security between states gets established.

Competition among states has become an established phenomenon as a result of social, political, economic, and technological competition among people, societies, and states. The competitive paradigm of security has intensified over the centuries, reaching new dimensions with the introduction of nuclear weapons into security equations. Nationalism, which is an intrinsic value that a sovereign nation state nurtures, added its dynamics to the competitiveness of national security. The primary reasons for this process may be summed up as follows:

- Sovereign nation state system in the twentieth century emphasized national sovereignty and security to a much greater level than before.

- Extra-territorial pursuit of ideological goals provided a sharp competitive edge.
- There was a speeding up of the effects of Industrial Revolution due to technological competition and potential superiority in the application of force offered by superior military technology.
- Free market economies were built on the principle of competitive advantage.
- Democracy encourages competitive politics, especially when it is still fragile.

Consequences of Competitive Security Paradigm

Serious thought must be given to the question whether the competitive security paradigm has provided greater potential for security or, in fact, created conditions for building security on the foundations of insecurity and generation of vulnerabilities. The consequences of competitive security paradigm include:

- Increase in the sense of insecurity of states because of the pressure of the drive towards an absolutist concept of security by a sovereign state.
- Vulnerability becomes an integral component of strategic stability under a competitive security paradigm. Security is built on generating and sustaining insecurity, at times, in profoundly threatening ways. Doctrines of aggressive maximum nuclear deterrence, for example, seek to institutionalize vulnerability.
- Endemic arms race, especially among hostile pairs of states (and their allies). A concurrent consequence is the high levels of military spending and militarization of states and societies. This, in turn, results in disproportionate amounts of resources being allocated to military means of security, often at the cost of more fundamental elements of security needs.
- Threat perceptions tend to be built on worse case scenarios and politico-military doctrines tend to centre around the principle that 'offence is the best means of defence', raising the risks and incidence of wars and armed conflicts.
- Competitive security paradigm intrinsically encourages militarization of interstate relations, and encourages hegemonism with states seeking to dominate/control the security environment.
- Ideological disputes and dissonance tend to deepen and drift to use of armed violence as the tool.

Collective Security

In the twentieth century, the search for collective security appeared to offer a way out of the competitive paradigm. The roots of collective security, of course, can be traced to the emergence of sovereign states after the Treaty of Westphalia (1648), which obligated all its signatories 'to defend and protect all and every article of the peace against anyone . . . and to join the injured party, and assist him with counsel and force to repel the injury'. In more recent times, the principle was enshrined in the Covenants of the League of Nations (especially Article 16, besides Articles 10 and 11). The failure of the League of Nations (primarily because of strategic and national interests of sovereign member states) to maintain international peace and security, and the World War II led to the establishment of the United Nations as the new peace organization. The record of the UN over the last half-century has been mixed. The single most important factor that came in the way has been the issue of sovereignty of the nation state system. The nature of power distribution resulted in the limitations on the UN itself, where many of the mechanisms visualized in the Charter for the implementation of Chapter VII provisions were never really instituted.

Collective security should logically be defined in universal terms. For application of collective security principle to the United Nations, it is clear that all members of the international body would be included in the framework of collective security. In such a case, collective security would be 'the guarantee of the territorial integrity and independence of each state by all states' (as defined in the *Dictionary of Political Science,* New York, 1964). On the other hand, a less than universal principle has sought to be used in many cases. For example, Hans Morgenthau defined the organizing principle of collective security as a 'moral and legal obligation to consider an attack by any nation upon any member of the alliance as an attack upon all members'. But this should logically be termed as collective defence rather than a collective security paradigm. Let us examine one trend of peace and security.

War and Society

Society has always been involved in war preparedness and contributing the means and manpower for wars. However, till the closing years of the eighteenth century, wars were less destructive especially in relation to society.[6] 'War was an exclusive undertaking of the armies and navies. Restraint was not only a characteristic of eighteenth-century battles and strategy, the attitudes towards civilian population had changed notably after the large-scale casualties of the Thirty Years War. Military planners and commanders made serious efforts to preserve society from the ravages of war. Pre-French Revolution assessments were that: 'At the present day war is carried on by regular armies; the people, the peasantry, the townsfolk take no part in it and as a rule have nothing to fear from the sword of the enemy.'[7] Fredrick the Great, in fact, even believed that 'when engaged in war, the civilian population should not even be aware that a State of war existed'.[8] Developments arising out of the Industrial Revolution (leading to the industrialization of war) and the French Revolution (with its revolutionary nationalism) resulted in society itself becoming inclusive to war and war-fighting. This also coincided with the beginning of the totalitarian nature of war, which finally culminated in the world wars of the last century. The American Civil War reinforced the model of mass armies pitted against each other in years of battle, with the societies (of North and South) mobilized behind them.

At the beginning of the nineteenth century, especially during Napoleonic Wars, mobilization of the nation for war had become an integral element in international security. At the same time, subjugation and destruction of the 'national will' had become one of the primary objectives of war and the application of military power. This brought society within the ambit of war and inter-state conflict. Targeting of the civilian population was increasingly seen as legitimate. Mobilization of the nation for war provided plentiful human resources, motivated by patriotic and ideological fervour. This provided the leadership with a margin of safety that the smaller professional military power was unable to provide. Progress in technology threatened to increase the ability to cause pain and punishment. Towards the end of the nineteenth century, serious international efforts to control the means of destruction, and keep them localized, through negotiated agreements (negotiations at the Hague convention, 1899) are typical of this trend, where aerial bombing was sought to be banned.

The World War I saw the total war model really coming into its own with the emergence of political economy of war on one side, and the expansion of military-technological means to bring society totally within the fold of war on the other. As Ludendorff was to write: 'The nature of totalitarian warfare literally demands the entire strength of the nation, *since such a war is directed against it*'[9] (emphasis added). Two developments were to intensify the inclusivity of population to war. The success of the Bolshevik Revolution in Russia established the foundations of not only a new revolutionary model, but one where the 'export of revolutions' was an integral component of the ideology. Its further evolution was to be based on the use of violence (and repression); and most of the century was to pass by before the Russians altered the basic ideology. However, the model of export of ideology still exists and has been pursued by other states and political entities. The second development concerned the extension of warfare into the third dimension through the advent of air power.

Released of the erstwhile limitations of having to necessarily destroy the adversary's military or conquer his territory first air warfare made it possible to target the adversary nation's society (and its 'will') *directly*. Early attempts to control the process failed. On the other hand, the strategists of Western Europe and the USA conceptualized that air-power will project the spear point of a nation's military force behind the frontlines of the battlefield (and thus escape the horrors and costs of trench warfare) into an army's vital areas to render it powerless to defend itself. Aerial bombing would cause such destruction and paralysis that 'resistance is no longer possible and capitation is the outcome'.[10] The essential target was the enemy nation. Douhet was forthright about inflicting terror from the skies when he prophesied that victory 'must depend upon smashing the material and moral resources of a people caught in a frightful cataclysm which haunts them everywhere without cease till the final collapse of all social organization'.[11] As technology advanced and nurtured, this was manifested in the 'strategic' bombings and city-busting of World War II, and its final culmination at Hiroshima and Nagasaki. Society had become totally inclusive to war in the total war paradigm. This is essentially the reason why civilian casualties in military conflicts have been on the increase.

A second phenomenon, equally disturbing but more debilitating, is the expansion of violence inside society especially for ideological and political purposes. This is one of the most serious problems of peace and security, since it not only undermines national and international security, but also threatens social peace. Such violence has been propelled by criminal activity as well as ideological goals. This violence can be purely domestic and within national boundaries, and it may have external linkages varying from sympathy to provision of sanctuaries, or moral political and material support. The most commonly recognizable form is militancy and terrorism. Modern means of communication, increased vulnerabilities of interdependent, integrated civil societies, and modem instruments of violence (of which the AK-47 Kalashnikov and sophisticated explosives are symbolic) provide a powerful combination for the spread of violence.

The motivations of state and non-state actors to expand violence in society are diverse, and vary from purely criminal intent to ethnonationalist fervour. Intra-state conflicts inevitably involve the society much more deeply into violence and accompanying brutalization. It is not intended here to go into the details of the roots, motivations, and nature of this violence. For our purpose, it would be sufficient to note that while trends of the past two centuries had made society inclusive to war, the trends of the past four decades are, in addition *making war inclusive to society.* Expansion of war (and violent conflict) in social depth is one of the most serious challenges to national-international peace and security. It is necessary, therefore, to reverse the competitive paradigm of security.

Paradigm Shift to Cooperative Security

The foregoing analysis points to the changing nature of armed conflict and war as well as the need for a paradigm shift, which would replace the competitive model of inter-state security. The concept of international security and its operationalization has to be based on the prevailing system of national and international organization. The issue, therefore, is not so much a question of dilution or removal of sovereignty, but more of harmonizing the contradictions of sovereignty directing national security and building international peace and security on more durable, less threatening foundations. This can be achieved by a conceptual shift from the current paradigm of competitive security to that of cooperative security.

Cooperative security requires a set of principles and guidelines for any policy, which may be summed up as follows:

1. An increasing level and scope of cooperation with other states in matters affecting security, especially with the (potential and existing) adversary. It may be recalled that even during the cold

war the two primary adversaries had instituted a significant element of mutual cooperation to ensure strategic stability. SALT I and II, ABM Treaty, INF Treaty, START 1, the Helsinki process, and other agreements were part of that cooperative framework, even if the basic goal was more to freeze existing capabilities rather than a step toward a more fundamental paradigm change.
2. Mutual and equal security of all states includes a recognition of not only the sovereignty of one's own state but also acknowledges respect for the sovereignty of potential adversary.
3. Renunciation of use and threat of use of force in international relations. Resolution of disputes and conflicts only through peaceful means and processes.
4. Strictly respect the inviolability of international borders and mutually agreed lines of control. Progressive contraction of the envelope of armed conflict and violence against states and societies. Civil society must be excluded from all forms of armed violence.
5. Harmonization of politico-military doctrines while adopting less threatening and non-offensive defence concepts and postures. Moving (conventional and nuclear) deterrence doctrines and practice progressively down to insurance and reassurance.
6. Institutionalized arms control and disarmament measures to reduce military forces in cooperation with the adversary.
7. Enhanced transparency in military postures, and confidence and security building as an integral component of state policy.

The paradigm of cooperative security would seek national security through a cooperative framework and process, which harmonizes the imperatives of one's own security with that of the needs of the adversary. The goal would be to decrease the threat levels rather than increase vulnerabilities, thereby achieving security at progressively lower costs—political, economic, and military. In the process, the principles of sovereignty of a nation state are to be reinforced rather than eroded; but in a way, that they lead to cooperation rather than competition and conflict. The end of cold war and changing strategic situations in many parts of the world have opened up new opportunities which need to be exploited for the broader goal of achieving more durable basis of security for the state as well as society.

It is, however, easier to define principles of cooperative security than implement them in real world since it requires a fundamental paradigm shift in the prevailing belief systems. On the other hand, objective reasons as well as significant trends already exist, which support such change. The actual implementation, by definition, would have to be adjusted to the specific realities of a region and the bilateral context of the countries concerned. In essence, there will be little chance of success if measures being instituted are not related and adapted to local conditions.

The aspect which is most likely to produce positive results is that of establishing the process and mechanism for a dialogue among states on political and security matters, which would help to build trust and confidence for the paradigm shift to take root. This can be bilateral, subregional, and/or regional. To achieve necessary support, it will have to be preceded by what has come to be known as Track-2 approach of informal semi-official dialogue on a continuing basis to improve understanding and evolve new approaches to issues and challenges. To a large extent, some clues on the approach which can be adopted may be obtained from the European experience in setting up formal mechanism for such dialogue through CSCE (Conference on Security and Confidence-building in Europe) and its formal follow up organization on one side and the ASEAN Regional Forum (ARF) on the other to the extent that these experiences are relevant to other areas. Bilateral dialogue on security and strategic issues is important whether the process needs to be expanded later or not.

International Institutions

The United Nations provides the most important vehicle for re-shaping and re-vectoring the international order, especially since it carries the primary responsibility for international peace and security through its Security Council. However, the UN was set up in 1945 essentially in tune with the geopolitical realities as witnessed at Yalta. But the world has altered in significant ways. The imperial age is now behind us and the membership of the UN now is more than three times that of 1950. The geopolitical architecture has also changed because of many other reasons. The defeated nations of World War II, who found little say in the dispensation after the war was over, are today major powers, especially in techno-economic terms so much so that many geopolitical issues appear to be resolved at the G7 forum rather than at the UN. The logic and process of 'globalization' itself requires a serious re-examination of the structure and procedures of the UN. In fact, there was a great deal of expectation across the world that reforms of the UN system would take place in harmony with the fiftieth year of the founding of the UN. But not only has very little happened in the shape of reforms of the UN even five years after that, but we have witnessed an increasing tendency toward marginalization of the UN due to the policies of the great powers of the Western world. The military operations by NATO in Yugoslavia during 1999 is a case in point.

But the UN is likely to become increasingly irrelevant unless serious efforts are made to redefine its functions and structure in consonance with the current and emerging realities of the international order. The structural problems that the UN faced in trying to implement a system of collective security can best be illustrated by the experience of the functioning of the UN Security Council which carries the primary responsibility to ensure international peace and security as the executive organ of the United Nations. The Security Council played an important role in easing or containing numerous crises, and it provided a high level for diplomatic contact and negotiations. The Charter provides for the decisions to be taken on the basis of unanimity among the five permanent members holding veto powers. This had been built into the Charter consciously through the compromise arrived at Yalta.[11] It was inevitable that the exercise of veto power by any of the permanent members, or the constant possibility of this happening, have dominated the functioning of the Security Council. Between 1945 and 1993, a total of 195 resolutions were vetoed, many by more than one permanent member. Figure 2 provides the correlation of vetoes by the US/NATO allies, USSR/Russia and China. It may be seen that throughout the history of the UN a very high number of vetoes were cast either by the Soviet Union (especially during the first two decades), or by the United States and its allies (during the remaining years). China stands out as the only permanent member which has been extremely economic with its vetoes.

Conventional wisdom claims that the UN was paralysed during the cold war era, especially after the mid-1970s. Empirical evidence above indicates that functioning of the Security Council was affected by vetoes by the Soviet Union during the early years when the General Assembly and the Security Council was dominated by the West. But from mid-1950s, the Western powers started to use veto extensively. While the USSR/Russian vetoes account for a little less than half the total number, the vetoes try the US, the UK, and France combined account for more than half. In terms of time horizon, 110

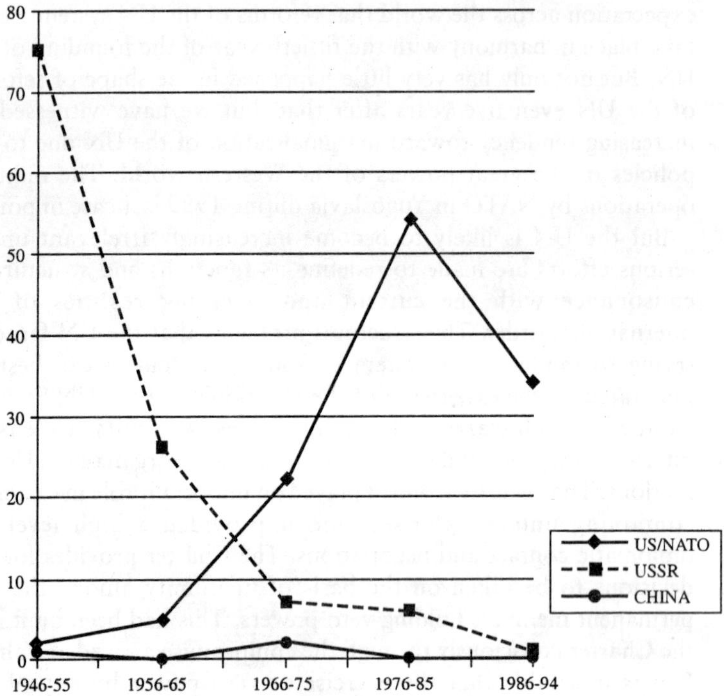

FIG. 2: NUMBER OF VETOES IN THE SECURITY COUNCIL 1945-94

out of the total (115 till 1994) Soviet vetoes, came in the first twenty years. The highest number of US vetoes (34) in any decade came during 1976-85. This also contributed significantly to the US distrust of the UN increasing. Interestingly, the number of vetoes cast came to its lowest figures in mid-1960s. This was also the period which was being described as the 'end of cold war'.

UN and Intra-state Conflicts

The birth of the UN was followed immediately by that of the cold war which stymied UN ability to deal with inter-state conflicts. Its record of managing intra-state conflicts has been mostly disappointing. The structural limitations, principles of sovereignty and non-intervention in domestic affairs were the major reasons. But more important was the fact that the five permanent members of the Security Council, especially the two superpowers, intervened in many of them directly or indirectly. As noted above, two-third of the conflicts between 1945 and 1982 were intra-state, and external intervention was a significant factor in over two-third of these.[12] Superpower involvement and interventions prolonged and vitiated many of these civil wars and intra-state conflicts of which the long wars in Vietnam, Afghanistan, and the Horn of Africa were typical examples. Only in some cases did the UN play a positive role, as in the Congo in 1960-1.

The UN was not really designed to address the problem of civil wars. To that extent, even where civil wars tended to expand and involve the interests of other great powers, the UN appears to have generally played a passive role. The provisions of the Charter itself inhibit the UN in playing an active role in civil wars and intra-state conflicts. The UN is a state-centred organization where the Charter establishes strong taboos against intervention in domestic affairs, and hence, 'civil wars'. The frequency of UN interventions in the name of 'peace keeping' have increased markedly since the end of the cold war. But this appears to be more a case of misplaced focus of the UN, unable to deal with inter-state conflicts (which is its primary role) attempting to expand its role into an even more complex field of human conflict.

Civil wars, more specifically, the internal breakdown of states, represent grave human tragedies. But their implications for 'international peace and security' are not always clearly established, except where there is an external involvement. It is specifically in such case that the UN has tended to shy away. Civil wars and militant violence (including sustained terrorism) of different types were going on in Afghanistan, Bosnia, Russia (Chechenya), Northern Ireland, India (Jammu and Kashmir), Pakistan (Sindh/Karachi), Sri Lanka, Yemen, Tajikistan, Angola, Rwanda, Somalia and other hot spots in Africa and a host of other places in 1994. But few, if any, were likely to escalate or spill over so as to endanger international peace and security. After the initial enthusiasm for interventions in civil wars and 'humanitarian' peace keeping, the United States has recognized this underlying reality as symbolized in President Clinton's address to the UN General Assembly on 27 September 1993: 'In recent weeks, in the Security Council, our nation has begun asking harder questions about proposals for new peace keeping missions: is there a real *threat to international peace?*. . . The United Nations simply cannot become engaged in every one of the world's conflicts. If the American people are to say yes to UN peace keeping, the Unites Nations must know when to say no' (emphasis added). This is equally applicable to all members of the United Nations. The answer, therefore, lies in the UN paying greater attention to prevention rather than post facto actions. The UN, for example, will need to consciously discourage ethno-nationalism, and be less permissive in providing legitimacy to separatism and secessionism.

The modification of the earlier peace keeping role into what has come to be called 'peace enforcement' role has many problems. But what is often ignored, and where the UN has not initiated any action (except in the case of the problem of landmines) is in relation to the means with which these 'civil wars', armed militancies, insurgencies, and other forms of armed violence including terrorism are fought that is, *small arms and light weapons.*[13] The landmines issue emerged on the international consciousness finally as a result of the attention focused by non-governmental, especially human rights, organizations.[14] But it is difficult to escape the conclusion that the attention was also made possible because the socialist countries had been primarily responsible for the spread of landmines. On the other hand, few governments, especially of the Western world, with the USA leading, are innocent of the proliferation of small but highly lethal weaponry across the globe which today threatens international peace and security, seriously challenges the stability of states in many cases, and is spreading like cancer into civil society. The democratic states are particularly vulnerable to the consequences of spread of small arms into their societies. The problem is that many states and substate groups have sought to use armed violence in pursuit of their own ideological (often based on ethno-nationalism or religious radicalism) or national goals and objectives. The UN has recognized the destabilizing influence of ethno-nationalism. But it has not come to grips with the problem of the emerging world in respect of political exploitation of religion. Even more significant has been its failure to address the serious threats to international peace and security caused by the global spread of small arms and light weapons, although the dramatic increase in the frequency and role of UN peace keeping missions has been caused by conflicts where ready availability of lethal weapons is a significant factor. Unfortunately, although this problem assumed acute proportions by early 1980s, and the superpowers left a great deal of such weaponry as a debris of the cold war they were prosecuting for four decades, the Secretary General's *Agenda for Peace* (1992) did not even mention the issue except in a passing reference in the follow on report of January 1995.[15] It is difficult to visualize effective measures for maintaining international peace and security today without a concerted attempt at dealing with the problem of proliferation of small arms and light weapons.

The world has been witnessing a phenomenal spread of small arms and light weapons during the past two decades. This spread has resulted in an overwhelming measure as a result of the proxy wars prosecuted by the super (and great) powers during the cold war. And the post-cold war spurt in civil wars was boosted by the tremendous debris of the cold war strewn all across the world in the shape of nearly 3 million Kalashnikov type assault rifles, hundreds of thousands of other automatic weapons, hundreds of shoulder-fired surface-to-air-missiles of the Stinger variety, besides tons of sophisticated explosives. An early establishment of a register of small arms by the UN (on the pattern of the Register for Conventional Arms) would go a long way in enhancing transparency.

The UN represents an evolutionary process in the efforts of the international community to seek ways and means of establishing international peace and security through resolution and harmonization of the numerous conflicting demands of the international political architecture founded on the principle of sovereign nation-state system. The record so far has been mixed, and the actual functioning deviated a great deal from the goals and objectives set by itself in the beginning. The UN will need to review its Charter and functioning if it is to meet the challenges to international peace and security in the twenty-first century. Among a large number of measures needed for restructuring the United Nations, two fundamental needs stand out.

Firstly, the conceptual base for addressing the issues of international peace and security has to be constructed so as to harmonize the contradictions of the sovereign state system with national security needs. The attempts to find a solution in collective security, as has been sought so far, is unlikely to provide real solutions. What is needed is a paradigm shift from competitive security to cooperative security. The former is generated and reinforced by the concept of national sovereignty, a principle enshrined in the foundations of the UN. The UN cannot change the international system of sovereign states, but it also remains a static organization structured to meet past threats in accordance with the geopolitical framework of the past. There is a view that sovereignty is a dying concept and this process must be speeded up. The example of West Europe is the easiest to cite. If this was the trend, peace and security in former

Yugoslavia should have been easily found. Theoretically, of course, dilution of sovereignty should reduce the demand for national security at the expense of security of another state. But, in reality, it will have to be diluted to an extent of making the existing system of states irrelevant before governments will be ready to forego their national security interests. The United Nations, by definition is a state-centred organization. Its role in maintaining international peace and security will have to remain within this framework.

But what is feasible is to move inter-state security into a co-operative paradigm. This would require cooperation on matters of peace and security not only with friendly states, but more so with unfriendly and adversary states at progressively higher levels. The broad principles for such cooperation exist in the UN Charter. There have other attempts to define the parameters and basis for cooperative security.[16] The fact that a level of cooperation among the two superpowers had existed even at the peak of the cold war confirms that it is feasible to move along this direction, and that this would establish stability (absence of war) and peace on a more durable basis than the model of collective and competitive security that has been sought so far.

Secondly, it has been apparent for many years that changes in the Security Council will be necessary if the UN is to meet the demands of international peace and security in future. The central role of the Security Council will have to continue, but its present composition reflects the geopolitical order obtaining at the close of World War II. The UN, on the other hand, must be able to respond adequately to the challenges of peace and security not only in the 1990s, but the early decades of the twenty-first century at the very minimum. This demands a Security Council that reflects the geopolitical realities of the coming decades, and the General Assembly's resolutions to be treated with greater respect to ensure that democratic (and normative) deficits of the UN are removed.[17]

International political architecture had been evolving into a polycentric framework even before the cold war ended. It can be hypothesized that this was an important factor in the demise of the cold war confrontation. The international order is likely to move towards multipolarity over a period of time. But this is also likely to bring about polarization in the international community. This is not likely to be helpful in the management of international peace and security even if provides a level of stability. The end of cold war has etched out the contours of the polycentric geopolitical order more clearly. There is a need, therefore, for the Security Council to transform into a structure that is more representative. It is obvious that countries like Japan, Germany, and India have to be included among the permanent members of the Security Council at an early date.[18] However, this cannot be the total list and the restructuring of the Council should be based on an objective criteria. The question of veto will have to be decided on the basis of equity among the permanent members, and the use of veto should be restricted only to enforcement provisions where military force is sought to be applied against the member state. There is also a need for greater public accountability of the UN, especially the Security Council and the requisite checks and balances in an institution where 'No organ exists that can call the Council to account under the rule of law to protect the interests of members, or to protect other persons with no voting power, or to protect the long-term interests of law itself'.[19]

Diffusion in the relative capabilities among significant powers was in evidence over the previous decade; and this was also manifested in the growing tri-lateralism of US-Japan-West Europe (with Germany central to it). The disintegration and collapse of the USSR expedited the rearrangement and realignment in the international political architecture towards a polycentric system. The end of the cold war marks the growing importance of centres of power (like Japan, Germany, and India), who have not built up their national strategies around military power and its projection as an instrument of policy. Going by conventional wisdom about attributes of national power, the half-a-dozen leading powers in the coming years would be the USA, Japan, European Union, India, China, and Russia. In this polycentric constellation of the global system, two states do not possess nuclear weapons. The current five permanent members of the UN Security Council also happen to be the five recognized nuclear weapon states. If non-nuclear weapon states like Japan and Germany, are admitted as permanent members of the UN Security Council, a profound shift away from military power as the central actor in the power and strategic, calculus would take place, especially since the UN offers new opportunities to improve international peace and security in future.

In the final analysis, it is clear that a comprehensive approach to reforms in the UN system are needed. Prime Minister Ingvar Carlsson of Sweden had cautioned that 'There is a risk, though, that changes would be made piecemeal in a way which would leave the United Nations much the same as it is now, and which would not address some of the urgent security demands of these closing years of the century.'[20] The organization will have to remain state-centred and managed by governments for a long time to come. The concept of 'strengthening' the UN has been proposed to overcome some of the existing deficiencies.[21] The key to reforms does not lie in merely tinkering with it under the rubric of 'strengthening' it. While some aspects require strengthening, there is a need for some basic changes. For example, the UN must set for itself a goal for abolishing war and armed conflict. As it is, war as an instrument of state policy is losing its nineteenth-century rationale and cannot be sustained into the twenty-first century. But what is needed is to move beyond that to ensure that norms against use and threat of use of force, by states or non-state actors, are strengthened to ensure durable and comprehensive international peace.

Conclusion

We can draw some broad conclusions related to the nature of the international order and its evolution in the coming years:

(i) The cold war was certainly bipolar in nature and content. But the international order during the cold war was not rigidly bipolar and its bipolarity was moderated by independent policies pursued by countries like India and France. There has been an inevitable uncertainty after the bipolarity of the cold war ended a decade ago.

(ii) There is a need to vector the international order toward a non-polarized non-hegemonic polycentric framework. Current trends indicate that the international order, in fact, is moving toward such a framework.

(iii) In order to sustain a polycentric international order it would be necessary to reform international institutions like the UN in consonance with the transformation taking place.

(iv) A paradigm shift from the traditional competitive security model in existing for a long time would be required. Cooperative security paradigm needs to be established at the global, regional and bilateral level constructed on sound principles of mutual and equal security which seek increasing levels of cooperation among potential adversaries.

(v) Transnational cooperative action is required against transnational challenges to peace, security and human development.

In specific, an international coalition needs to be built up against transnational terrorism and transnational crime (like narcotics trafficking).

(vi) Respect for sovereignty of states must continue to remain the central principle of inter-state relations, and intervention in the internal affairs of sovereign states should be carefully calibrated under the legitimate authority and organization of the UN.

NOTES

1. Subimal Dutt, *With Nehru in the Foreign Office*, Calcutta, 1977, p. 22.
2. Jawaharlal Nehru, *Discovery of India*, Bombay: Asia Publishing House, 1966 rpt., pp. 575, 579.
3. Jawaharlal Nehru, *India's Foreign Policy: Selected Speeches, September 1946-April 1961*, New Delhi, 1961, pp. 2-3.
4. Nehru, *India's Foreign Policy*, p. 2. See also his speech on 13 December 1946, in *Jawaharlal Nehru's Speeches*, vol. 1, pp. 5-16.
5. *Jawaharlal Nehru's Speeches*, vol. 1, p. 241.
6. Vattel in *Laws of Nations*, cited by Sir Basil Liddell Hart, *The Sword and the Pen*, London: Book Club Associates, 1978, p. 85.
7. Geoffrey Treasure, *The Making of Modern Europe 1648-1780*, London: Metheum, 1985.
8. Erich Ludendorff, in *The Nation at War*, cited by Liddell Hart, op. cit., n. 12.
9. W.F. Craven and J.B. Cate (eds), *The Army Air Forces in World War II*, Chicago: University of Chicago Press, 1948.
10. Lee Kennett, *A History of Strategic Bombing*, New York: Charles Scriber, 1982.
11. Bruno Simma, ed., *The Charter of the United Nations: A Commentary*, Oxford University Press, 1994, pp. 9-10.
12. Istvan Kende, op. cit., n. 17.
13. See Prashant Dikshit, 'Proliferation of Small Arms and Minor Weapons', *Asian Strategic Review 1992-93*, New Delhi: IDSA, 1993, pp. 205-31.
14 *Landmines: A Deadly Legacy*, New York: The Arms Project, Human Rights Watch, 1993.
15 Boutros Boutros-Ghali, *Agenda for Peace 1995* (2nd edn), New York: United Nations, 1995.
16. See the Panchsheel agreement between India and China, 27 June 1954; the Simla Agreement between India and Pakistan, 2 July 1972; India-China agreement on maintaining peace and tranquillity on the borders, 18 December 1988, and mutual and equal security agreement of September 1993. For one outline of cooperative peace and security, see *Towards a New Asia*, Report of the Commission for a New Asia, 1994, pp. 11-19.
17. J.D. Sethi recommended some changes in the statute to rectify this. See J.D. Sethi, 'A Broken Totality', in U.S. Bajpai, *Forty Years of the United Nations*, New Delhi: Lancer International, 1987, p. 38.

18. Coral Ball, 'The Fall and Rise of the United Nations', in Coral Ball, ed., *The United Nations and Crisis Management: Six Studies,* Canberra: Strategic and Defence Studies Centre, 1994, p. 16.
19. Jose E. Alvarez, 'Me Once and Future Security Council', *The Washington Quarterly,* 18:2, Spring 1995, p. 18.
20. Ingvar Carlsson, 'Roles for the UN in International Security After the Cold War', *Security Dialogue*, vol. 26 (1), pp. 7-18.
21. Anthony Parsons, *From Cold War to Hot Peace,* London: Michael Joseph, 1995, pp. 244-60.

DISCUSSION 1

Participant: I have one question for any of the two speakers. First of all, Jean-Marie, you raised so many issues and so many ideas that I am tempted to reduce the complexities of your talk to something simpler, as you yourself recommended. Do I understand you correctly if I say that in your view, multipolarity will work in the sense of a world more peaceful and more stable only if there is some kind of redefinition of power in international politics, and if such is the case, how do you think the countries are able to implement these redefinitions? This is the question I had for you. Now concerning Mr Calleo. You described, at the very beginning of your talk, the United States as an indispensable nation and I would like to say that I tend to agree with this definition, and coming from a French citizen, I am sure you will appreciate that. The reason why I tend to agree, is that if one only imagined the world without America or if one would imagine what would have been the end of the cold war with either Russia or China as arena, this is certainly not a world I would have preferred myself. Now with this kind introduction I have a question which is less kind. There is something I never understood in the American Foreign Policy since the end of the cold war and this is related to your relation with this country. I never understood why since the end of the cold war, Washington has never articulated the very simple sentence that India will become a grand democracy, a major democracy, may be in the next century—I mean, this century—the major stable pole in the world to come.

Participant: I think I have an observation-linked question to both the speakers. The first speaker would like to continue the discussion from the earlier session about what our understanding of the free market economy is. It seems to me that whether we discuss either unipolarity or multipolarity, the coming future for the world system is envisaged in terms basically of a market system as opposed to a state, intervening state-controlled economy, which was characteristic of an earlier phase or global economic development. But an understanding of a free market economy seems to me that there is one extreme view where the government and the state find virtually no role whatsoever. As it was pointed out in the morning that if the Third World is not getting enough capital flows commensurate to its requirements even after multipolarity has developed, then it is the responsibility of Third World policies alone. I think that this view of a free market economy is probably slightly at variance with the way the weaker half of the world-views the transitions to a market system. And there again, one would like to know whether institutional finance has a role to play in this free market system or not. Certainly, whether the IMF and the World Bank or the Asian Development Bank would be able to make loans as I said in Euro and Yen or only in Dollar. It is just a very symptomatic question, still to be answered. To the next speaker, the other question: The US has seen previous periods of boom, the post-Second World War period, of the US economy in my view was a tremendous period of growth. And, at the same time, it was a period in which Japanese competition was developing alongside. So that after a number of years, i.e. after about 15 or 20 years of such growth, suddenly the US found that while it was a much more self-sufficient part of the world economy, the Japanese companies were able to offer a sort of competition which the American companies started complaining about, the whole negotiation between Japan and the US and the whole question of tariffs being used to protect American industry. At the same time, I think there are many American companies who are much more alert, who have learnt, in a view, the lessons from the past and who are not prepared to see this as salvation in itself, who are prepared to see that there is much more competition around the corner and that is why we see this process of merger. I think one of the major factors determining global investments today is what are known as mergers, capital moving from one place to the other in search of larger company sizes, larger mergers. And, I think, this has a particular relevance for Third World countries. They can hope to benefit from this process in a way that previous periods of US isolationism did not help them to benefit. So I think would we look at this process of globalization, which is going on simultaneously with the growth of the US economy, as perhaps a new phase of development in the system of multipolarity.

Participant: I have two quick questions. The first one is: Does it really make sense to think about the polarity issue on a global level? In fact, if one looks at it, the experience of most states is that it is the local great power distribution of power which really matters. So that, in Latin America it has always been fairly painfully clear that there is only one power, that is, the United States and it has always been a kind of unipolar system for the Latin. In Europe, we have had, during the cold war, a classical bipolar system with the Soviet Union and the United States. In parts of Africa, France was, in effect, perhaps the only power. In Southern Africa during the seventies, there were three or four powers that were the most important. In most of Asia, from 1949 onwards, it has almost always been a tripolar system; the Chinese, the United States and the Soviet Union being the primary powers. One could go on. In that sense nothing much seems to have changed after the cold war. Every region has, in effect, in the most practical sense of foreign policy very different configurations of great power relations to deal with. So, my first question to either panelist is in effect: Isn't it better to really see a far more differentiated broken up discontinuous world? The second question is on the issue of multipolarity, which presumably is at least a normative goal that we all like. Surely this does depend on whether China stays united and continues to accrue power, whether Japan gives up its kind of self-abnegation of power, whether the European Union coheres in foreign policy and security policy, whether Russia comes back, as it were, from the ashes and not least whether India sustains economic growth and develops its military potential. So it seems to me that in respect of those 4 or 5 units or entities, at least prima facie, the trends don't look very good so that multipolarity really looks quite distant.

Participant: I fully agree with the idea that if we do not redefine power, indeed, the multipolar world can be a very dangerous world. One can see power as a way to move up in the pecking order of nations and to have control and domination over other nations, to be the dominant power, for instance, in one region. This is a hierarchical view of the world. That view of power, I think, leads us to disaster. When we talk about the Europe that has to be a power, there is an ambiguity in that expression that I think I ought to clarify here. I think when we say, we, the French, want Europe that has power, I think, we see it as an aspiration, a democratic aspiration. Power is needed if you want to have control over your own future. If you have no power, you are dependent without having any way to assure mutual interdependence. So, I think, power is legitimate when it is the expression of a democratic aspiration not to use power, then, in a sort on unlimited way, which brings us back to the first definition of power but in a self-constrained, organized way whereby power is a way to share responsibility with others. So, I think, the key word here is the idea of power with the idea of responsibility. The more power you have, the more responsibility, free market and the state. I am not by profession a specialist of development in economics, so I will tread cautiously on that issue. But what I would like to say is that, I think in all our countries we see, we witness a redefinition of the respective role of state and market. We are convinced and not just the Europeans, I think, the Americans would also agree with that, that there is no free market without an efficient state. The free market is not the law of the jungle, nobody or very few people believe that. A free market requires institutions, requires enforcement so that market is not abused, dominant position, etc. In the EU for instance, the EU Commission plays a very important institutional role in making sure that the free market functions in an equitable way. That being said, there is an agreement in, I think, that the idea of competition that we first tested in the democratic process is good. Indeed, this is also in the economic area and in a way it is good in the political arena in the sense that institutions, up to a point, may compete with each other. And, in the EU, we accept the idea that we are not building a sort of super government of the EU but there is a measure of competition between the various nations within the agreed framework of the EU. The political question becomes: What level of competition, for instance, is acceptable and what level is not acceptable? That is a political issue. Now, if I broaden the perspective to look at the global picture, I think that when we look at the future of the economics of development, we see a big role for non-governmental forces, for independent forces. Private capital flows have a major role to play. In a country like India which has the assets of democracy and a functioning legal system and a very well trained elite, the problem is quite different from countries where there is no legal functioning system. You can much more easily get into the world capital market here than in many countries. I think one has to differentiate. There are countries in the developing world which need a much more active involvement of governments to bring capital there because the private forces will not trust the legal system in the country to move it. With a country like India, the case is different and I think the kind of negotiations we must have is where political institutions can play a role is the mutual opening of markets which, of course, is in our best long-term interests on both sides but since it is, in fact, quite different on particular segments of the economy, you can have contingencies here or there which see the short negative aspects of that opening up of markets. But when I think of the economic relationship between India and Europe I think it is in the mutual opening of the market at various levels. I would add one last point. A difference has to be made between the opening of the markets for goods and the capital market. An economist, actually a famous Indian economist, a professor at Columbia, Mr Bhagwati, a great promoter of free trade, has made the point and he is not suspect of being a protectionist, has made the point that there are specific constraints for capital markets. I think when we look into the future in that respect we should take that into account. Poles and regions, I think I disagree, Latin America and the cold war, the support to military regimes by the United States was linked obviously to the cold war. In Africa, up to a point, South Africa, it was the same issue so I think as the cold war ended there is much more flexibility, much greater margin for manoeuvre, for the better, for the worse sometimes. I don't want to come back to what I was saying, but I think there is a difference.

Prof. Calleo: The idea that United States should leave Europe, as a good American European, seems to me an unpleasant prospect. Of course, the United States does have a continuing role in Europe. Why have we never articulated the importance of India? I am not a great expert on this topic. All I can say is wait till the President comes. I don't really have anything to add to what Jean-Marie Guehenno said about the importance of the state and free markets and so on. I would like to point out something I didn't mention. One of the reasons American business is so strong at the moment is because it did go through a terrible time in the 1980s, a period when interest rates were sky rocketing, the Dollar was very high and so on. It was a kind of purgatory for American corporations and I think they learnt a great deal from that period. One of the reasons that many American companies are very strong is because of that experience. Arguably, Europe has been through something of the same nature through the 1990s and particularly the requirements for getting rid of fiscal deficits in order to install the Euro. Mergers, on the other hand, seem to be another question. There are many fads in business as everything else and seems to me that not too long ago we were saying to ourselves we were clever enough not to have such large mergers any more because they are essentially unmanageable. It remains to be seen whether this present enthusiasm for these colossal mergers is, in fact, wise from a managerial or economic point of view. Perhaps, it is my imagination, but I simply can't believe that there are too many companies in the world worth 100 billion Dollars or whatever. So I am rather suspicious of these mega mergers. I think there is another point which hasn't been brought up while we are talking about these economic questions which should be for purposes of general honesty all-round. There is a large opposition in the United States, which is growing through trade with Asia and this has to do with the labour question. Seattle, after all, was not in a developing country so the groups which came to Seattle to demonstrate against the WTO were essentially American unions who were becoming increasingly troubled by the prospect that there would be direct competition between labour in the United States and labour in India or China. So, you have all these little games about freedom of workers, freedom to organize, all these things which are, in a sense, protectionist measures. They may have other virtues but they are also designed to protect. Now, this is a case where complete free trade obviously cannot be allowed to prevail. It won't prevail and rather than pretend, which only parliaments can do it at will, it is better to try and make a kind of political arrangement which is in everybody's interest but something like that will I think have to happen. On the point that the prospects for this consolidation of these regional systems is less than brilliant in some cases, we might not have and even Europe may not succeed in these big ambitions to form a European bloc, let alone recreating some kind of system like that in Asia in the long run or indeed even the big individual Asian countries may not succeed as well as they would like. China itself may come apart, etc. Doesn't that mean that the unipolar world will remain? I guess my answer is, if all those things go wrong, the unipolar world won't mean much either. It is not as if the United States is a sort of world manager by default and any problem which anyone else can't take care of, we somehow will. In fact, such a world will be completely ungovernable by the United States or by anybody else and this will have little to do with our own views about these things. But even if we were determined to become the Roman Empire, which is I try to suggest here we are not, we would not be able to deal with that kind of breakdown. Now this whole question of tripolar Europe and Russia is a large topic which I perhaps wisely decided to leave out of this talk. The linkage is essentially what Mr François-Poncet mentioned this morning. The United States will increasingly be caught up in trying to maintain some kind of regional balance in Asia. And this does mean primarily a balance with China, with the ideal arrangement of some kind of cooperative security system in which China is involved itself rather than some recreational bipolar conflictual relationship. But whether that idea will be achieved, who can say. But, in any case, even China is already a major or semi major nuclear power and has every capability of becoming a more serious one if it chooses. By serious, in this case I mean able to attack the United States directly and again as Mr François-Poncet mentioned this morning when that situation develops then the level of danger for the country which is extending nuclear deterrents to others increases enormously and we wiggle and squirm about how to reduce that danger as we did also during the cold war in Europe and the solution which we came to is flexible response, that is to say not being put in the situation where the only response we have to an aggression is to start a nuclear war when we know a nuclear war will mean an attack on the homeland. This is a pastiche which no country, no matter how imperial it may be in its mentality, can contemplate with equanimity. In that situation you look for conventional options which is what is meant by flexible response. The problem with this is that it costs a great deal of money, especially if you have to maintain large military forces an ocean away from your own homeland. So you need allies to get into all the territory, which will presumably be discussed tomorrow. If you look around for allies in Asia, Russia is an obvious candidate. Russia is a country which is very exposed to China, which has an enormously rich territory, which doesn't have too many people in it, which has been invaded demographically by the Chinese, at least the Russians think so. And, therefore, Russia is a sort of natural ally. As this Asian past becomes more important for the United States over a period of time, then the policy of the United States in Europe of recent years, that is to say, not just NATO enlargements but the sort of NATO enlargements we have pursued an open ended enlargement, today Poland, tomorrow maybe Ukraine, the Baltic States and so on, combined with a great deal of military activity in Central Asia and the Caucuses and so on, seems a policy almost calculated to enrage the Russians. So we have managed by this policy of strategic dissonance, you might say, to alienate in Asia the most obvious ally in the pursuit of this policy of NATO expansion in this particular fashion inside Europe. This doesn't seem to be even for a policy as disconnected, even for a country as disconnected as we are. This is not a policy which will endure and where it leads to an appreciation of the importance of bringing Russia into some European system, making peace with Russia and Europe and this involves probably a retreat of the United States from its overwhelming predominance in this NATO system into what we were talking about earlier, a much more self-sufficient Europe, a NATO which is in itself organized to encourage European military self-sufficiency. Now I don't think this goes to the extent of talking about an American withdrawal from Europe. It is not as is often said, that Europe is somehow much less important to the United States than Asia. That is not true. But, it is true no doubt, that in Asia, there is no indigenous structure like the European Union or even like NATO, which will permit the United States to take a much lesser role and, therefore, the United States will be drawn more and more to Asia; not because Asia is more important but more necessary. In Europe, this move, this point stored if the world is rational and, of course, often it is not, especially in Europe. This point stored, I guess, is a tripolar Europe in which Russia, the United States and the European Union are present in a common pan-European system. The Americans have a role to play, even if it is rather a passive one as a kind of reinsurance treaty against a resurgence of some kind of aggressiveness in Russia, which, after all, is not totally impossible. And indeed, against the resurgence of aggressiveness on the part of anybody in this European complex, there is a German problem still in Europe, which has nothing to do with the wickedness of the Germans but does have something to do with the fact that Eastern Europe is very weak, Russia is very weak and so there is a vacuum there. Again, the United States can play a certain stabilizing role in preventing these fears and competitions from getting out of hand. For that reason, I think, a tripolar Europe is in everybody's interest.

Participant: I have a question for both our speakers today. Why is it that since morning, whenever we have referred to pole or poles, the references have been restricted to a nation or a group of nations? Why is it, for example, that we haven't really spoken of whether or not certain conglomerates, which have risen or about to rise would not constitute interesting poles themselves? Particularly after the AOL Times Warner merger, there is a feeling that could possibly constitute a different kind of a pole and have an impact elsewhere. Secondly, we have not really discussed pan-national terrorism. High tech terrorism is again, one of the poles that is going to guide the destinies of the planet, whether we want it or not. Religious extremism is yet another incipient kind of a pole in the making and sometimes religious extremism cuts across nations to constitute a certain amount of threat to all kinds of things we have been talking about. And, finally, we haven't really focused attention on a whole brand of activity which is behind the scene so to speak about the black economy or the parallel economy which is fuelled by crime, drugs, arms and so on and so forth. Does this enter into the picture at all in this overall discussion of what multipolar would mean in the years to come?

Participant: I take off from what Mr Guehenno and what Kanti Bajpai said, which is something awfully important. We need to be really looking at even the risk of being slightly theoretical in some places. The question is: Is the world as unipolar as it looks? I got the answers, but let me make my comment on that. Yes and no. There is unipolarity that United States exercises whether you explain that in terms of realism, imperialism or a combination of whatever else we can put through, but there is also multilateralism which exists between the European nations, United States, Japan and the US allies. It is a multipolar world or a much smaller world than the real world but it exists. So, in a way, the United States in its unipolarity is supported by at least 24 developed countries in a process of multipolarity. Now, whatever name you want to give it and that cuts across the globe and that is not recent in that sense. Let me give two examples of that. Are we talking about a world where x number of powers will have their zones of influence and control? Is India ready to create a zone of influence around itself, not necessarily geographically so, but in the world and then to deal with the others? Where do the lesser smaller countries as powerful countries, however large they may be, fit into this construct? But, more important than this will a multipolar world unlike a bipolar world, be non-hegemonic or hegemonic? The question is: who will exercise the hegemony? So, instead of one country or source or a set of countries exercising their hegemony, are we suggesting that there will be multiple countries in a multipolar world which would exercise hegemony. The second question is, in fact, which Mr Guehenno himself raised on the question of stability. Can a multipolar world remain non-conflictual? It is constructed on the basis of the theory of a pole and a balance of power amongst the poles. Thirdly, can a multipolar world avoid the risk of movement towards increasing polarization, either towards, once again, a bipolarity or intensifying a multipolar competition and conflict? I think these are fundamental points that we need to be thinking about and that is what raises a lot of doubts in my mind in tune with what Mr Guehenno says, except that my answers are not the same as his. I will give some answers tomorrow, but at the moment I want to be as brief as I can because the question then comes in, is where does sovereignty fit into the multipolar construct? We need to be very careful before we write off sovereignty or start diluting it as an institutional process, because for most of the world it is not just a question of any one set of countries, although there is a very clear example of those set of countries. Europe is coming together increasingly into a European Union where a supranational sovereignty is being established, not at a cost of a national sovereignty but by the willing surrender of national sovereignties in selected areas by coming together into a larger one. But the decision is a sovereign decision. It is not forced by any other system which is a different issue then sovereignty being subjected or subjugated by the sheer fact of another power trying to impose its will on another set of countries. What we are looking at, then, is a framework where what we argue otherwise. What I heard this morning and in the afternoon was a more democratic international order. Even in a democracy there are leaders, so it is not a question of what framework we adopt or what is the nature of the functioning of that leadership. There are democratic leaders who have been known in the world to act as dictators and dictators who have been known to act democratically. So, I think, we need to actually look at this framework as to what is it that we are looking for under a label or under a flag of a multipolar world because there a series of interpretations that can actually come through. My last little point on this is that are we looking for multipolarity or are we looking for multilateralism?

Participant: I really think a couple of comments of Air Commodore Jasjit Singh were right on the head as it were. I really feel that we need to, in some ways, define what we mean by a pole. If we use a definition of military significance, a militarily significant cluster of units as a working definition, in some ways, almost needs to reflect where the concept of the pole comes from, where does the concept of the pole really enter the discipline of international relations. It really comes from physics and electromagnetism. Now that is true if indeed around the concept of the pole there is a certain sense, the sense that Air Commodore Jasjit Singh also mentioned the notion of attractional/repulsion then almost by definition a polarity cannot be a singularity. In that sense then, to talk about a unipolar world is almost nonsensical by definition. Any militarily significant cluster of units would, in time, create at least one opposing cluster if not more. So that would be one way in which we could approach this whole question. I think there is another fascinating way one could look at this whole question of poles. I was fascinated about the description about the web-site page under construction on multipolarity because if you were to look at what the Pentagon says, they are really dividing the world into four category of states. These are the core states; the core really being liberal democratic capitalist states, there are the transition states, those states that are in some way making a transition to the core; there are the rogue states those states that are willy-nilly absolutely opposed to the interest of the core and then there are the failed states, those states that are not able to do the basic functions of the state. Look at this kind of US state on how the international system has in some ways, how the state in the international system can be classified after the end of the cold war. It is quite fascinating, this is a definition that has ultimately very little to do with military capability or any other type of capability. In other words, we are not looking at all at militarily significant clusters of units or any such thing. What we are looking at is ideas here, it is almost a kind of notion like at the end of history, the triumph of liberal democracy, the notion that really, at the ideational level, there is no challenge to the liberal democratic idea. All that you can see is states, at their own pace, cohering to their core. Some might take their time doing it, some very large states like China, Russia and India being transition states or Brazil for that matter, all the more important because they shouldn't become rogues obviously. But there is a certain cluster of ideas that, in some ways, has already won the war. My only point is, is this really so and I would like both the speakers to reflect on that, the notion there is a thesis now that dominates and this thesis really cannot produce an antithesis like the theses in the past have.

J.M. Guehenno: These are very difficult questions. I think there is one set of questions which is about poles. In my presentation, I made the point that we should question the notion of a pole the end of one pillar changing the nature of the other pillar and by implication this is the very idea of a pole. The third question is the appearance of non-governmental actors. It might be more fruitful to look at the notion of power, the various aspects of power rather than the idea of a pole which prejudges that power is organized in a certain type of entity. But there are various facets of power, which means, the states are not disappearing but they are in competition with new actors which, is as I said for Europe, a good thing if it challenges to improve their ways. At the same time, you need institutions if you want to precisely organize power and introduce the idea of legitimacy. And that brings me to the set of issues brought by Jasjit Singh. I am not sure I am going to answer all his questions. First, on the nuclear issue, I would say that we, all the nations of the world—India, France, countries that have no nuclear weapons, all the nations of the world today have a stake in the success of non-proliferation, that nuclear anarchy is in the interests of nobody. We are in a very complex situation where you have a non-proliferation treaty that should not be opened without getting the system unraveled. We have other treaties on the contrary like the CTBT that can be joined without rocking the boat in any way, that can prove the strengthened as they are if the membership is broadened. But the fundamental point is there that we have to strengthen the legal order in terms of nuclear affairs. We all know the complexities of the nuclear order that I just mentioned, so we have to work around that but I think it is in the interests of all of us for the stability of the world that there is not a multiplication of proliferation. Each of us has his own strategic circumstances and we have our opinion of what is right and what is wrong, but that is what it is. What is essential for the future is that we move in that narrow path where we do not destroy what exists in terms of legal order frameworks. Sometimes they are formal treaties, sometimes they are arrangements that depends on the political circumstances. We have not been able to go all the way on all fronts but I think it should be understood in India that there is a difference there. Then the idea that Europe on that matter will be just sort of led by the United States is completely wrong. On the non-proliferation issue, we have a lot at stake in Europe on those matters, which is agreed with some aspects of American policy, we think it is extremely unhelpful that the US Senate has not ratified. We have our differences with the United States and we tell them very frankly that we have those differences but we have one common objective which, I think, we share with you as responsible countries who want a stable order which brings me to the broader point on hegemony and can a multipolar world, or, will a multipolar world be more conflictual or not. Hegemony brings us back to the question raised by power. I think, if we had around this table a representative of Belgium or the Netherlands, he would tell you how institutions have been essential in equalizing power, not that Belgium has as much influence on European institutions than France has or Germany has, but the Belgians or the Dutch—and I don't think any citizen of this country will contradict me, the Belgians and the Dutch—feel they have a say in their future because they are members of the European Union and this organization has not been created to impose the power of a few big European countries over the smaller ones. It has been a way to integrate and equalize power between the various countries. Institutions, when they are well defined, can accommodate differences in an acceptable way. That is what we should work at. And, I think, if we do not build that kind of institution we will be heading towards a very conflictual world where big powers will think their power is just their created zone of influence. The last question: Multipolarity or multilateralism? I have no hesitation, I think it is multilateralism because it is precisely the organization of the permanent negotiation on a variety of issues where we create our own constraints. There we come to this problem of sovereignty. I think we really have to agree on principles where there are procedures to adjudicate differences in the World Trade Organization. We may discuss the principles, we may even disprove them, but the idea that they are procedures through which we adjudicate is essential. I think we have to work towards that, otherwise it is going to lead us towards a vicious circle of unilateral measures which are in the interest of nobody. But even multilateralism can be a fraud. As we all know, there can be multilateral organizations in which one country is predominant or a group of countries is predominant and the others are just forced to go along, no matter what the structure is. So, a European miracle is something different. It is, as I said earlier, a practice of formulating national zones, with the interests of neighbours in mind. This is a kind of political miracle in a sense that the Europeans have managed to do this. It doesn't mean there is no conflict amongst the European states. Obviously, there is a great deal of friction among the European states and it doesn't mean incidentally that there is no balance of power. The European Community, I think, has many subtle balances within it and there is always the right of revolution so to speak, the right of small states who feel they are being pushed around and they suddenly start to alienate in a very negative way. It is something like the European structure. Every region will have to have its own version of these things. The European structure has taken a long time to develop. That is the model for us, for Americans in our own continent, with our own neighbours and perhaps a model in Asia as well.

Participant: I am a retired government officer. I would submit that in a multipolar world the concerned powers have to behave like poles if they are to attract influence and attract power. And I would try to relate this to France in particular. Rightly or wrongly, we in South Asia have the perception that France is obsessed with Africa and turns a more or less blind eye towards the needs of Asia and particularly, South Asia. This perception is reinforced to some extent by treaties like the Convention which allows duty-free import of African goods into the European Common Market and acts very much to our detriment. It seems to me that France should pay more attention to the problems of South Asia in particular because our problems are, in fact, really much more intractable than those of comparatively resource rich Africa. Our land to population ratio is enormous. We don't have much scope for improvement in the administrative practices unlike the African countries. France has got a very large and modern industrial base and I would submit that it would be desirable if France invested much more in India compared to say the UK or the USA. I don't think that France's record of foreign direct investment is particularly good. Peugeot walked in at Bombay and walked out again. Alcatel, at one time, was quite active in the telecommunications industry but it is no longer so. It seems to me that companies like Alstom and so on have a much bigger role to play compared, say with Siemens. Siemens has entered into agreements with BHEL and other companies and I was wondering why Alstom does not do the same thing. Similarly, Airbus industries and perhaps Mirage could collaborate with Hindustan Aeronauticals both with regard to aircraft parts and ground-to-air missiles and other armaments. I would submit that France is one of the unique countries which generates quite a substantial proportion of its power from nuclear energy and perhaps a worthwhile thing would be for the French industry to put up a nuclear power station on a build, operate, lease and transfer basis. This would help us and it would certainly also help the French nuclear industry. Finally, I have a question for the second panelist. I think he mentioned that the United States has built up a large external deficit and, as a corollary to that, he said that this may result in rather rocky prospects for the Asian exporters in the sense that the exports from Asia would dry up. May I pose the counter question that there's a lack of confidence in the American Dollar? And may it not also reflect on the strength of the Dollar? I would love to have your reactions on that.

Participant: I am an unemployed journalist sometimes masquerading as a scholar. I want to make one brief statement but I do want to preface it with a remark that I agree very broadly with most of what Mr Guehenno has said. I admire the lucidity with which he has said it except on one point where I noticed that in his very major presentation he suddenly got a little emotional. It is the nuclear issue. And if I may say so with all respect and great friendliness, I think that answer to Jasjit's question on the nuclear issue became a classic example of what hegemonism, not by one single country acting unilaterally, but by a group of countries acting together can be. When France was going nuclear, everybody was trying to tell them not to do so, it was a bad thing, we all wanted non-proliferation, etc., etc. The point I wish to emphasize is that if non-proliferation has any meaning, then it should be non-proliferation, not proliferation by the five privileged ones in which the French forget all their differences with the other four and certainly with the United States. This is the grandest illusion that you can have of non-proliferation in this world while the five nuclear weapon powers can go on holding on to their nuclear weaponry in perpetuity and go on talking, go on refusing. The world would be certainly a better world with no nuclear weapon at all. We will be delighted if France joins us to start an initiative towards that. Let the French, as a nuclear power, do what the South Africans did. Let them say we built the nuclear weapons in a different kind of a context, now the context has changed, non-proliferation is important. It is regrettable that other nuclear weapon powers are not agreeing to a total elimination of nuclear weapons, we take the initiative and we are destroying our nuclear weapons. I will applaud it and I will certainly accept that non-proliferation is important, not until then.

Participant: As I spoke in the morning, I have only two points to make. I think the afternoon discussion has been pretty sophisticated and I attach a lot of importance to the statements which came from our French colleague, that in a situation of globalization and interdependent economies, can there be a unipolar world? Isn't there a basic contradiction between the two? Thereby hangs many a question. One of them is: Are we not in a transition period where a multipolar world is emerging? Secondly, I want to cite two examples to you, for how important American hegemony or superpower is. I was speaking, two days ago, to a very senior Japanese diplomat and we talked about a possible flare-up in the South China Seas if the present incumbent in Taiwan declares independence. Will the Chinese intervene? They are committed to invade if there is a declaration of independence in Taiwan and suppose they do, what will Japan do? And he said categorically, 'I can assure you, Japan will not join that war. If there is a war between Taiwan and the mainland in which America is present, Japan will not be present.' 'But will you give logistic support?' I asked. He said, 'Yes, to a limited extent to meet the requirements of the security treaty but our joining, our bombing China or attacking China will be so unpopular in the country. It will be such an upheaval of public opinion that we cannot even think about it.' Now the Americans have been pressing us for a pretty long time to sign the CTBT and enter into a dialogue with Pakistan since the Kargil war and Clinton had made it very clear that this would be his two targets when he arrived here. A little while before his final departure from power, you will get nothing. We will get very little from them, I am sure about that. But he will not get it from India, which is not an economic giant and which has many economic problems, mass poverty, etc. But the Americans do not have the clout here that they can exact a price from us which we are not prepared to yield. That is the story about American hegemonism or unipolar world.

Participant: I was just wondering that in talking about multipolarity, multilateralism and so on and so forth, we seem to be getting into a theoretical discussion of models of international relations and getting away from the here and now, the realistic aspects of policy. What is the ends to which a multipolar world would address itself? I recall here Jean Kirkpatrick's very famous slant on what was more important in the early 1980s, whether it was democracy or order, and she said that order was more important. If order is what is to be achieved, if that is the end result that needs to be achieved, then the question is: What will achieve that goal better? Shouldn't that be the concern rather than worrying about the kind of international system that may eventuate? That is getting into abstractions and speculations and looking into the crystal ball which may be intellectually invigorating but not helpful. So, I suggest, in some sense, that perhaps the two panelists would address what it is that a future world order would seek to achieve.

Participant: I think there are questions here which, in fact, go back to ask what is the Chinese concept of multipolarity. Their concept of a multipolar world, I am sure, is quite different from the concept elsewhere. That is exactly why it is also necessary to at least look at some of the theoretical constructs on which one can build the practical side of it. Primakov came here and promptly talked about Russia, China, India strategic alliance. The Chinese had talked in Moscow about the strategic partnership in opposing hegemony. The Chinese have talked at length about multipolarity to oppose a hegemony. In all cases, the common denominator is the United States and, obviously, India has not given any indication that they are willing to join that type of multipolarity which is in opposition to another power or a set of powers. That really gets the defining issue then and I will go along much more with Mr Guehenno, rather than the issues of power. I talk more in terms of centres of powers and their relationship rather than multipolarity, because I have great difficulty, may be, in my two classes at school where I learnt some physics which I think of poles as something quite different. But there is a reality here that what are we meaning by this? In that context, Mr Guehenno, I say that there is a multipolarity that exists between the transatlantic alliance. It is a multipolarity. It is not a question of saying that Europe is a subgroup of the United States, but to say that there is a multipolarity operating there where even Belgium has a say. India may not have the same say in that matter because we are not part of that club, whatever the shape and form of the club may be. But why it is not part of the club is a different issue altogether. But then, when we are talking of it, are we creating a new club of multipolar world? In which case, what happens to the others? The OIC can turn around and say that they are multipolar in a different framework and you have to deal with the OIC and they have been active, not very influential, but active. OPEC is another multipolar grouping. So you can carry on. There are lots of these which are in a different form and shape.

Participant: I think it is a very interesting question and one I would like to respond to, because I think, in many ways, the Indian Foreign Policy has evolved at several levels. So, to me, as an independent nation state and a large one, the bilateral component has been important but India was the first country to choose to remain within the British Commonwealth and begin from there as far as multilateralism is concerned, the main country to build a non-aligned movement with Egypt and Yugoslavia as the core of the non-aligned movement and continue to do so. One of the main countries to move on the disarmament issues in the United Nations or build up the Group of 77 and so on and so forth. That so far the Indian effort has been to represent the developing world's point of view has certainly provided the real need to define a multipolar construct and that remains the project. After all, as I said in the first session, multipolarity must mean equality and prosperity for all and everybody tended to agree with that. It cannot be that only the European Union and NAFTA emerge as the biggest beneficiaries of a multipolar order, which is quite likely also to be the case and Russia and India and parts of Asia and Africa are left out of it. I think this is a very serious issue which those who are advocating a multipolar democratic world order should see that it is an inherently contradictory situation because some parts of the world are racing ahead, while other parts of the world are falling behind. That is not a multipolar world order. It has seeds of grave instability because now conflicts are getting interlinked. There are going to be perhaps more nuclear powers around and conflicts of this kind can be global, whereas the multipolar world is tending to be regional. What do we mean by multilateralism and the objects of multipolarity? The goals have to be common goals in many ways even though it is a multipolar world. To that extent, India's multilateralism can be understood in terms of that framework which does not contradict bilateralism but tries to build upon it towards common global goals.

Participant: France, Africa and Asia, the first question. I think France feels it has a responsibility *vis-à-vis* the countries where it was present for sometimes centuries, sometimes several decades. I would immediately add one thing that when I observe the way French business looks at the world today, I notice that it is mainly the French that still spend money in Africa because it feels that it can't let some of those countries down at the very delicate moment in their process of development and the French companies are investing all around the world: first in the OECD and then in Asia. The take off of investments in India has been a little behind the investments in other Asian countries. I think it is just on the verge of taking off and there is a rebalancing of perspectives that is taking place, that should make all of us rather optimistic. On the nuclear issue, I would say after the French there are two countries that have made significant moves reducing their arsenal as part of the fundamental bargain of the NPC, that is Britain and France. There has been a very significant reduction in the number of weapons. And I would add, when I look at India today, I think honesty has more to do with China and Pakistan than it has to do with the number of nuclear weapons that Britain or France have. I think few people would question that basic statement. So I think we are prepared to move along further in disarmament as the other nuclear countries move in that direction. We have taken a lead with Britain in that respect. We will go further when we see that there is a broader movement but it doesn't make sense today to do that sort of thing as we see that the key issue today is to kick start the process between the two superpowers in the nuclear area. So, I don't think that it is useful to point at us on that respect. In my opinion we must all work together constructively to see how we can manage this nuclear world so that nuclear weapons have less and less relevance and will be lesser and lesser symbols of status of a country. They were acquired by France in a particular strategic circumstance of the East-West confrontation, of the relationship with the linkage with the United States, the question on that linkage, the overwhelming threat of the Warsaw Pact. I am not going to give a history course on that. I think the trend is clear. We have to make the nuclear weapons less relevant. That does not mean that we are prepared to abandon them tomorrow. I think we will make the world safer and we will make the goal of a multipolar world central for security because there was a point on that but I think India and France are two great democracies, with great democratic traditions. So we should agree on one fundamental point, that order without legitimacy is not sustainable. That is a key point for a sustainable multipolar world. A sustainable multipolar world is a world where there are shared responsibilities and institutions that organize that responsibility. If we just live in a world where the weaker are crossed by the stronger, this leads to confrontation and war.

Prof. Calleo: I have little to add as I agree through the most part. There was a particular question about the Dollar and whether it is weak or strong depends a great deal on which formula is being used. The first point to make is that in many respects, as a participant said this morning, we, like the Europeans now with the Euro, don't really care very much whether the Dollar is weak or strong. Of course, there are people who benefit from the strong Dollar but there are also people in our economy who benefit from a weak Dollar for the usual reasons. As I say, whether the Dollar is weak or strong depends a great deal on the formula being used to finance deficits. If the deficit is reduced presumably, I guess it would strengthen the Dollar. Financing through debt also serves, all other things being equal to strengthen the Dollar because it requires higher interest rates and in flow of capital and so on which is the formula we have been using recently. The one thing that would weaken the Dollar, I suppose, is financing by inflation which we have also done in the past. We did it in the 1970s but as I say, up to a point anyway, this is not something we are particularly frightened of. Perhaps we should be. It may be that our policy has been much more inflationary than we think. What seems remarkable about the present world economy is, on the one hand the presence of an enormous mass of money floating around the world and the fact that somehow it seems insulated from effects upon real economies. A large part of it is, as you know, tied up in hedging of one sort or another, it is essentially a monster chasing its own tail. The trouble is, occasionally it breaks loose from these constraints and starts affecting exchange rates as we know. Then, of course, it does have real effects on real economies. So, it may well be that our stock market boom is financed not only by foreign money coming in but by an inflation in the United States. An inflation that is distributed, however, in such a way that it doesn't produce inflation in the way that we are used to seeing it, that is to say, higher prices or higher wages, instead of that it is asset inflation and certainly if you were looking for an example of asset inflation you might look at the stock market in the United States. Democracy or order is rather fundamental, especially in the nuclear world, especially if we are dealing with nuclear powers. We like to believe, as Mr Guehenno suggested, that there really can't be stable order that is illegitimate but, of course, an extreme is we know perfectly well that there can be order that is not legitimate. We don't think it can last and anyway, we don't want it if we can possibly avoid it. We want a society which is not only stable but democratic and has respect for rights, which is not necessarily the same thing as being democratic. And we also want societies that are prosperous. It seems to me idle to list these things in some kind of order. We basically want to have it all and any order which is seriously deficient in any of these things becomes unstable as well as undesirable. One last point about hegemony and leadership. In the real world, as we know perfectly well, there is always some form of hegemony. There is hegemony inside political systems, natural political systems. There is always a party or a coalition which, for the moment anyway, has the initiative in running the country. In groups of states there is also hegemony. The question is whether it is a civilized kind of hegemony, whether it is based on the consent of other people, whether it is recognized to have a kind of legitimacy or whether it is something more ugly and imposed by force.

Certainly, in this European construction that we have all been busy praising and recommending to everyone else, there is a form of hegemony. It is a highly complex combination of things. There is respect for the rights of smaller countries. It is a very civilized institution. Everybody talks forever in the European Union until finally people are sufficiently exhausted so they arrive at a solution. Small countries talk as much as anyone else and, therefore, have this sense that this is their institution and that they are taken seriously in it. There is also a very high degree of convergence among these member states. They do have interests which are very similar, that is not an accident, that is something that has been worked at over the course of several decades but there is also a kind of hegemony, there is leadership and it has come essentially from France and Germany in the sense that the two of them have taken on the task of managing Europe, which neither one of them was able to do by itself. That is a kind of hybrid hegemony, if you like, within this very civilized system. Arguably, there are limits to how far hegemony can extend. Final point, to go back to physics, you may come to chaos theory but beyond a certain size it is simply impossible for leadership to be very effective. That is another limitation on international organizations and on regional systems. They have to have many of these elements of convergence and they may take a long time to create. But they do need leadership.

Participant: I used to belong to the Foreign Service. I have not listened to the mornings discussion but for the afternoon's discussions I have the following responses. Order without legitimacy cannot be sustained. Point no.1. Legitimacy without objective criteria on the basis of unilateral declarations is not legitimacy, that was the basic point. Legitimacy has to be on the basis of objective criteria, equilibrium and justice in every dimension, that is my response. The second point which I wish to make is an attempt at self-evaluation. I think this tendency on the part of all of us from

Asia and India to constantly whine about certain iniquities to those who do not feel that those are iniquities, to me, is a futile exercise because it has no meaning and also because there are element on impulses and power equations whether they are unipolar or multipolar which govern attitudes and policies. If either we or the Asian countries are a mature and practical group of people, we should calculate what the implications are and try to act accordingly. My third point is an answer to our friend from Geneva. He asked whether India wants to be bilateral or multilateral. My response is that they are not mutually exclusive phenomena. In terms of national reactions from a country like India, the bilateral prism would be used for those objectives which we think will be best met through the bilateral processes and where multilateralism of whatever category, as Air Commodore Jasjit Singh mentioned, whatever category is. If it is useful, we will participate in the process. If it is detrimental to our interest, we would like to call to the process by creating competitive multilateralisms of one kind or the other. And let me remind the very distinguished audience that these highly theoretical phenomena are not static in nature, or content orientations where multipolarities will change. My last point is, the question was asked as to what kind of cross currents of influence, hegemony, what kind of multipolarity will govern international equations and national policies. My simple response is, those who have the money, those who have the resources, those who have the technologies and those who have the armed power, weapons systems, they shall dominate the world system. Where there is a complimentarity between people so endowed that multipolarity as it was rightly pointed out, there are hegemonies. This is an objective reality and in this context, the only other point I wish to make is that theoretically the demise of the nation state is going to be a slow process because the sense of self of collective entities as nations though sovereignty can be self-abnegated. It cannot disappear in terms of any theoretical models or external pressures beyond a certain point in the foreseeable future.

Participant: I must say that we have been listening to very wise and scholarly presentations by our two colleagues and I think they have brought out certain basic concepts relating to multilateralism, bilateralism, the bipolar world and the unipolar world. They have made it very clear that we have arrived at that stage of history now where the bipolar world has in a way ended and according to our

French colleague, the bipolar world was dangerous and immoral. So if it has broken up, the bipolar world, it follows that we are getting into a world which will be more moral and less dangerous. And I do not know whether this can be said and sustained at all but then, certainly, we are moving ahead. I think it was Kanti who said that we are entering into the world which is more broken and disconnected than we had inherited before the end of the cold war. That is a very important point which we have got to keep in mind. Proceeding from there, if the bipolar world has come to an end, where are we moving? This was a question that two of our colleagues and all of you handled. One was that we are going to be more unipolar or we will have a unipolar world. The second was that in some form, the bipolar world exists in certain areas. The third is that it will be a multipolar world. Now the first day we took up the question of unipolar world and they said immediately when you think of a unipolar world you think of a superpower and with the Soviet Union demise, America comes to your mind and you start thinking that when you are talking of the unipolar world you are really talking of the hegemony of one country. You call it a superpower. You call it the only power or global power, whatever that may be it is there. I think Mr Calleo told us in a very descriptive manner as to why it has become the most important power today. Because, if you look at it from the military point of view or the economic point of view or even the technological point of view, surely the answer is that America is that particular one power. Now, the question that they discussed was: Is the world proceeding in a particular direction? The answer which was given was no, because they pointed out as to how there are other forms of polarism appearing on the scene. The European model was given by everybody by saying that how a regional continental state, from the national state, it is moving into a continental state. How do you synthesize these with a globalization, the forces which are being activated by science and technology? I would rather say more by technology relating to communication and transportation. So the question is that how do you really synthesize the two. There they took up two important issues which I think are very vital. One: when you deal with a state the power becomes an important factor. The power of the state, if it is not distributed evenly, it cannot give you a balanced state in the multipolar world. And, therefore, one has got to see as to what is happening. I think a question of a state sovereignty also comes in there. I agree with you that the sovereignty will not disappear and Jasjit has also said about that particular thing but I think sovereignty is undergoing a big change. The qualitative change, the type of interventions which are taking place today, clearly shows that the sovereignty has receded to certain extent, there was a time when we openly used to say that you cannot interfere in the internal or the domestic affairs of the other countries but today we are seeing that such interventions are taking place. So, therefore, one will have to draw a line of limits where the sovereignty can recede but to what extent and how. The other important thing which was being said and is really worth consideration are the economic issues which were raised and market economy, liberal democracy and globalization. They definitely go hand in hand but the question arises as to what are some of the injustices which are born with a type of multipolar economic development which is taking place. I am not bringing monopoly or the other but certainly there are losers in this particular game and there are winners, so what do you do? I don't go into that question but I quote your Prime Minister in this particular regard when he says, 'Market economy, yes, but market society, no', which really means that you have got to concede this particular point that the forces of economic globalization are there but it has got also certain challenges before us as to what happens to those who are the losers in this knowledge game. We definitely concede this particular point that tomorrow's world is going to be the knowledge world. Tomorrow's worker is going to be the knowledge worker. Tomorrow's products are going to be the knowledge products. But, having said that, there would certainly be a class of people who will not be benefited by it as we would like them to. So, therefore, that particular question comes in and we have definitely got to consider. And you raised the third dimension of this particular triangle by saying that is unilateralism like it what appears to be. I think the answer is no. The second question which you raised was whether multilateralism was desirable. It is certainly desirable minus some of the problems which have been discussed around this particular table. Now the conditions which are necessary in order to make multilateralism more feasible and more acceptable to the world which will be the harbinger of peace and order in this particular society. You suggested that there have got to be institutions and synthesis between the regions of the globe. Absolutely correct. But here I would only draw your attention to what Havel said in his speech in America that until and unless there is a spiritual force which dominates, legality by itself will not solve the problem. Both of them have said that unless and until the ethical and moral concepts are grasped you will never be able to get the type of world that you are wanting only through mechanisms and institutions. Dr Heptulla ended her speech beautifully by reminding everyone of what Gandhi had said. Gandhi had said that ultimately, democracy, peace, prosperity will depend if the institutions are pushed on the rock of non-violence and truth. Now this might sound very abstract and, as Havel says that people might be ashamed of saying that I am for love and I am for friendship and I am for relationship, but he says those are the essential qualities which have got to be inducted in order if the institutions may work properly. So I would like to add that particular point to your presentation. The last point which I make would be, however good the whole system may be, unless and until you have leaders with a vision, you will never be able to achieve this because that is where the whole chemistry and the chemical action take place. It is this particular leadership and vision which is necessary to be emphasized and with that I would say today's discussions lead us to a very positive position in history, that we are moving towards more democracy, we are moving towards more multilateralism and though a multiculture always existed but it has existed side by side. It is the first time that there is a merger which is taking place between the nations and between the cultures and between the spiritual values which are being shared by most of the sensitive people interested in this particular game.

Multipolarity and International Security

Multipolarity and Security

RAJA RAMANNA

In the history of nations, the domination of a single power by virtue of enormous military and economic might has always given the impression that it is likely to last almost for ever. There have always been groups of nations who have dominated others by virtue of greater muscle power over considerable periods of time, mostly connected with economic exploitation usually under cover of evangelization. They have, however, disappeared on account of their own inherent weaknesses. In more recent times, the world has witnessed a bipolar assertion of power, based on nuclear strength. The countries concerned are large in size and have had enormous power of mass destruction. However, one of them being economically unstable, was unable to obtain its status and collapsed over a short period of time and this, in spite of the large nuclear arsenal it still possesses. The collapse of this system has now resulted in a unipolar world with all the attendant dangers that the situation will become both permanent and inevitable, unless there is a regrouping of the balance of power in the rest of the world.

The aftermath of the two world wars in the last century clearly pointed to the need of a global system for achieving sustained security. It was for this reason the League of Nations and later, the United Nations came into existence. The former failed miserably, as it was essentially a European creation with its justifications for an imperialist role. The UN, though it was created for a more universal and a balanced global role, because of the immediate needs of the period, specified that the five victorious countries of the World War II be given a special status having powers, without any time limit in its most important body, the Security Council.

In the first flush of the workings of the United Nations, it was expected that the veto powers would eventually go and the deliberations of the UN would be more transparent and evenly balanced. But this has not happened and in a sense the UN seems emasculated to the extent that nations have preferred to depend on military bodies like the NATO to implement their decisions. The NATO has all the semblance of a 'private' army of the past, and also has the highest possible striking power that it is greatly feared by many countries. It is hardly a satisfactory solution to the problems of the present world and if there are to be alternatives for the future, an analysis is required as to why unipolarity and 'private armies' have come into being.

Some of the difficulties the UN has had to face belong to a period even before its inception as a battleground between the superpowers. It became a regular feature of the cold war and continued until the collapse of the Soviet Union. During this period, the most tragic development that has come to pass, is that developing countries, which would have liked to be left alone, have been forced to take sides, for fear of the slogan 'that those who are not with us are against us'. This meant that the newer nations, which had yet to reach stability in the post-colonial period, had to face the possibility of an inner split. More often than not, it led to a highly involved, self-destructive arms race and ended up in a total subservience to one or either of the superpowers.

The cold war is over, but unipolarity has come to stay and all matters of importance have now to be approved by a single power, whose decisions are final as in a court of justice. As we shall see, unipolarity has serious consequences because of new developments taking place all over the world.

The forces that have come about, which complicate world stability, are the appearance of religious fundamentalism and state-sponsored terrorism. Fundamentalism and terrorism have always been there, but supported as they are, by drug trade and by states that are usually under military dictatorships, they have become a nefarious threat to all peaceful states. It is known that terrorists somehow manage to get the most sophisticated arms, which can only come from powerful countries. It has made the maintenance of law and order within law-abiding nations a difficult and expensive operation. By themselves, these forces would have died out, but for the fact that they have become pawns in the great power game and gained legitimacy in a unipolar world. Just as in the world of single human beings, even among countries, power breeds sycophancy and this has led to a weakening of international decision-making.

Over the centuries, countries have maintained their socio-cultural identities in some sort of equilibrium through checks and balances. Checks and balances derive their power from multiple sources. A single check suitable for one country or one aspect of a problem can be disastrous to another. A unipolar world, however well it is informed, tends to destroy this. The world has had enough experience of a totalitarian system forcing itself on others even in our own lifetimes, resulting in tearful genocide programmers and a loss of about 21 million lives.

In recent years, there has been a reversal in the value systems of countries of the world. At the end of every world war, the meaningless killing of people produced strong reactions in the world community against all future wars. But as it happens, it does not take long to revert back from total disarmament to domination by threat of arms.

Technology is fast changing the nature of domination by the threat of arms. New systems are being developed by powerful military complexes specially automated to destroy and kill and in a unidirectional way. The people who are the victims can never retaliate as the attackers are far away from the scene, controlling the campaign from great distances through satellite, surveillance, command and control. If this capability is in the hands of one country, it will have complete control over the whole world, irrespective of the values involved.

Can a country possessing all the military power enhanced by modem technology determine value systems for the future, which will protect the world? Or will their military complexes take control of all value systems developed in a small world of their own? The end of World War II saw the actual use of nuclear weapons and its fearsome nature. Yet, at that time the chances of World Disarmament seemed promising, but that opportunity has been lost. On the contrary, a little later during the time of the cold war, a nuclear arms race of unbelievable magnitude came into existence. In spite of all this, several countries, including India, continued to hope for total nuclear disarmament, but the hope has dissolved into a dream. A fragmented version is now being sold to the world, which perpetuates the control by a few nations for all time to come.

Among the nuclear powers, France has shown great understanding of these problems in all its totality from the very beginning, specially concerning developing countries and India in particular. Under the leadership of de Gaulle, a clear policy was evolved for deterrence and even considered nuclear weapons as a blessing in disguise. As an example of divergence in thinking, Table 1 lists the views of India, France and the US.

TABLE 1

	Policy	India	France	USA
1.	Possession of Nuclear Weapons	Only deterrence for National Security	Blessing in disguise as insurance	Ultimate evil
2.	Total disarmament in Unipolar world	Yes, if all agree	Yes, if all agree	Not possible in unipolar world
3.	As deterrence only	As deterrence national (regional/ global)	As local deterrence, protecting French interests	Global security
4.	Nuclear Forces	Triad	Triad	Triad
5.	Adversary identified	Yes	No	Not clear after the cold war
6.	No First Use	Yes	No, since results in loss of deterrence value	No
7.	War fighting options	SRBM/IRBM	SLBM, Air launched nuclear capability	ICBM
8.	Reaction to NPT	Not to sign	Delayed agreement (1992)	Strong pressure on all to sign
9.	CTBT	Agree to sign under conditions*	Signed and ratified	Rejected
10.	Reaction to FMCT	No restraints on fuel use for peaceful uses like in power reactors	No restraints on fuel use for peaceful uses like in power reactors	Stored as spent fuel without reprocessing
11.	Reaction to NATO	Unfavourable	Ambivalent response to NATO	Consider NATO essential for security of Europe
12.	Budget	Reducing	Reducing	Reducing

Note: *(1) All countries to sign, (2) Sanctions to be lifted, (3) Reliable verification, (4) Consensus in country.

As a guide to priorities in a discussion on unipolarity and security, the following points are placed for a discussion in view of the existing tensions in the South Asian neighbourhood:

1. The position of the UN in providing security and the decision-making processes to avoid conclusions arising from unipolarity;
2. Combating terrorism and fundamentalism;
3. On the limits of automated weapons both conventional and those of mass destruction;
4. Avoiding conflicts arising from ethnic distinctions.

My own personal reaction would be, however difficult the above problems are, the two countries namely, France and India, should open a world debate on these matters, and expose the dangers of suppressing them.

Democracy and Security in the Twenty-first Century

THÉRÈSE DELPECH

On the brink of this new century, much is said and written about economics, economic revolution, globalization, and its double-edged potential. Less so about policy and political regimes. States and politicians do not have a very good press nowadays. And very little is articulated about strategy. We used to have 'think tanks' in the good old days; we now have to be content with 'networks'. In a country where about twenty million human beings are being added to the nation every year, it would be absurd not to understand the primary importance of economics. The purpose of my talk is certainly not to dismiss it. Without a strong productive and technological base, India cannot secure its future. Nor can Europe, by the same token. The very concept of development and the vision of a powerful India without poverty is probably at the very core of the aspiration of most Indians, and rightly so. There is even an important security dimension in technological development: India has been invaded repeatedly by hordes smaller in numbers than their own forces, yet they lost because its technology was critically inferior, historians conclude. Today, technological strengths are especially crucial not only in order to create more productive employment in a very competitive world ('You adapt and you adapt quickly, or you get toasted', David Dorman) and to upgrade human skills. The advent of the information age has also dramatically enhanced the role of technology in combat, deterrence and conflict prevention. The security dimension of economics and technology is, therefore, well taken.

But the pursuit of growth and technology alone cannot hold societies together, whether developed or developing, whether European or Asian. At a time when the global balance of power equation is being reconfigured, when market forces and large corporations seem to have a bigger impact on people's lives than governments and international institutions, we also have to acknowledge that economics and politics are still very difficult to separate. To put it bluntly, bad politics can still ruin powerful and wealthy countries. And, useless to say, it is equally effective at ruining developing countries. Part of the anxiety of societies around the world is based on entering the new century with first class security problems and less than first class politicians. Perhaps the time has come for the people itself to debate in a more creative way on not only the goals of economic progress, but also the importance of good governance based on popular participation, management of diversities, respect for fundamental rights and equitable distribution of national wealth. What kind of society is being created by the new forces at work? What kind of society do we want for the new generations? How can violence and injustice be limited? Which multipolarity, if such is the world we are heading towards, is best able to prevent confrontation among the different poles? Which countries or bigger entities are going to constitute the future poles? Such are the major questions ahead of us. Politics can no longer be understood in a vulgar machiavellian way (as a machinery producing power) after the violent century we have just left. Responsibility, accountability, and legitimacy are at the core of the matter. This is not a way of assuming some historic victory of Western ideology or some 'expansion of the West' in the rest of the world. For instance, the Soviet Union probably died out of exhaustion and not because the West actually won the battle. And today, Russia is one of the best examples that Western values have not taken root. She still lives in a different world when it comes to respect for basic human rights, or indeed, simply for human life. *The International Herald Tribune* recently published an article entitled, 'The end of the beginning for a newly democratizing Russia'. The importance of the time needed for real changes to occur should not be underestimated. And the creativity, the resilience, the individuality of non-Western cultures should not be put aside either. In one word, the concepts themselves—accountability, responsibility, legitimacy, ability to deal with minorities—will be increasingly important throughout the world, but they will take different forms, according to different cultures. And in some places, they will be defeated.

The preservation of international peace and security and of fundamental human rights and freedoms are two equally important aims of the UN Charter and can hardly be separated. The UN Secretary General has repeatedly insisted on the moral dimension of international relations. He did so at this point in time in particular, where powerful destructive forces are at hand. He wants governments to recognize that human rights are interrelated, indivisible, universal, that they cannot be separated from the first goal of the United Nations: to preserve peace and stability. He also underlines the great dangers of unequal development. Why does he? Probably because failing to address the political and ethical dimensions of the globalization process, the economic revolution of our age would mean entering the new century with eyes wide shut. As Mahatma Gandhi used to say, industrialism can be a curse for mankind, if not properly understood as a revolution in human affairs. What he had in mind essentially was the increasing gap between the rich and poor (still a major problem). We now have to add the incredible destructive weapons the twentieth century has been able to produce. Survival itself is at stake. Ivan Bloch said it already in 1899, with the technologies of his time. He was convinced that Europe would not commit suicide. What would he say today?

Technological and economic revolutions have always generated social, political, and military backlash. With the experience of the twentieth century, it would be wise to include them in our thoughts now and not simply to submit to them when they appear: the backlash can be extremely violent, as the industrial revolution has shown with lesser means. For those who seek larger roles for themselves in the new international order—which is roughly what multipolarity means for many—the political responsibility to avoid devastating conflicts will continue to be the essential element of success or failure, of stability or instability, and of war and peace. Whether the Permanent Members of the Security Council understand this as their primary task is an interesting question, as the too polite British would say.

The twentieth century has amply demonstrated the possible strategic consequences of political systems. A terrible dynamic of revolutions and wars drenched it in blood. That lesson should not be forgotten as we enter the twenty-first century. Unlearned history lessons usually prove very costly. Even if history does not repeat itself, it does take revenge on those who fail to heed its lessons. Even if, as the Chinese proverb goes, experience is a lantern one carries on one's back, we should never forget the link between the deeply murderous nature of the twentieth century and the success of totalitarian regimes. That link is so close that the autonomy of politics as established since Renaissance days, particularly with respect to ethics, is now being challenged. The wars and revolutions which shook the last century, at the risk of annihilating civilization itself, were largely the result of authoritarian regimes which gradually pushed back the limits of destruction on their own societies and on those they had invaded. The past histories of Hitler's Germany, and Stalin's Russia, and of Mao's China abundantly prove this point. This has prompted some historians to remark that in the twentieth century, there were countries where, to quote Clausewitz in reverse, politics was sometimes the continuation of war through other means.

Europe and India, although in very different contexts, are both large democratic entities and open societies in a world where such entities are all too few, especially in Asia. India has chosen and kept democracy as its method of governance. The Indians have never derailed from their decision to remain democratic whatever the political instability, the difficulty of defining an economic strategy, or the often unclear regional and global policy of their successive governments. In the twentieth century, many nations contended that they should give precedence to economic development over political freedom. India, with its huge problem of development, would have had all the possible justifications to choose such a path. But it never did. The benefits are here today. India will be free from the terrible cost that authoritarian countries have to pay when their political utopia is revealed for what it is: a utopia. As George Orwell used to say, 'All the revolutions fail, but they do not all fail in the same manner'. Think of Russia, where generations were thought worthless unless they served the state. Social misery is now matched by endemic lawlessness, blatant corruption and political gloom. China will encounter similar difficulties: social and political unrest, angry minorities and huge unemployment. The exit from communism bears a heavy price: social, political, economical. In the coming decades, India will have to go through a huge revolution in order to empower people, but it will most probably be a peaceful one, in agreement with India's own way. It was, therefore, appropriate for the United States to recognize India as 'one of the most vibrant democracies' during President Clinton's visit in March 2000.

In a part of the world where democracy is still a rarity (even if the call for democracy is growing in Asia), India can be a major pole of stability in the new century. Indians chose the freedom of democracy for their own sakes. Still, it would be fair to remember that one would have much more to worry about the world's security if an authoritarian axis were to run from Afghanistan to New Delhi and Beijing. Therefore, paying homage to India's democracy is not superfluous: the price to pay for any other choice would be considerable. The United States probably understands it better than any other country at this point in time. National Security Advisor Sandy Berger declared on 16 March 2000, a few days before President Clinton left for South Asia: 'For fifty years, America's relationship with India has been viewed through the prism of the cold war and its aftermath'. Time has now come to deepen ties between two large democracies. Such was the main significance of the US President's visit, the first in 22 years. It may start for America a dramatic new relationship in South Asia, even if such a diplomatic change is not yet officially acknowledged in Washington.

In order to measure the rarity of the Indian political choice, think of most of India's neighbours. The military coup in Pakistan is raising new concerns, particularly concerning the future of the rancorous dispute over the Himalayan territory of Kashmir and terrorism. President Clinton, while in Islamabad in March, declared that the Line of Control should be respected. He also deprecated 'violence and extremism'. The most telling story concerning America's new relationship with Pakistan was the impressive deception. A decoy plane and decoy men were used when President Clinton arrived in Islamabad. The message could not be clearer. The cold war strategic alliance between Pakistan and the United States is over. Eastward, Burma's dictatorship makes also a difficult partner, in spite of India's efforts to improve relations during the last years. A number of official statements made it clear that Myanmar should take note of the large public support to democracy in India. Finally, as far as India's biggest neighbour is concerned, China, its autocratic regime, is one of the major problems tomorrow's world security will have to face. Far from being an island of stability, China relies on shaky foundations and could encourage nationalism in order to save the regime from huge internal pressures. Ten of millions of Chinese workers are angry about corruption and poverty. In February 2000, there was a violent protest by 20,000 miners discharged from their jobs. According to official estimates, 11 million workers will lose their jobs in state industries this year. Beijing's hard line against Taiwan is partly an attempt to divert popular hostility. The pressing need for political reform becomes more and more obvious, but Chinese scholars who argue in its favour are removed from their position. Old-fashioned purges of intellectuals indicate of how deeply the regime feels threatened by the changes occurring in the country in the last two decades since economic reforms began. At the same time, on the other side of the Strait, Taiwan has just passed the real test of a democratic system—the peaceful alternation of the parties in power. With the election of Chen Shui Bian, a lifelong advocate of independence, China and Taiwan are still further apart. Tensions between them may increase, leading to dangerous paths. As a commentator put it recently in Hong Kong, 'If China takes military action against Taiwan, the whole of Asia is going to collapse like a house of cards.'

Substantial differences in the political systems notwithstanding, the democratic choice is viewed as an essential element of stability in both Europe and India. Having built its democratic institutions over the centuries, Europe is still flanked on its Balkan southern side by a whole zone which has yet to learn to abide by democratic rules, especially if its ambition is to join the European Union. Looking East, Europe is confronted with a major unknown, namely the future of Russia, whose recent actions and even atrocities in Chechnya show evidence that basic rules are still far from being respected. And finally, on the other side of the Mediterranean, emerging nations are going through radical changes, sometimes causing concerns for their future. As for India, its difficult strategic environment has already been described briefly and only emphasizes the stabilizing strategic dimension of the Indian democracy. Tolerance has a long history here, rooted in the diversity of religions which the country has always valued as an essential asset and will hopefully continue to prevail in the future. Attacks against Muslims or Christians in India should be seen for what they actually are: an internal threat to democracy, which has to be contained. Tolerance may also stem from the necessity to run a huge, multifaceted territory, even if other countries, faced with the same problem and immensity, have chosen authoritarian states to keep the country together. All the more remarkable that this has not been the Indian choice. India also has a flair for compromise, and a passion for debate, which are fertile grounds for democracy.

In the establishment of a new regime of global security, it seems entirely justified to discriminate between democratic and despotic polities, as Professor Sondhi suggests in his book devoted to India's foreign policy. Why is it so?

First, as he himself recalls, political science and history teach us that the closest thing we have to a law of international politics is that modern democracies seldom fight each other.

Secondly, despotic regimes, having little respect for internal laws and regulations, are probably even less inclined to respect international law; in particular, good governance based on popular citizen participation and accountability is likely to provide a good basis for compliance with international commitments in particular arms control agreements.

Thirdly, contempt for human rights at home often goes hand-in-hand with reckless policies abroad. The ability to take risks appears to be much more pronounced in non-libertarian states. More generally, lack of domestic restraints made them dangerous both at home and abroad.

Finally, the most dangerous hot spots of the planet today include conflicts between democracies and despotic regimes. Such is the case for China and Taiwan, where rival nationalisms are increasingly intertwined with a political competition between the mainland's large autocracy and the island's young democracy. Such is also the case concerning the two Koreas, where the costs of the end of partition might be much greater than those for German reunification. Such is also the case in the rivalry opposing India and China, and the latter's determination to prevent India from emerging as a major pole in this century. India is convinced that China is seeking to deny India its proper stakes in the game of international politics.

In a way, Europe and India share a common understanding of some of the Enlightenment concepts, despite having followed very different paths. But democracy, as all precious things, is fragile, and its continued welfare in the twenty-first century is not assured. It is being threatened from different directions:

- By the persistence of authoritarian regimes,
- By on-going civil wars and weak states (weak states could mean weak liberties),
- By the emergence of powerful subnational actors,
- By some aspects of globalization, notably if it increases the gap between rich and poor. Globalization should include some dose of democracy as well,
- And mostly, perhaps, by the weakness of democratic convictions in those countries fortunate enough to enjoy the benefits of basic liberties. The West now has a superficial grasp of its own freedom.

> Our liberties, like our democracies, are becoming rhetorical and taken for granted. The human rights' compromises we engineer to protect our business interests show what values we really believe in—shareholder values. Such is the main danger before us. When communism collapsed, the reunification of Europe was expected to result in moral revolution and spiritual revival. But the West offered a new materialism which cannot meet the enormous challenges of the traumatized Russian society. The same could be said of the Chinese. Replacing utopian politics with utopian economics is a poor recipe.

To ensure a democratic tradition, there are some conditions that must be respected:

The first is to be convinced that there are values superior to the state. Higher to the state is humanity. This is something apparently impossible for any communist party to admit. However, the experience is there. Repeated attempts to neglect it bring to mind a line by the Irish writer Samuel Beckett: 'Ever tried, ever failed. Never mind. Try again. Fail again. Fail better.'

The second is to respect the law. There has constantly been in the Soviet Union and Communist China the idea that the Party was above the law. This has resulted in an arbitrary domestic legal system run by the party. The legal system in China is still stacked overwhelmingly in favour of the prosecution. China's conviction rate today is 99.7 per cent.

The third is to consider power with an 'Einstein' philosophy, as a relative value. Quite often, European states are told that they are not 'great powers'. In a sense, it is quite legitimate to sustain, for instance, that France and the UK are no longer great powers. But European countries, having been the initiators of two world wars in the twentieth century, have probably lost interest in 'great power' status. Since 1945, the European countries have voluntarily ceded aspects of their sovereignty in the shared belief that only interdependence would bring security. Power is no longer at the core of relations among states in Europe. As far as India is concerned, power has probably never been at the centre of its political thought, unlike in China, for instance, who has a deep-rooted tendency to divide the world into two categories—adversaries and subordinates. In the twenty-first century, major powers will not be those with huge military means but those who care about the main security problems of the future.

Europeans and Indians probably share the thought that there are values superior to the state, that law should be respected and that power is as relative as all other human inventions. We both respect our citizens and adhere to the provisions of international treaties we have signed. India is a modern, secular, democratic and internationalist state. What India has perhaps, in addition, is the strength of its spirituality. This can be a significant barrier against the idea that absolute power can ever be in human hands.

In order to conclude, India best illustrates that democracy is also an 'Asian value'. This is being further demonstrated by a growing number of Asian countries. In 1998, just when the nuclear tests took place in India and Pakistan, Indonesia had its students' revolution, ten years after Myanmar and nine years after China. Asians' values seem much like everyone else's in this respect. On some points Asians may even diverge more from one another than they do from Americans and Western Europeans. The dividing line is not about political values. And new converts are often more convinced and convincing than old believers. Few Europeans would be able to stand up in front of a column of tanks, to spend seven years in a psychiatric hospital after having unfurled a protest banner in Tienanmen Square in 1992 (Wang Wanxing) or to stay imprisoned for seventeen years for having asked for the fifth modernization: democracy (Wei). As Nietzsche wrote at the end of the last century, 'Freedom is not something one inherits, but something one conquers and defends.' In this respect, some in Asia might even help Europe (or more broadly 'the West') to rejuvenate its old democracies. We need to recapture a compelling purpose in world affairs.

We also require great changes in the way nations conduct their relationships. Only an international order based on human rights, justice and arbitration might head off crashes liable to unleash the devastating potential of the twenty-first century's technologies of war. We should not forget what Donald Kagan has written: 'The only thing more common than predictions about the end of war has been war itself.' If there is one means to change this course, it is what has come to be called 'democratic peace'. To achieve it, there is no other way than to unite our energies. We all need to nurture democracy to restore faith in its institutions. The largest advance in human well being involves the explosion of freedom. But again, freedom has never been easy to conquer, and never easy to keep. And to empower people, especially in developing countries, might be seen as the main goal in the years to come to become a major power in the next century. To define the twenty-first century as a democratic century will require more than fine speeches.

The New Nuclear Question and Regional Security: The Chinese View

LANXIN XIANG

In May 1998, India and Pakistan tested a series of nuclear devices, signalling the dawn of a new era in nuclear arms race, an era described by American political scientist Paul Bracken as 'the Second Nuclear Age'. What are the characteristics of this Second Nuclear Age? What is the Chinese view of this new development, which will not only change the nuclear non-proliferation regime in the world, but also change the geopolitical landscape of South Asian regional security? This paper intends to explore the Chinese response and analysis concerning the subcontinent's nuclearization and to explain the differences and possible common grounds between China and these two new nuclear powers.

China and India's Nuclear Tests

China's reaction to India's nuclear tests reflects less panic than ambiguity. It does not happen very often that China openly agrees with the absolute majority of the countries in the world, who participate in the international non-proliferation regime, on a major issue such as the India-Pakistan nuclear tests. The international consensus seems to be: first, the nuclear tension in South Asia was initiated by India and Pakistan only reluctantly followed suit. Second, the nuclear tests have not necessarily enhanced national security of these two countries. Third, the regional tension has been enhanced and the risk of war increased and fourth, the international non-proliferation regime must be maintained.[1] The official Chinese response to the nuclear tests falls one way or another into the similar lines paraphrased by the US Deputy Secretary of State, Strobe Talbott. Despite the provocative statements made by the Indian politicians that the decision to go nuclear was primarily prompted by a 'China Threat', the Chinese reaction was characterized as cautious and restrained. Although the nuclear tests took China, as well as the United States, by surprise, China did not panic, like many other countries. The Indian Defence Minister George Fernandes may be the new bogie man in the Chinese press. Foreign Minister Jaswant Singh's argument 'against nuclear apartheid'[2] has received some sympathetic echoes from China, as it sounds somewhat like General de Gaulle and Mao in the 1960s. China is ambiguous about the nuclear tests in South Asia because China has lost very little and gained a lot by siding with the mainstream international public opinion.

First of all, India clearly failed in its efforts to play the 'China Threat' card. The China Threat thesis, though it is crucially important in political psychology of India, has never been built on a solid basis. China and India do not have a long history of cultural, ethnic, religious and strategic animosity. Except for a very brief war in 1962, neither side has drawn the blood of the other as a habitual pattern of solving mutual disputes. Moreover, China has never exercised nuclear blackmail against India since its 1964 explosion of the nuclear bomb. India's calculation seemed to have banked on the difficult relationship between the United States and China and to ride the wave stirred up by the widespread China Threat Debate in the United States. India intended to prove its indispensable strategic value in containing the rise of China, yet the Western world, on the whole, stubbornly considers India's role in a regional framework. Even after the nuclear tests, no member of the nuclear club accepts India's membership. To blast itself into a nuclear power status is quite different from joining the club. In a word, despite the shock to the international non-proliferation regime, India has failed to globalize the significance of its nuclear test.

Secondly, China is not entirely unsympathetic to India's logic of argument. Although China has joined the international non-proliferation regime, it has consistently placed the main blame of nuclear proliferation of the superpowers. China, in fact, agrees with India that the West, the United States in particular, is pursuing a kind of 'power nuclear politics'. According to an authoritative Chinese view, 'Arms control and disarmament are the major instruments after the cold war, for the United States to intervene in other countries' internal affairs.' The authors pointed out further three forms of this new interventionism:

1. A 'stick-and-carrot' method to 'use political pressure, economic sanction, military punishment and coercive diplomacy with

force. . . .' The American idea to induce China into a nuclear disarmament scheme is 'to maintain its own nuclear superiority and weaken China's limited nuclear deterrence capability'.

2. A 'destroy-the-bridge-after-crossing-it' method to 'prevent others to follow suit and to develop its own'. That is to say, to forbid others to use the technology that has been outdated by the new US technology.
3. Sanction others for weapons sales and technology transfer while allowing itself to become the number one arms dealer in the world.[3]

The official Chinese rhetoric aside, India's action is perceived as more anti-America than anti-China. China is not the leader of the non-proliferation regime. It is merely a reluctant participant. More importantly, China's long-term strategy is to forge a multipolar world against the American hegemony. India's action has done little damage to, if not helped, that strategy.

Thirdly, like some experts in the West, China believes that India's nuclear tests were primarily motivated by domestic considerations. The kind of secular nationalism that had been exercised by the Congress party for decades since independence has broken down in recent years. India is different from China in a number of important ways. It is not an ethnically and religiously united political entity. For a long time, secular nationalism was the only way to hold the country together. However, Nehru's economic development strategy had bogged down, because it embraced certain socialist elements in stressing market control and protectionism. It resulted in widespread corruption and economic inefficiency. One irony that appears embarrassing to New Delhi is the fact that India's parliamentary democracy, often labelled the biggest democracy in the world, has not successfully managed the national economy the way the biggest communist country China has. The Indian democratic procedure has led to constant political instability due to the internal political division. India's political system is not plagued by too little political participation. On the contrary, as one Indian scholar pointed out, India is the most politicized country on earth. India is not content to just 'have politics, but to be molded by politics'.[4] Almost every issue and sector of administration, with notable exception of the judicial system, is politicized. With thousands of political parties and independent candidates contesting the local and national elections, India remains as it has always been—a country characteristic of highly divisive cultural, ethnic, religious and hierarchical political landscape. While for the Chinese government, the central question is how to govern better. Deng Xiaoping's philosophy was, 'No matter the cat is black or white, it is a good cat if it catches mice.' India lacks a pragmatic philosophy of government. Indian political leadership is often demanded by the voters simply to govern.[5] The rise of the BJP and its native ethnic and religious fundamentalism are analysed by many in the West as the new, darker form of nationalism.[6] In sharp contrast, many Chinese experts have viewed the Vajpayee government in less unfavourable terms. According to two leading India experts in Beijing, Prime Minister A.B. Vajpayee's success in the last election represents a new era of political stability in India. The authors showed great admiration of Vajpayee's mature political experience, superb diplomatic manoeuvre and the ability of managing crisis such as the India-Pakistan confrontation in Kashmir.[7] The Chinese calculation seems to be that a stable India would lead to a more stable foreign policy. So long as China does not perceive a real 'India Threat', stable and consistent bilateral ties are of crucial importance.

Another domestic factor that prompted the Indian nuclear decision was undoubtedly the difficult relationship between the civilian government and the military. The Indian military has long been considered a repressive force used by the colonial government. Since India's independence, the military is often looked upon with suspicion by politicians and civil servants. The service chiefs are rarely consulted on key security issues. They were informed about the 1998 nuclear tests only shortly before it took place. The tug of war between the Ministry of Defence and the military often ended up with the military on the losing side. Moreover, the Indian military is well known for another war, an uncontrollable turf war among the services. The bad collaboration between the Army and the Air Force in a recent conflict with Pakistan is just one of the numerous examples. Building a nuclear force is, therefore, aimed at eliminating these internal bickerings and creating a more efficient national security mechanism, which is entirely compatible with the BJP's new nationalism emphasizing great power status and internal unity. But India has a long way to go to achieve that objective. The jostling for position has just begun. There should be serious doubts about whether the new superstructure in national security system in India can perform effectively.

The Chinese nuclear programme, on the contrary, has little to do with domestic stability question. Starting in 1964, the nuclear force has always been the integral part of the People's Liberation Army which, as the name suggests, is not affiliated with an inglorious colonial history. For most periods of the People's Republic, the military is under the control of one governing party. The nuclear force is useful neither for internal security, nor for settling turf wars. The military was, in fact, invited to participate in politics under Mao. But Deng Xiaoping was determined, during the reform period, to send it back to the barracks. Moreover, the Chinese nuclear decision was primarily influenced by repeated US threats of atomic attack.[8] India has never faced any nuclear blackmail. From the Chinese perspective, those domestic factors that led to the Indian nuclear decision thus reflect more internal weakness than strength. Chinese analysts often take for granted the views expressed by some Western observers, such as Zbigniew Brzezinski, that India has constantly overestimated its long-term capability. There is, in fact, no 'India Threat Debate' among experts and politicians alike in China.

Last but not the least, the declared nuclear doctrine by India, minimum deterrence and 'No First Use' doctrine, sounds eerily familiar to Beijing. Minimum deterrence is the only strategic choice for a secondary nuclear power such as China or India. The 'No First Use' doctrine was invented by the Chinese in the old days when China was resisting the test ban treaty regime vehemently. It is, in fact, a quite meaningless doctrine in operational terms. The Chinese use this doctrine more for diplomatic purposes than for actual military and strategic planning. Since the UN Charter grants sovereign country rights of defending itself with all the means available, the 'No First Use' doctrine can be violated both in theory and practice. So far, India has not come up with anything fundamentally new in its strategic thinking.

China and Pakistan's Nuclear Tests

China's reaction to Pakistan's nuclear tests is equally ambiguous. With or without a nuclear bomb, China and Pakistan are natural allies. This alliance was a direct product of the 1962 Sino-Indian border conflict and was substantially extended during the cold war. From Beijing's perspective, the most fundamental geopolitical utility of this alliance is to create a two-front threat to India. A strong and hostile Pakistan restrains the capability of India to fight a war with China. Indian defence planners have to take into account the possibility that Pakistan will enter a large-scale Sino-Indian war. India has to deploy a large force away from the disputed border region with China. India's de facto alliance with the Soviet Union during the cold war further enhanced Pakistan's strategic value to China. However, the end of cold war not only diminished the value of the Indo-Soviet alliance, but also the Sino-Pakistan alliance. In the past decade, China has begun striving for some form of equidistant position between India and Pakistan.

The close relationship with Pakistan also serves another important purpose for China. Pakistan is a major country in the Islamic world. China needs Pakistan to facilitate good rapport with the rest of the Islamic world. Moreover, Pakistan is useful for China's internal security. A good relationship with Pakistan helps to convince the Muslims within China that the Chinese regime is not anti-Muslim. Since Xinjiang is of critical importance in China's national security system, its agitated Muslim population can be appeased by Islamabad, where many Central Asian Muslims look to for support and guidance.

China's reported nuclear and missile technology transfer to Pakistan was a direct reaction to India's nuclear test in 1974. It has served the double purpose of containing India and maintaining internal security. But the Chinese policy was aimed at maintaining a non-declared balance in South Asia. This was the option the Pakistan leadership had preferred as well. While India's motivation to go nuclear had global impact in mind, Pakistan, however, opted for overt nuclear status only because of the regional environment. The international factors, which came into play only after the tests, were inevitably negative and unwelcome. A sanction regime did more damage to Pakistan's economy than India's. This had, in part, prompted a major political backlash, culminating in the return of the military to power. Therefore, Pakistan's nuclear tests do not serve China's long-term interest.

China's major concern was the erosion of political stability and economic conditions in Pakistan. China considered the open nuclear race as too costly an option for such a poor country. In sharp contrast to India, Pakistani politics has long been marked by a weak representative government, a divided political leadership, and the tendency towards direct or indirect authoritarian rule. The constant internal instability has helped perpetuate the military's control over security policies. Since Pakistan's security doctrine is India-centric, the military not only strives for a large conventional force, but also an adequate nuclear programme. These prove far beyond Pakistan's means to achieve. But China was in a dilemma concerning Pakistan's nuclear tests. On the one hand, China found no way to convince Pakistan not to follow India's footsteps in its nuclear tests. Shortly after the Indian tests, Pakistani Foreign Minister Shamshad Ahmed met his Chinese counterpart Tang Jiaxuan in Beijing. While both sides declared the same position concerning the Indian tests, the Pakistanis failed to persuade China to declare a nuclear umbrella over Pakistan. China, apparently, showed no interest in extending its own nuclear deterrence. All China could do was to assure Pakistan that it would not impose sanctions should Pakistan conduct a nuclear test. It is probable that China had tried but failed to convince Pakistan to remain a covert nuclear power. When asked by reporters whether China had urged Pakistan not to go nuclear, Foreign Minister Ahmed merely said, 'China has not asked us do anything which is not in our national interest.'[9]

On the other hand, China was intensely interested in improving Sino-Indian relations. China and India had repaired some damage in border disputes since a 1993 agreement to reduce tension in the Himalayas. Confidence-building measures were already well under way before the Indian tests. Despite the harsh criticism of India's nuclear option, China's action was more moderate and cautious. The Indian decision for nuclear tests had forced China to make a clear stand on the side of its old ally in Islamabad. Pakistan's immediate nuclear response to India, however, may make things even more complicated. Under the circumstances, China's safe policy went with international public opinion. China not only supported the UN resolution condemning India and Pakistan, but also signed joint communiqués with the US president and Russian government to urge restraint on both sides and return to international non-proliferation regime 'unconditionally'. While criticizing both countries on a high moral ground, China was not prepared for any concrete punitive action to further alienate either country.

What is slowly changing, however, is the nature of the Sino-Pakistani relationship. Chinese commentators in recent years are concerned with Islamic fundamentalist movement in Pakistan and worried about Pakistan's active role in installing Taliban to power in Afghanistan. Pakistan was dismayed to see that China refused to side with Islamabad on the nuclear question. So far China has not helped Pakistan to break its diplomatic isolation. Moreover, Pakistan had hoped that China and its Islamic Middle Eastern allies, especially

Saudi Arabia, Kuwait and the United Arab Emirates, would help it overcome the difficulties caused by international sanctions. There is no such help forthcoming. The leadership in Pakistan painfully realizes that the country cannot afford a nuclear race. It can hardly find adequate funds to start a full-scale programme of nuclear weaponization and deployment. Even China has publicly vowed to stop missile cooperation with Pakistan. Nevertheless, given the durable nature of this relationship, China is unlikely to allow Pakistan's internal and external weakness to perpetuate. China will continue to need Pakistan for strategic reasons, if much less for internal security reasons.

Regional Security Implications

1. Nuclear Instability?

Most Western analysts tend to believe that the nuclearization of South Asia will inevitably lead to more regional tensions. In Paul Bracken's words,

> The most important issue of the twenty-first century is understanding how nationalism combines with the newly destructive technologies appearing in Asia. If energies in these examples become harnessed to this firepower, then the world could be in for a very dangerous era that the West is ill prepared to understand.[10]

What Bracken tries to imply is that the kind of nationalism, from China, Pakistan to India, will not tolerate the Western concept of rational calculation of deterrence. Thus, the world has to shudder at the thought that a real nuclear war may take place in this very region. The cold war logic of nuclear deterrence and strategic parity may not be applied to South Asia at all because the rivals are close neighbours and have drawn each other's blood in the battlefield for decades. Talbott also made the same point about the differences between superpower nuclear confrontation and the current situation in South Asia.

These alarming analyses are, perhaps, only half correct. The assumption that Asian ethnic nationalism pays less attention to the value of human life has been a long-standing argument by the international NPT regime dominated by the United States. It demonstrates a tendency to undervalue the Asian civilization and statesmanship. The reality is that China has become steadily more responsible in nuclear matters since joining the club. Not even during the heyday of the Cultural Revolution did Mao consider a nuclear war operational. It is hard to imagine that a democratic India and a semi-authoritarian Pakistan will become even less rational after the nuclear tests. The simultaneous declaration of the nuclear status has actually enhanced the strategic stability between India and Pakistan. The progress made so far by India and Pakistan in establishing a nuclear restraint regime in South Asia will serve to reinforce the symbiotic relationship between India's and Pakistan's nuclear programmes.

From China's perspective, the South Asian nuclearization has long been a fait accompli. In strategic terms, there is no qualitative difference between covert and overt nuclear status. Chinese analysts are far more optimistic about the regional stability than their colleagues in the West. In one expert's words,

> The two countries now begin to realize that maintaining nuclear balance and coexistence is the only way to survive. Thus the two countries will not launch casual nuclear strikes to let South Asian security go out of control. From a long-run perspective, the relationship between the two countries will improve.[11]

The Chinese analysis is partly supported by at least one Western expert, François Heisbourg, who argued that, 'The strategic communities of the new nuclear states are cognizant of deterrence theory, and their political and military masters do not have prima facie reasons for departing from a deterrence stance.'[12]

One problem for China, however, is the uneven nuclear arms race in South Asia. Pakistan's nuclear programme is India-centric and its decision on nuclear arms race is entirely on ad hoc and reactive basis. It is, therefore, predictable. Moreover, the Chinese are encouraged by Pakistan's nuclear policy, which was announced by the new military ruler General Pervez Musharraf. In one statement he declared, 'For our security, we will ensure minimum deterrence in the unconventional and conventional fields.' In another, he stated, 'Pakistan would not try to match India in respect of the number of missiles produced, but would retain just enough missile capacity to reach anywhere in India and destroy a few cities, if required.'[13] India's nuclear programme, however, includes China's nuclear capability. It is an open-ended programme evolving on a long-term, systematic basis. It is highly unpredictable. China is sympathetic with Pakistan's perspective that the minimum deterrence doctrine announced by India is essentially meaningless. Lawrence Freedman's definition of minimum deterrence as 'the possession of sufficient nuclear weapons to inflict grievous harm on the enemy in retaliation an *no more* [italics added]'[14] cannot be taken for granted in South Asia. Because India's minimum deterrence is China-centric, there will be 'no more' limitation after sufficient deterrence is established against Pakistan. Under the circumstances, Pakistan may have to enter the race with India, because, as one Pakistani analyst argued, the drafted nuclear doctrine by India has in effect 'deposited the concept of minimum deterrence into the morgue'.[15] Since Pakistan will never expect to be able to match India's nuclear programme, Islamabad is much more willing to cooperate with the nuclear arms control regime than India. China supports Pakistan's efforts to initiate a regional solution to the nuclear arms race, while India makes clear that its nuclear programme is not country-specific. Therefore, there is no chance at the moment that India will participate in any South Asian nuclear arms control mechanism.

2. *The Prospect of Sino-Indian Conflict*

In the area of nuclear weapons, China is worried about India's superiority to Pakistan as well as about the pronounced desire to reach nuclear parity with China. There is little doubt that India's long-term goal is to reach nuclear parity with China and to extend its nuclear deterrence to cover the whole of China. India considers China the 'main potential threat', and Pakistan 'the main immediate threat'. Three arguments have been advanced to support the China Threat theory. First, China and India are fundamentally different in ideology and their strategic interests are incompatible. Second, the two countries are faced with fundamental conflict in a 1,25,000 sq. km disputed border area. And third, China's efforts to establish good relationships with other countries in South Asia are designed to isolate and encircle India.

How realistic are these arguments? To begin with, the ideological differences never prevent a good relationship between states. What India resents most is, perhaps, the fact that a biggest democracy, or exactly because it is already a democracy, is not being taken seriously by the Western world. While China, as the biggest communist and 'rogue' country, has been elevated to the top five power position in the world. Playing 'rogue' to defy the non-proliferation regime is thought to be more effective to draw attention. This is a misplaced prestige-building effort. It has often been argued that China always adopts an arrogant and condescending attitude towards India. In reality, China does see long-term clash with India in strategic issues. Both are 'rogues' in term of challenging the unipolar world dominated by the United States, and both consider economic development to be the top priority.

At the regional level, it is not China's fault that India has not become more 'Asian' since its independence. The irony is that, China and India almost decided to withdraw from Asia at the same time in the late 1940s. After the founding of the People's Republic in 1949, Mao refused to integrate with the Asian economic and political trends by creating a tightly controlled communist autarchy. India, too, turned its back on Asia since its independence from the British colonial rule in 1947. Isolated by tradition and politics (being the only democracy aside from Japan in Asia), India did not need Asia for its socialist-oriented economic development strategy. The Non-Aligned Movement led by India received lukewarm response in an Asia that was fragmented by the cold war alliances. Surrounded by a hostile Muslim world and a less hostile Confucian world, India, for decades, was content with a position of no durable friends, no serious competitors, and no strategic partners in Asia. India's only durable partnership was with the former Soviet Union. Its strategic ambition was thus limited to a South Asian hegemon. China and India had enjoyed a reasonable and amicable relationship in the 1950s. After the war in 1962, they turned their backs on each other.

The economic opening up of China has changed the picture. Once again, China and India decided to reintegrate with Asia almost simultaneously. Beijing started the process a bit earlier in the late while India began to return to Asia in the late 1980s. This phenomenon, termed by a French expert as 'joint return to Asia',[16] has caused certain apprehension in India, though not so much in China. The roots of this apprehension is that China has reintegrated with the Pacific Asia or mainly with the Confucian (or chopstick) Asia, where the economic dynamism was the most impressive and its cultural tradition was familiar at the time when China made the decision to return. China's relationship with its neighbours, from Moscow, to Seoul to Bangkok has improved a great deal since the 1980s. Even with a hostile Taiwan, the economic ties are becoming too important to be abandoned.

From New Delhi's perspective, a prosperous China, once again turned its back on India. More seriously, the rise of China means the relative decline of India in the international political arena. A 'catching-up' mentality has prevailed in Indian politics. This is not at all a bad thing, as the Chinese experience showed that the rapid development of its economy hinged upon a more relaxed and less hostile international environment. India started serious economic reforms in the late 1980s, culminating in the new development strategy in 1991. Major progress has been made since in industrial deregulation, removal of barriers to domestic and foreign investment and liberalization of trade. The results are impressive. The recent years see sustained growth rates of 7 per cent. However, the Chinese economy is still 35 per cent faster than India's and India's imports are a quarter the size of China's. More importantly, China receives twenty times more foreign direct investment than India. One problem is that India's economic reform is not Asia-oriented. According to Western commentators who made a loud call for 'taking India seriously', India does at least as well as China in attracting non-Asian investors,[17] but this has said a lot of the Indian approach to reintegrate with Asia. It has never been very successful. Since the end of the cold war, India has made some progress in improving relations with the neighbouring countries on the subcontinent, namely Bangladesh, Bhutan, Sri Lanka, and Nepal. But it has failed to establish close relationship with the Pacific Asia. It would be gross exaggeration to argue that China's reintegration has hindered India's efforts. Many Asian countries—for example, the ASEAN countries—actually welcomed India into such organization as ASEAN Regional Forum, to pose as a counterweight to China's influence. But only recently Indian elite began to appreciate the so-called 'Asian values' and to cast off the 'dependency theory'. However, the continued confrontation with Muslim Pakistan and Communist China will certainly not help India's position in Asia. The decision to go nuclear has resulted in a double isolation. In the democratic world, India is now considered at the best a 'rogue' democracy, while in Asia, doubts and suspicions have grown as to India's real intentions. The Indo-Japanese relationship, which had a promising start after the cold war, is now in difficulties. As a non-nuclear great power, Japan is extremely sensitive to any nuclear proliferation case. Japan's policy of changing the existing composition of the permanent members in the United Nations' Security Council coincided with the Indian policy. The nuclear tests changed the prospect of any such cooperation. There is little chance that India's membership at the UN Security Council will be supported by major powers. Culture and tradition aside, India is too preoccupation with a global role as to allow paranoia to distort priorities.

As far as the Sino-Indian border disputes are concerned, there is, of course, no easy solution. But both sides seem to have realized in recent years that neither would gain from a renewed confrontation. Limited confidence-building measures have already been in place since the early 1990s. India's efforts to reach nuclear and missile, especially short and intermediate range missile, parity with China may not necessarily lead to destabilization of the disputed frontier. India's anxiety about China's deployment of nuclear weapons in Tibet will be lessened. China cannot stop the Indian nuclear plan, but it does feel a nuclear threat by it either. In fact, the new Vajpayee government has already downgraded the China Threat thesis and made some efforts to return the Sino-Indian relationship back to a normal status. Chinese analysts considered the recent trend as helpful and hailed Foreign Minister Jaswant Singh's recent visit to China as a great success.[18]

China's alleged plan to encircle and contain India in the Indian Ocean area is also overstated. India is a great power in the Indian Ocean region. It enjoys a unique geopolitical advantage that is beyond China's means to challenge. Its overwhelming size, population and economy have prevented the emergence of a normal balance of power. India's South Asian neighbours, even Pakistan, realize that India is a predominant power in the region. This imbalance has often called for the participation of another big power, China, for the maintenance of a balance of power, a fact that India has vehemently resisted. A unique geopolitical feature of the subcontinent is that India is the only country that shares borders with the other states. India has direct borders with Pakistan, Bangladesh, Nepal and Bhutan and is separated from Sri Lanka only by a narrow strait. It also faces the Maldives across a channel. But India's six neighbours have no common borders. This had made inter-state communications among them difficult. At the same time, the multiethnic and religious composition of India has determined that whatever kind of ethnic or religious conflict in the neighbouring countries will in one way or another, involve India.

China's main concern in this region is not to challenge India's de facto supremacy in South Asia. On the contrary, it is in China's interest that India will play a responsible role in its surrounding area. Moreover, China does not have a long-term strategy in this region.

China is yet to come up with an integrated regional policy. For a long time since 1949, China was seen as a regional power without a regional policy. The constant internal political turmoil and its crucial position during the cold war prevented China to pursue a coherent regional policy. More importantly, the uncertain nature of the Chinese policy towards its neighbouring countries is caused by the fact that China is more than a regional actor, but not quite yet a global power. Only in recent years the Chinese began to develop what it termed 'Zhoubian Zhengce' (periphery policy). But the cold war has forged the traditional Chinese habit of seeing security in global, not regional terms. Even now, China and India are not pursuing the same agenda in the region. China's reaction to India's active regional policy in the last few years is not always negative. According to an internal Chinese analysis, India's regional policy is to 'link the West and pull the East, stabilize the North and settle the South'. Such a strategy does not necessarily undermine China's global and regional concerns. The author further argued that, 'India's multifaceted diplomacy in recent years has actually improved a great deal its military relations with the neighbours, and established India as a military great power and the mainstay of the regional security in the Indian Ocean and South Asia'.[19]

The most effective approach to Sino-India relationship is, therefore, close and friendly consultations and negotiations. Arms race, nuclear or conventional, will only result in China's re-adjustment of its regional policy during this fluid, uncertain and transitional period. It must be pointed out that Pakistan's nuclear programme is India-specific, India's is China-specific, but China's is US-specific. These three nuclear powers are not converging in their long-term strategic perspectives. A nuclear arms race in the region is essentially wasteful and meaningless. It may, in fact, help those Chinese strategic Hawks who are promoting the new nuclear strategy of 'limited deterrence', which is something between minimum and maximum deterrence. 'Limited deterrence' requires an early nuclear attack and negates the 'No first use' principle.[20] If China seriously considers this doctrine, India will be unsettled once again and it will have to entirely revise its nuclear doctrine.

It has often been argued that the Chinese naval presence in Myanmar will unsettle India's sense of coastal security. But one should not forget the fact that India's naval programme is a few steps ahead of China, because of its acquisition of an aircraft carrier, while China has none. Moreover, there is a real prospect of friendly cooperation between India and some South-eastern countries, namely, Indonesia, Philippines or Singapore, in naval affairs to keep the sea-line open in the South China Sea where the dispute between China and the South-eastern countries over the Spratleys may become explosive at some future point. Nevertheless, India should not expect an overt anti-Chinese naval policy to be supported by other Asian countries.

It is significant that India's old ally, Russia, seems to hold the same position as China. Primakov's proposal of a China-Russia-India triangle has received enormous attention in China. At one point, it was even under serious consideration to be a possible cornerstone of the entire Chinese 'periphery policy'. The Indian nuclear tests, of course, have blown this option away. The Primakov proposal fits very well with the Russian desire that constructive bilateral negotiations should play the predominant role in this region. According to two Russian Defence Ministry officials, 'In our opinion, any Chinese threat to India is more hypothetical than real. In real terms, the most important issue for Sino-Indian negotiations may be the termination of Chinese missile and technology transfer to Pakistan.'[21] It is obvious that the more India exploits the China Threat thesis, the less likely China will stop these transfers. Although India and Russia remain very close in military cooperations, a vehement anti-Chinese policy is considered by Moscow as detrimental to its long-term strategy to dominate the US-dominated unipolar world system.

3. *The Prospect of Regional Security Arrangement*

The prospect of regional security arrangement is not bright, but hardly hopeless. Both China and India are members of the ASEAN Regional Forum, while Pakistan is not. China, like India, is traditionally wary about any multilateral security arrangement. In recent years, however, China has become more and more comfortable to work in a multilateral setting. It has participated in many international organizations and security forums. For the foreseeable future, China's major security concerns will continue to focus on the United States. Its relatively benign neglect of the subcontinent will provide India with a good opportunity for developing its military power and economy. To be sure, the China factor will continue to bedevil India and its security policy. But as long as the two countries carry on the constructive dialogue, their regional rivalry will remain manageable and a secondary priority for China. For India, China is also the source of envy and emulation. Since 1999, India has carried on its ambitious economic reform. Two key measures adopted by the Vajpayee government are very similar to ones taken by China. The first is the economic liberalization. The second is to do away with the Nehruvian socialism. China has over twenty years' experience in pursuing these twin objectives. The two Asian giants are moving fast to converge their development philosophy. They have a lot to learn from each other.

The nuclearization of South Asia has made the idea of regional security arrangement more a possibility, not less. Nuclear ambiguity in the past created uncertainty and miscalculation. Most major powers involved in South Asia, namely, the US, Russia, China and Pakistan are warm to the idea of regional arrangements. India's opposition represents a rather isolated case. Pakistan and China always propose the third power involvement in the volatile region of Kashmir. The United States and Russia have no objection. As conventional war can no longer escalate indefinitely as a result of their nuclear tests, a real chance may arrive in Kashmir. India's traditional approach is to deal only with Pakistan. But three wars and the recent skirmish have proved that emotions could run amuck without a reliable management system. India may have to readjust its Kashmir policy to defuse tension. Recent trends seem to indicate that India is moving slowly towards a more flexible position. Since the Lahore Summit of February 1999, New Delhi no longer insists on a no-negotiation policy while Islamabad has downgraded the Kashmir settlement as the precondition for improving relations. It is not clear, however, that India will ever accept a third party mediation à la the Israeli-Palestinian model.

In conclusion, the recent tension on the subcontinent will not go away easily, but conditions for regional stability already exist. Since its opening up, China has adopted a comprehensive view on national security. This involves giving priority to sustained economic development and building up its military might that has to be based on real economic strength. Since the NATO action in Kosovo, China has been completely preoccupied with the prospect of defending itself against a high-tech war. China is not going to spend itself into bankruptcy to reach nuclear parity with the United States. The gap between China and the United States cannot be filled in the foreseeable future. To China, the subcontinent is, as usual, of secondary importance. China hopes that India also adopts a comprehensive perspective on its national security and focuses on economic reform.

Many Indian politicians and strategists are responding to Beijing's message. Inder Kumar Gujral, a former Prime Minister of India, has argued that India should be totally concentrated on putting its economy in order, and not waste its precious resources on the military build-up. He stated that, 'I don't think India should be concerned about matching missile-for-missile and ship-for-ship with China or Pakistan. We should be assiduously working to expand our economic growth.'[22]

Pakistan has never been enthusiastic about nuclear arms race. Its foreign debt has reached the level that can hardly be reduced and its foreign exchange reserve can sustain but one month's import needs. For the foreseeable future, Pakistan has to be content with the fact that its new nuclear status has undermined India's long-standing conventional arms superiority over Pakistan. Pakistan's future largely depends upon its ability to restore economic health. It is not surprising that, though both India and Pakistan had pledged to join the Comprehensive Test Ban Treaty in the near future, Pakistan is willing to take a further step by offering to sign the Comprehensive Test Ban Treaty independently of India's action. Given the symbiotic relationship between the two nuclear programmes, Pakistan's move is unusual. It reflects a desperate desire to end the international sanction regime.

Traditional militarism, i.e. the triumph of the generals over civilians whose main interest is promoting economic development, is over in Asia. Despite religious and ethnic differences, China, India and Pakistan are moving closer in their philosophy of government, and economic development. The weapons of mass destruction are not likely to alter that trend.

NOTES

1. For a summary of this consensus, see, Strobe Talbott, 'Dealing with the Bomb in South Asia', *Foreign Affairs*, March/April 1999, pp. 110-22.
2. See, Jaswant Singh, 'Against Nuclear Apartheid', *Foreign Affairs*, September/October 1998, pp. 41-52.
3. Xiaobin Wang, et al., 'Junkong Caijun zou Xiang Hefang' (Where Will the

Arms Control and Disarmament Go?), an editorial in *The PLA Daily*, 20 October 1999.

4. S. Khilnani, 'The Idea of India', Penguin, New Delhi, p. 9.
5. Indira Gandhi's 1980 campaign slogan was 'A Government that Governs'. The BJP's 1998 campaign slogan was 'For Good Governance'. The BJP's use of the archaic English word 'governance' instead of 'government' reflected, as one French scholar pointed out, a popular call for a government that actually governs. See, Bernard, Jean Alphonse, *L'Inde, la Chine et le nucléaire*, p. 44, *Defense National*, November 1998.
6. See, for example, Bracken Paul, 'Asia's Militaries and the New Nuclear Age', *Current History*, December 1999, p. 421.
7. Jiali Ma and Xiaoqiang Fu, 'Vajpayee New Government's Internal and External Policies', *Xiandai Guoji Guanxi* (Contemporary International Relations), Beijing, vol. 11, 1999, p. 9. The Chinese military, however, is more critical of the Vajpayee government, see, for example, Xishen Hua and Minming Zhang, 'New Indian Government Remains Facing Mounting Problems', *The PLA Daily*, 24 October 1999.
8. For an authoritative account, see, J.W. Lewis and Litai Xue, *China Builds the Bomb*, Stanford University Press, 1988, pp. 11-34.
9. For Sino-Pakistan talks, see, 'Chinese Delegation Seems to Deny Pakistan a Nuclear Umbrella', *New York Times*, 21 May 1998 and 'Pakistan, China Slate India's Reckless Action', *Dawn* (Islamabad), 21 May 1998.
10. Bracken, op. cit., p. 420.
11. Jieyun Liang, *Indian National Security Strategy at the Turn of the Century, Contemporary International Relations*, vol. 5, 1999, p. 26.
12. François Heisbourg, 'The Prospects for Nuclear Stability between India and Pakistan', *Survival*, Winter 1998-9, p. 83
13. Quoted by Pravin Sawhney, 'How Inevitable is an Asian "Missile Race"?', *Jane's Intelligence Review*, January 2000, p. 30.
14. Lawrence Freedman, *Evolution of Nuclear Strategy*, New York: St. Martin, 1989, p. 207.
15. Farah Zahra, 'Pakistan's Road to a Minimum Nuclear Deterrent', *Arms Control Today*, July/August 1999, p. 10.
16. Jean Alphonse Bernard, op. cit., p. 38.
17. James Manor and Gerald Segal, 'Taking India Seriously', *Survival*, Summer 1998, p. 53.
18. Ma and Fu, op. cit., p. 10.
19. Xiaozhuo Zhao, 'India's National Security Strategy', *Qingkuang Tongbao* (Situations Reports, secret, internal circulation), May 1999, p. 7.
20. M. Ehsan Ahrari, Growing Strong: 'The Nuclear Genie in South Asia', *Security Dialogue*, vol. 30, no. 4, December 1999, p. 440.
21. Alex Andronov and Boris Maximov, 'Is Security Regime Possible?', *Security Dialogue*, vol. 30, no. 3, September 1999, p. 334.
22. Quoted from Ahrari, op. cit., p. 435.

DISCUSSION 2

Participant: Yesterday and today we have heard very reassuring, I would say, even comforting arguments explaining the convergence of perspectives, European perspectives, particularly, French perspectives and Indian perspectives. My question is to what extent is this convergence a hostage to the outcome of the Indo-American dialogue going on where there also are convergences brought out but all of them are, in fact, if not so stated make hostage to the outcome of the talks about CTBT. That outcome is still very uncertain at the moment. Sometimes it looks promising, sometimes not. But whatever the outcome of that might be, is there any kind of a bilateral level framework at which the convergence at least between India and France can be rescued from that particular risk to it? The French spokesman, particularly Mr Poncet, has mentioned yesterday that you have commitments to various other partners in the P5 Club and that those commitments are a constraint upon France. I presume the same would be true of Europe. Is there any kind of a level of discussion or a level of agreement between these two countries which would survive, whatever might be the outcome of the Indo-US dialogue?

Participant: The starting point was the table of convergence about the French and the Indian position on nuclear issues. The question is: Is there a similar development in relation to the United States in this respect? If I may clarify my question, is this convergence that we have been speaking about, very encouraging and comforting convergence between India and France, rather India and Europe, more particularly India and France, is that also a hostage to whatever might be the outcome of the Indo-US dialogue taking place specifically about CTBT, because there are similar convergences seen at another level between India and America. But these certainly are a hostage to that outcome, which at the moment, is very uncertain as far as the public knows. Or is there a level of discussion between India and France at which, there can be a sufficient degree of agreement which rescues this convergence between India and France from the perils of that outcome?

Participant: First, we are not looking for exclusivity in a polycentric world. So, India has to develop dialogue with major countries. Second, we discussed that last week with Mr Mishra and we hope that after President Clinton's visit in India, what we did in the last two years will follow and we are absolutely convinced that our Indian friends will continue with this strategic dialogue we set up two years ago, which is very useful. Somehow, we were anticipating as a precursor in this new kind of dialogue between centres, between poles because it is the right way to deal with very complicated issues and it is true that we have gained within Europe a more than four decades long experience as it was put in many presentations yesterday and this morning of dialogue to try to get compromise. It was a case not only between Germany and France but also perhaps within the Union. We are not only intellectually, but practically also prepared to dialogue with all the major countries on an equal basis. And my own conviction is precisely that which was put yesterday by Jean François Poncet, that Europe has to do with not only an institutional laboratory but with a redefinition of what national interest means. I think a new model or a new geopolitical model has been invented in Western Europe, so we are very open to this kind of continuous dialogue with major countries. And as far as France and United States are concerned, for example, in European defence, we have accepted in the last years to promote an European defence which is articulated to the United States. Why? Because we were alone among the 15 to have a kind of Gaullist view of what European defence should be. It was not possible to duplicate our nuclear view on collective defence in Europe, so we have accepted to take into account our neighbours' perspectives and this made possible a kind of very effective deal first with Britain, after that, with Germany, Italy and this became a new concept of European defence. We don't think that anybody should be afraid of being hostages of such countries, we are not interested in that.

Participant: I just want to come back for a second to your point because you referred to my presentation yesterday. My answer is very short. It is, of course, that CTBT is an important issue and as I said, we have international obligations in that respect which we cannot just disregard. I don't consider CTBT as, let us say, a key that opens the door towards discussions and convergence. For instance, it has nothing to do in my mind with the World Trade Organization and the reverse is true. We could finally come to some agreement on non-proliferation and not agree on what has to be done in the World Trade Organization. So let us not say that everything is hostage to CTBT. It is important enough but there are many other important things. And when we speak of the multipolar world, which is our subject, it is not all dependent on what India finally decides to do on CTBT, especially since the American Congress has not ratified CTBT. That makes CTBT, I think, much more relative than it looked before. So important, yes, obligations, yes, stumbling block, no.

Participant: I will have a very brief comment as a completely irresponsible citizen. Unlike my two predecessors, I would like to say a few things. First of all, Europe probably is in a much better situation to talk with India on CTBT than the United States. Why? Because at least we ratified the treaty and this is the very first point I want to make. Secondly, if India does not need more tests it could help to sign the CTBT and in particular since Pakistan usually follows what India does, it would be interesting, then, to look at what Pakistan would do, that is my second point. My third point is that France, from the very beginning, in 1998, started a very large dialogue with India. Why? It was not on the CTBT, it was not on the NPT. Why? Because we took some of Indian security concerns seriously. So this means that whatever is done on signing the CTBT is certainly not a condition on the French side to have further dialogue. And lastly, concerning the relations India has with the United States on these broad issues, it seems to me that the French perfectly understand that Indian relation with the United States are extremely important and if India's talks with Talbot goes in the right direction, all the best, we are happy about that, it is good for you.

Participant: I am very glad that in the three things the question has been faced, it has not been faced fully. Therefore if you will permit me, I will formulate it a little more crudely than in the sophisticated manner in which one of the previous speakers had formulated it. On our inability to sign the CTBT immediately, I think you made a very pertinent point that we say we need no further tests, that we have put a voluntary moratorium on further tests, that we are willing to give a de jure international effect to this and that we will not stand in the way after CTBT coming into force. So you can see the significance and meaning of it. Why it can't be signed today has a number of reasons. One is a lack of consensus in this country. There are distinguished scientists sitting here. Dr P.K. Iyengar, a former chairman, has written an article this morning. You might see why our signing the CTBT on the dotted line cannot be accepted by many. Then there are operatical difficulties. Another big difficulty is that India does not want to get into what happened to it in relation to the chemical weapons convention, which was, as you know, signed in Paris and we were the first to sign it. We were also foolishly the first to ratify it. Then we found that the US Congress ratified it with 20 conditions. We have to be watchful whether the CTBT is ratified eventually if ever it is ratified by the United States with about a dozen conditions. So, with that apart, there isn't going to be an immediate signing by India of the CTBT. Will this or will this not prevent cooperation in the civilian nuclear field, is a very simple question.

Participant: I was, in fact, quite glad to hear Dr Raja Ramanna speak about the word disarmament, which is these days a very unpopular expression. I think that focus, which has been a major element of India's policy, has apparently not got articulated in the recent past. Disarmament remains of primary importance not only for global, regional, I would say, India's national security, even in the narrow sphere of pure military capabilities. I would also like to submit one step ahead of this process of disarmament. May I speak about another unfashionable area, the concept of 'no first use'. If we are looking at disarmament as unacceptable to the so-called multipolar configuration within the unipolar framework to which Air Commodore Jasjit referred yesterday, may I suggest another route? Why not start if the process is delegitimization of nuclear weapons? Why not start with 'no first use' and eventually come to the end point of disarmament through the route of delegitimization of nuclear weapons? The second point is that I am not quite clear as to why—although we have almost finished two days of discussions—not much has been said about the initiatives that are being taken, or, I should say, unleashed in the realm of national missile defences and theatre missile defences. I think this is something in the nature of a drastic transformation of the nuclear order and the impact it will have on international security because if we are looking at a Japanese American congruence on establishment of theatre missile defences in the eastern areas of the world, then you look at what impact it will have on China's perception of its own nuclear security and the kind of pressures it will generate on India to go beyond, possibly the minimum credible deterrent that we have been talking about. My last point is, of course, in relation to Mr Xiang's very interesting summary of points on India-China relations and if he has given an impression that the situation is hunky-dory, let me correct him. He referred to the fact that there has been no blackmail by the Chinese in so far as nuclear weapons is concerned. May I draw your attention to a reported incidents in the media about undercurrents of blackmail of the United States by the Chinese in recent years? You mentioned that nuclear weapons are not related to neighbourhood of China. May I suggest to you that while nuclear, we are talking about tactical nuclear weapons are passe as far as the rest of the world is concerned? India's articulated position at least, not in the nuclear security doctrine but general consensus, is that tactical nuclear weapons must not be employed and must not be developed. China is the only country which even today believes in a very major component of its nuclear arsenal being tactical nuclear weapons and this, obviously, will have ramifications in the region. And may I say that about 90 per cent or more of China's nuclear weapons are related to possible employment in the regional context, in which neighbours get directly involved? These are issues which I thought you may like to clarify because there are a whole range of. It is not a border dispute between India and China, you made a reference to that, it is a territorial dispute. There are far too many complexities in that relationship which bring us out to the point that it constitutes a strategic challenge to India in the long-term and, therefore, talks of there being no threat to or a challenge to India from China may be perhaps out of place.

Participant: I think that we must note in relation to CTBT, it is not only the USA which has not ratified it, it is the Russian Duma and the Chinese parliament also which has not ratified it. Which means, three countries possessing almost 85 per cent of the nuclear weapons have not ratified CTBT. So how important it is that France and Britain have ratified it? A treaty does not go into effect even if you ratify it if you don't have to abide by it. So, clearly unless and until there is a move on the part of the bigger nuclear powers and it is a paradox that they have not ratified it when they possess most of the nuclear weapons, and Britain and France have ratified it when they possess a very small quantity of nuclear weapons. So, I think that clearly, India has to take this into account. The reasons that have been put forward in the US Senate as to why they have not ratified the CTBT. A lot of technical arguments have been brought out about ageing of nuclear weapons, countries having more experience with that, about the need to build more compact nuclear weapons in the future, all those are points that go beyond only the issue of a political consensus. There are points relating to nuclear weapons technology as such and in a country like USA, which has the longest experience of operating with nuclear weapons, it is not constant. If the experts are split down the middle on the technical aspects then where does a country like India stand, which has experience of nuclear weapons of only 5, 6, 7 years? Those are issues which are not a question of willingness. They are question of the way the debate has shaped up on nuclear weapons after the CTBT was initialed by heads of states but not ratified by their parliaments. After all, the essential signature is the ratification. Parliament signature, the other one, is the leader's signature. I don't think the CTBT has, in effect, been signed by the major powers. You can talk about ratification as being something totally after signature, but I think that is a real, in a way, verbal distinction. So ratification is the real signature. That is one point. Secondly, the Indo-French dialogue precedes the Indo-American dialogue. So, in that sense, there is no linkage between the two dialogues. In fact, after our nuclear tests there was a violent international reaction and it is the French government, the French President who opened the door to a dialogue with India. And then the French role in trying to moderate international reaction to India's tests, whether within the G7 or the European Union or even in the United Nations discussions, in particular, in the South Asia task-force that was created as a result of the G7 meeting in Birmingham. I can say with confidence that the French have played an extremely helpful and positive role in trying to moderate the discussions within this group. In fact, the French have fairly openly expressed their desire to see this group wound up. We must also bear in mind that when President Chirac came to India in January 1998, one of the important items on the agenda was opening the door to possibilities of cooperation with India in its civilian nuclear power programme. Then our test occurred and the initiative that was taken by the French side got complicated but the French did not allow our decision to conduct nuclear tests to divert them from their decision to continue the dialogue and on this subject too, which has continued since. In the meantime, we announced certain decisions that we were willing to take in the non-proliferation field. On the CTBT we announced a voluntary moratorium and then we said we were willing to convert it into a de jure obligation and then we also made it known that we were willing to sign the CTBT subject to evolving a national consensus. We also said we are willing to participate in the FMCT negotiations and that we are willing to tighten our export controls. So these were the three significant items on our non-proliferation agenda. On the CTBT, I think the expectation has been not only of the French but of others that we were steadily moving in the direction of signing the CTBT. On the FMCT side, the whole issue has got blocked in Geneva, so there is no realistic expectation amongst the countries we are having a dialogue with that anything can emerge from that in the short to medium term, which will allow the international community to positively judge India's role in a FMCT negotiation and then see how this can help them to alter or modify their policies. Insofar as export control is concerned, I think, neither for the Americans nor for the French, it is really a major issue because they all accept that India has been very responsible in terms of safeguarding its nuclear programme and preventing any flow of technology out of India. Now the CTBT issue has become complicated because of the rejection by the US Senate and that what seemed to be, I think in the understanding of the French, one decision which would then enable them to dialogue with their partners and see how India could be, I won't say rewarded, but how the partners could be convinced to look at the entire issue of cooperation in developing India's civilian nuclear problem differently. Now we must remember that the French position has always been as follows, that we understand the reasons why India undertook its nuclear tests even if we don't agree. Even if we regret India's decision, but we understand the security reasons why India undertook these tests. A big country like India is entitled to an independent defence, we understand that. At the same time, we are committed to the nuclear non-proliferation regime, now how do we marry these two, so that we allow India the autonomy to take decisions in the defence area? We have a dialogue with India, but at the same time, ensure that the entire non-proliferation regime doesn't collapse. In this context, it was felt that if a gesture came from India in terms of signing the CTBT, that may give the French reason and the leverage to talk with partners. Now that has not happened and that is where the issue is stuck. I think you are quite right in saying that there is a linkage ultimately between our dialogue with the United States and our dialogue with France because it would be unrealistic to expect, unless the French tell us this that they are willing to do it alone, they are willing to disregard their commitments to the NST or to the nuclear non-proliferation regime, they are willing to have this serious point of difference with the Americans. It is for them to answer that question. Therefore, what we are able to achieve with the Americans, either during Clinton's visit or afterwards, or as a result of our dialogue with them will certainly have a bearing on our discussions with France. Finally, I would say that this entire question is definitely linked to the subject we are discussing today, the creation of a multipolar world, because if India and France are committed to a multipolar world, then this multipolar world will necessarily entail a stronger India and an acceptance of India as a nuclear power, one way or the other. It would also mean that at some stage, there has to be an easing of restrictions on the flow of technologies to India. In other words, the entire subject of application of certain regimes to India has to be reconsidered, whether or not France is willing to move in that direction, what will be the base of moving in that direction will continue to be a subject of our dialogue with the French. Certainly, the question of NPT is totally not on the agenda, neither on the French side nor on the Indian side. Basically, this sums up the way we are in terms of our dialogue.

Participant: I have only three points to make. First of all, on 'no first use'. Here, I wish to say that in Europe, after what we have discovered in the Soviet plans, we do consider that 'no first use' is about lying. It is politically interesting, but militarily it is about lying. It is even more so about lying when you have a lot of tactical nuclear weapons as someone has said before. So as far as I am concerned, this is my own position. Now everything the Germans want to talk about we are ready to talk about with them. Second point concerning CTBT, we could, us French or us British, we could have said exactly what you said, that the United States have not ratified, the Russians have not ratified, that the Chinese have not ratified and so go to hell the CTBT, we don't ratify it either. We didn't do that. Why? Because we thought it was important to be seen as responsible partners because we do believe that to be a major power in the present century is not to have a lot of weapons, it is to deal with important security issues and to be seen as responsible partners. This is my answer to the CTBT. I leave India with its own problems. It is for you to decide.

Participant: My comment is about CTBT. Now, CTBT means stopping, a cessation of testing. Why do you want to test because some countries believe that they have tested enough? What now remains is, well, we have all tested now, stop. There are other people saying, 'well there is more to learn from these tests from the point of view of deterrents'. We should continue testing, that is the feeling that is available in India and we have to draw the line when will you stop testing, because every test costs a lot of money, costs a lot of fuel which will disappear. All this has to be taken into account when you take the economic condition of the whole country. We are not going to have a nuclear war. But one of the things that have always impressed me, especially now that Gen. Nambiar, who is here with me today, used to say, 'How can I maintain the morale of my army, which is fighting on conventional lines with a country which has already got nuclear weapons? We just can't keep the morale because they are sure to end up with a situation that you may have the best. If they are beginning to lose they will probably use the final weapon that they have.' It was a question of morale and I remember, he made a very strong point on some other occasion, I don't know whether you still hold on to it. It is a rather important aspect of deterrents. Another aspect, of course, of deterrents is how far is India going to lead the world—which is a terrible thing to do on disarmament—on keeping Gandhian values, on saying CTBT must come mainly because testing is bad. Of course, it is a very unpopular thing in a group like this which is talking of deterrents, 'no first use'. As the lady correctly said, first use could be a lie in the sense because you have submarines which can be hiding anywhere in the sea and fire off. You don't know who has done it, you may have done it yourself, or the people you trust may have done it; 'no first use' is an answer to a question about first use by itself which is good in the Gandhian sense, but not in the tactical sense. So one has to be careful. Now the last word is about a philosophical question, which my old friend Air Chief Marshall Suri raised, and that is the meeting of minds. On the meeting of minds immediately, you don't give a consensus. You have the first meeting, you see the differences and it goes on. So it has to be a step-by-step affair. Now I am rather surprised on your saying that you expect to get final solutions from all these discussions as this is the beginning of the meeting of the minds. Minds cannot completely get a total picture of the entire situation until this goes on over a long period of time.

Economic Multipolarity and Globalization

Globalization, Economic Order and Multipolarity

PETER R. WEILEMANN

The topic of this third panel actually should have been dealt with at the beginning of this conference on multipolarity and a new international order. Even a political realist who believes in the future of nation states that try to maximize their own interests and remains convinced that politics will control the economy, will have to admit that the impact of economic globalization on the world of nation states and, therefore, on the future international order and multipolarity, is much greater than he likes to realize.

This paper will concentrate on three aspects:

1. The main characteristics of globalization to make it that new political and economic challenge at the beginning of this century;
2. The impact globalization will have on the traditional nation state; and
3. The consequences for the international economic order and its institutions.

Globalization as a Political Challenge

In contrast to some economist's view maintaining that in comparison to the late nineteenth century, globalization basically is nothing new, there are some characteristics that give globalization at the beginning of the twenty-first century a different quality. Not only has mobility of goods and capital increased, but distances and time spaces have decreased. Globalization goes along with a new age of economic civilization.

The common notion of globalization concentrates on the first aspect. New technologies have led to new forms of transnational interaction. Due to high-tech communication and transportation facilities, there is a growing mobility of goods and capital as well as investments. Product markets grow together irrespective of national boundaries and companies are more directly interconnected with foreign countries.

The indicators for that development are well known.

(*a*) *International trade:* The volume of manufactured goods has doubled over the last decade (1999: US $ 5,225 billion; 1990 3, 5 billion services 1,290 billion; 800 in 1990); the growth rate of international trade is twice that of global economic output (7-8 per cent; GNP in real terms 2.3/3.2 per cent).
(*b*) *Direct foreign investment:* Direct foreign investment has tripled over the last 10 years from $ 56 billion in the mid-eighties to $ 208 billion in the mid-nineties.
(*c*) *International capital flow:* In the mid-seventies, foreign exchange trade per day amounted to $ 40 billion approx. In the mid-eighties, this amount had already doubled. In the mid-nineties it is estimated at $ 600 billion per day. In addition, currency trading is 70 times higher than merchandise trade.
(*d*) *Transnationalization:* In the early sixties the number of transnational actors (multinational cooperations, Banks or NGOs) was estimated at 3,500. In the late nineties, UNCTAD counted 44,000 transnational companies alone.

While already these indicators—others might be cited in addition—show that the quantitative growth and the acceleration of international economic and financial processes have a dimension of qualitative change, there is further dimension of technological evolution that brings in additional momentum to the dynamics of international order.

At least, Western economies are undergoing a dramatic structural change. The percentage share of the original primary sector—agricultural production—on the Gross National Product today is well under 5 per cent. In addition to that, 'smokestack' industry has to cede to services industry and new technologies like information technology, bio- and gene-technology, new energy systems, space technology and so on. We are leaving the industrial age and enter-ing the information society, a new world of 'e-commerce' or the 'e-economy'. The implications for the nation state, therefore, are twofold.

The Impact of Globalization on the Nation State

In public general debate, two theses dominate the discussion on the impact of globalization on nation states. The first maintains that globalization widens the unequal distribution of wealth not only between states but also inside the nations. The second argument fears or supports the idea that globalization will undermine the territorial state, that borders will become meaningless and governments will lose control over economic processes. Some go as far as to predict the demise of the modern state as such (Creveld).

As far as the first thesis is concerned, there is some evidence that not as many people benefit from globalization as one would like to see. UNCTAD maintains that in comparison to the seventies, economic growth in developing countries today is 2 per cent lower, while at the same time trade deficits have increased by 3 per cent. Terms of Trade have deteriorated. In addition, liberalization of capital markets has brought fresh private capital, but according to UNTACD, 40 per cent of it is to be considered as 'hot money' that does not help financing long-term growth. In Third World countries as well as in transformation countries, there seems to be only a small group that can participate in international economic transactions while the number of those excluded from economic wealth is growing. From an economic point of view, the balance sheet of globalization is still open. Paul Krugman, at the Davos-Meeting in February 2000, identified two group of people: The Davos-men and the Seattle-men, the immediate beneficiaries of globalization and those who will earn the fruits only at a later stage. To bring the groups together is at the core of any future economic policy.

In Western industrialized countries, too, criticism on globalism is rising partly footing on the same arguments. But the main challenge in those countries lies in preserving their living standards and especially their social welfare systems. Due to factor and capital mobility, a competition of economic systems within and among industrialized countries, transformation in Third World states has started. Production goes to low wage countries with the consequence of high unemployment rates, at least in Europe, and dwindling tax revenues (corporate as well as income taxes) for the state. Combined with demographic trends, these developments put the traditional welfare state under pressure and challenge its legitimacy. This crisis of legitimacy, combined with feared loss of control over the main economic transactions is seen by many as a threat to the modern state in general. This, however, has to be put into perspective. The challenge of transnational actors is there. However, while the turnover of big multinational companies might equal the GNP of medium-sized powers (Ford/Norway; Exxon/Indonesia), it is small in relation to big industrialized countries. (The output of General

Motors, the biggest of the multinational corporations, equals only one-sixth of the Gross national product of Great Britain, the smallest of the 'Big Five'.) While trade protection by tariff has gone down dramatically, grey zones of protectionism are increasing at the same rate. So, boundaries still count. In addition, domestic direct investment is still much higher than foreign investment. Finally, many governments viewing globalization as a chance have embarked on the path of reform and international cooperation without jeopardizing their capacity to control.

The structural change of the economy too, is a challenge as well as a chance for the nation states. It has certainly some truth in it that no longer the rulers of land and material resources will be the leading nations but the rulers of ideas and technologies. Bio- or gene-technology might lead to better use of land and more efficient agricultural production. The quest for territory will be less urgent. National possession of energy or raw-material resources becomes less important than the command of technologies and know-how to exploit and use them more efficiently. Growth rates in the future will be induced by replacement of capital-stock. That means the strong economics will be those where the old industrial infrastructure gives place to new technologies. In addition, one should not neglect the implications of modern technologies on warfare and military power. More nations than before gain relatively easy access to high tech military technology at relatively low prices (Internet; revolution of military affairs). Certainly, one has to hold against this projection that knowledge that does not lead to new technology is *l'art pour l'art*. New technologies need industrialized manufacturing capacities. One must also not forget the question of financing. To take part in the game, a sound fiscal and economic policy—in order to have the stable currency and to attract money—is necessary. Political power depends on financial power. Both support each other. Therefore, the well-established powers already commanding more men and resources than ever before in history. Performing a sound fiscal and economic policy and possessing a good functioning educational system will benefit more from globalization than others. It will be hard for newcomers to join the club. But there are opportunities for new rankings in power status and therewith changes in international power distribution.

The revolution in international economics, therefore, poses challenges for the individual states but not for the nation state as such. The state is not powerless but confronted with additional tasks.

Individual states might get loose or even disappear if they do not adapt to those changes by appropriate economic and political inner reforms and adjust to the international environment. In addition to urgent inner reforms (revamping the welfare systems, structural economic reforms in the industrialized countries or borrowing less in foreign currencies and establishing proper supervisory systems for the banking sector while slowly open up capital markets in developing or threshold countries), all nations will have to reorient their concept of sovereignty and independence. The future lies with those nations which are fit for cooperation not for isolation or going it alone.

Aspects of a New International Economic Order

In the last fifty years (1948-99), 185 economic regional organizations came into being to facilitate economic exchange and promote political cooperation, 100 of them since 1990 only. The success story of the large majority of them has been mixed if not a failure. Most of them are free trade areas whose members are not ready to really pool or share sovereignty. Their organization lacks good working political institutional arrangements. The question of inner coherence, identity and outer boundaries, are not fully addressed. Member States cannot agree on what the regional order should be. And political, if not military, conflicts exist on who is the leading power or should be the hegemon. While with the end of the cold war the influence of great powers on regional arrangements might have declined, the more successful of those organizations have benefited from existence of an external 'federator'. It could well turn out that the structural pressure of globalism might become such a force that leads to a rethinking of traditional concepts of sovereignty. For modern states the prevailing paradigm should be: in order to keep sovereignty you pool or share it. This means, however, for the coming shape of political as well as economic international order that the future lies not with globalization in the sense of one-world-society but with an ever more complex system of interaction between nation states, regional organizations and global institutions. In the context of the topic of multipolarity, two issues arise here: If there is a need for global institutions, how should we manage the interaction between the blocs, the regional and the global level? A second working hypothesis goes like this: Such a system will not be a self-governed but needs legitimate political regulation. The question, therefore, arises: Who should manage it? Who is stabilizing the 'world of trade', the international economic and financial order?

The need for global institutions is obvious. Today's international economy needs an order of competition, including a dispute settlement body as it is known on a national level. Given the growing interdependence of national economies, there is a need for global economic policy. To close the gap between rich and poor countries, a framework for a global adjustment policy must be there. Finally, to manage international monetary liquidity, an international financial structure is needed. The institutions to cope with these challenges exists. The founding of the World Trade Organization was a good step forward to an international order of competition. Guidelines for cooperation in global economic policy are worked out and partly managed by the G7/8. The World Bank (partly in cooperation with the International Monetary Fund) as well as other UN-bodies are responsible for a global development policy. And the International Monetary Fund as well as the BIS (Bank for International Settlement) a charged to manage international liquidity. In comparison to the international political order after the end of the cold war with its anarchical traits, the world of international economy seems rather structured.

However, the present international economic order is challenged conceptually as well as politically. Not only fundamentalists question the basic philosophy of free trade and liberalization, but also the protagonists of the latter see a need for adjusting the existing institutions and arrangements. From a conceptional point of view, the strategic guidelines for reforms are defined. A reform of the global financial system has to heed at least the following three concerns: the frequency and intensity of financial crisis must be minimized. Because of the speed of financial crises there must be sturdier defenses against contagion. Finally, the 'innocent', those who are the bystanders or victims, must be 'better protected from financial hurricanes' (Bindler). The agenda for the next international trade round is well known but, as Seattle has shown, heavily disputed. Access to markets for goods and services must be further liberalized on the basis of predicable and non-discriminatory rules. Social, labour and environmental standards must be integrated into a concept of free trade that is acceptable to all, preferably, a social market economy on a global scale. All this requires global institutions whose decisions are accepted and seen as legitimate. As it would be wrong to discard the philosophy of free trade and free capital flow by going back to protectionism and isolationism, it would also be unwise to completely alter the existing international economic and financial institutions.

Today's international political order suffers because the structure of the cold war disappeared and with it the old military alliances—with the exception of NATO—or groupings like the non-aligned movements that came into being after World War II. But what is often overlooked, however, is that the economic international system, in principle, dates from the same time. Actually, it was an US-design conceived as a corollary to the political Pax Americana. Despite some adjustments, it still is strongly influenced by the United States or—depending on the perspective—dominated by the 'clique of developed countries' (Murasoli Maran). Developing countries are not part of the decision making process in those institutions. Even Europeans complain that while the United States looks for as much unilateralism as possible, they accept only as much multilaterlism as necessary. But it would be wrong to make the US the only scapegoat or to believe it would be better without it. The reform of the political aspects of international economic order should be dealt with from four perspectives.

1. The most fashionable reform proposals concern the role of private international economic actors and NGOs. After Seattle, there is a tendency to offer them new fora (yearly meetings, consultative processes, some sort of consultative parliamentary assembly, etc.) with established international (governmental) organizations. There are many proposals in this respect but no convincing concept exists. Their rights and duties still have to be defined. The fact is, that from the point of legitimacy they have very undemocratic inner structures. In whose name do they act? Who is giving the mandate? So one has to ask seriously whether or not we want to extend the concept of multipolarity to non-state actors. The interests of consumers, industry or banking associations, of trade unions seem still be best represented through the intermediary level of the nation state.
2. The basis of a successful reform starts at home. While the nature of the nation state is changing, it remains still at the same stage. The idea of a world state or world society is an illusion. The main responsibilities for sound economic and financial policy lie with

national governments. This attitude also fits into the logic of subsidiarity as one of the guiding principles of national, regional and global order.

3. But as the idea of world society is a dream, so have the concepts of isolationism or the ideas of unilateral hegemony outlived their practicability in today's world. To the degree individual states pool their resources new forms of horizontal as well vertical coordination among regional bodies and global institutions have to be developed. From an economic point of view this poses challenges of a rather technical nature. The rules as laid down in the GATT or, more recently, the World Trade Organizations agreements, give enough room to accommodate those developments. As long as economic blocs, so the theory goes are spearheads or the avant-garde for a global free trade, they can be accepted. Although in praxis regional economic blocs do not always behave that way the general thrust over the last four decades has gone in the direction of more liberalization in world trade and services as well as financial transactions. What kind of political and economic impact the introduction of the EURO will have in this respect is still an open question.

    - From a political perspective, regional blocs have not yet become a real issue. There is much talk about a new area of Geo-economics, where new blocs in world politics structured around technological leadership compete in world politics. But so far economic competition, even between the most advanced nations, has produced certainly many conflicts but not power-conflicts or even wars. Most of the regional organizations have no political infrastructure to act externally. And if they do so, like ASEAN, it is very weak. Even the European Union, which has turned a Common European Market into a Political Union, still is no active strategic political player in world politics, and certainly not an aggressive one.
    - On the other hand, there is already a structure of political dialogue among important regional blocs: ASEM (EU with ASEAN-countries), the dialogue of the EU with Latin America or transatlantic processes in the framework of the Trans-atlantic Agenda. In reaction to this Asian nations in 1989 established APEC (the Asia Pacific Economic Cooperation Council). This list is far from being complete. What is of interest, though, is that almost all of those intra-regional

cooperations include the United States. This leads to the last point.

4. Global international economic order cannot be upheld without political backing. It was the main advantage of the Bretton Woods order that it was backed up by one strategic power that combined the resources for political leadership as well as economic wealth and technological know how for economic leadership—the United States. A continuation of this is disputed today but mostly for the wrong reasons. Today, the political players are still not present in international economic institutions basically due to their own economic backwardness as a result of many decades of wrong economic policy. An economically weak Russia is not even member of the WTO and only recently member of the G7/8. China's membership in the World Trade Organization is still on hold (not the least due to its lack to play by the rules). Nor is Beijing represented in the IMF and the possibility of its becoming a member of the G7/8 has only recently been put on the air, interestingly enough, by the German Chancellor and now by the Japanese Prime Minister. Countries of the Third World, unlike in the seventies, have no structure of political communication in this field, not to speak of a political leader. Many eyes lie on the European Union, which could take more leadership in international economic institutions to counterbalance the United States. There are not a few indications that the Europeans are in position to act in that way. During the preparation for the new WTO negotiation round Brussels could form a new consensus on many issues, but it still has deficits with respect to its agricultural policies, its behaviour in the banana conflict (more ready to accept sanctions than to submit to international rules) and its policies towards a multilateral agreement on investment (MAI). European insistence on social standards are not greeted by Third World countries. In addition, the rather cumbersome decision-making process within the European Union will become more difficult after enlargement in the next couple of years. With the coming of the Euro many see the dominance of the Dollar challenged. However, this will take time. It took decades for the Dollar to replace the Pound Sterling as the worldwide reserve currency. And, partly due to missing of structural inner reforms, the external value of the Euro today lags far behind the expectations. In addition, there is a European Central Bank responsible for

monetary policy but not for international financial politics. There is no economic government in Europe; the EURO-Council is outside the institutional system of the European Union. And external representation for example in the IMF (which knows only nations states as members) or the G7/8 is not yet settled. But still, in the field of international trade as well as global financial architecture, the European Union is already a heavy weight. And yet, it would be unwise if the EU would exercise that leadership in confrontation with the United States and not in a complementary way within the body of the Atlantic Community, notwithstanding economic competition.

Economic multipolarity is not only a question of institutional reforms. Sticking to a concept of equality of each nation, irrespective of the economic input, might even hamper legitimate distribution of power. Multipolarity is also a question of political will and diplomatic skill. The case of the European development shows some of the basic ingredients of a mature multipolarity. Accepting the challenge of globalization positively, sharing sovereignty, differing on issues but within a shared common value basis and exercising leadership by consensus building and not coercion.

Economic Multipolarity and Globalization: An Indian Perception

MONTEK SINGH AHLUWALIA

Thank you, Mr Chairman. I know that lots of people want to ask questions, and we have had two very thorough and very comprehensive presentation of the issues—certainly the general issues on globalization. I think that they've laid out the ground quite well so I won't give you my view on globalization because there will be a lot of overlap. I mean, the most important thing is to recognize that it is a phenomenon that goes beyond economic interaction, as has already been pointed out. I thought that I would use this time simply to respond to the globalization related issues really from the point of view of where India stands on some of these things. I really can't claim that I am speaking for the southern world as a whole. I mean it's too diverse a group. But I thought it might be useful just to lay out how we perceive some of these things.

Like most countries in the developing world—one of the issues, of course, in India is that the perception that the globalization agenda is not really being set in the developing world—the globalization agenda is being set in the developed world and the developing world has to more or less cope with it. I mean, whatever the issues are and those issues that the developing world wants to put on the agenda may or may not be addressed, and since we don't have much economic clout, to make sure that they are addressed, there's a very fundamental asymmetry as to why people are a little unhappy and uncomfortable with the way globalization is being handled. I think there is a perception around the world that there are some real issues in globalization. It's understandable that developing countries have all kinds of hesitation. I would say that in the last two decades, most developing countries have addressed these issues and moved very substantially forward and I think that's certainly true of India. At any given time, we may be taking positions that appear, certainly to outside observers, as somewhat negative, and maybe not even in our best interests. But I think that simply reflects the fact that this is a very disputatious kind of country where people like having arguments with each other, but if you forget about the noise that is generated on any debate and look back where it is going and what is the trend, then I would say, at least in India, there is a very clear acceptance that globalization, at least in economic terms which means opening up, integrating with the world and coping with the kinds of strains and stresses that poses, this is being accepted as a policy. We have moved in that direction and even though there are tremendous vested interests and so on the way policies have moved, it has been somehow possible to build a consensus in favour of that change towards openness. I just sort of identify for our guests from abroad, some of whom (probably all of whom) are very familiar with what I am going to say. Well, just to put it on the record, I just thought I'd make a few comments on what is happening in India on trade, on technology and on investment capital. These are the economic dimensions of globalization. There are actually other dimensions that I wasn't planning to deal with. Now clearly, as far as trade is concerned, India has, in fact, moved very dramatically from what I think is a traditional suspicion of trade approach. The kind of belief that a highly protectionist regime is good for a developing country to a recognition that we need to open up. The only questions that have been raised are the pace at which that have been done and I think the good news really is we are now pretty much at the end of that pipeline. Till very recently, we used to have a lot of quantitative restrictions, we didn't allow many of our consumer goods to be imported, and somehow, many of our people in the industries used to regard this virtually as a natural policy. They used to think that it's perfectly alright to import capital goods, raw materials and intermediate goods but certainly consumer goods should be protected. It's amazing how widespread this feeling was and despite that kind of attitude, the present position is that we have agreed to eliminate all quantitative restrictions on all kind of commodities, including consumer goods, by April next year. And, in fact, by April 2000, the remaining restrictions will be cut in half, so we will see a very quick transition. In addition to that, the government has been lowering tariff rates, they're still high, but the state position of the government is that within about three years, we want to go down to the tariff levels existing in East Asia which would be, by and large, regarded as one of the open parts of the world. So, the complete elimination of quantitative restriction on trade and a shift to tariffs at about East Asian levels, really means that by the year 2001 or by the year 2002 at the latest, on the trade front, India would have done everything that's really needed to make a very substantial movement on the trade side. As far as technology is concerned, we have been very open and it can be liberalized even further and as far as adherence to international intellectual property regimes. This was an issue that was regarded to be very controversial two or three years ago, but we have now said that we will be fully in line with the Uruguay Round commitments by the year 2005. So that's also another area where the process is well underway. We have made big changes in the investment policy. The government now is to welcome foreign investment in large areas. There's a lot of investment welcome in manufacturing. Not just manufacturing, also in servicing which are quite crucial actually for globalization because whether you look at telecommunication services or financial services. I mean, these areas where opening up foreign investments, bringing up foreign investments is quite crucial in determining the pace of globalization. Both these areas have really opened up. In fact, the one big block in India used to be the area of insurance and it is this year that the government has opened that up as well. So, we expect to have, during the course of the year, joint ventures with foreign companies operating in the area of insurance.

That brings me to the fourth very broad area—the free flow of capita—other than foreign direct investment. Now, here we do tend to have a mixed regime. It's not that free flow of financial capital is not allowed, but firms need to get permission to bring money in the form of debt. The government does not allow short-term debt to be incurred. It encourages long-term debt. I think that area could be liberalized progressively, while keeping short-term debt somewhat restricted and that is more or less the direction in which the policy has been moving.

The last difficult area really is the retention of control outward domestic capital. The present Indian policy is that when a foreigner brings money in, he is free to take it out. So any foreign investor who comes in, can exit whenever he likes. But domestic residents are not able to exit by investing abroad, so there continue to be restrictions on the ability of the Indian companies or Indian individuals, to take money out for whatever purpose. This is being progressively liberalized for investment by companies that are interested in export and also in software hi-technology companies. So, here again is a slightly restrictive policy. I think, policy is following the East Asian crises, when there was a lot of nervousness on what could happen if there is a sudden loss of investor confidence. The desire to maintain a more gradual pace of opening up both for short-term capital inflows and for outflows of domestic capital, is quite likely to continue. But, I think, these are areas where the broad direction is quite clear but we need to move further in the direction of opening up, which means, globalization. The only thing is that the pace is as yet a little bit uncertain. Having said that, in our own areas, many people have doubts about how the end result will be, the policy decision clearly is that globalization is inescapable. The issue really is not whether you hold it back, but how you make a transition. Secondly, what's the best way of managing it? I think, this is really the crux of the thing. Clearly, there are lot of things that we have to do ourselves to manage the globalization process and part of the debate really is on the relative importance of what you have to do yourself and what has to be done by the international committee. My suspicion is on the big difference between the 1990s and the 1970s. I think in the 1970s, there was a perception that opening up and globalization and integration might actually be bad for developing countries. There were schools of thought in some of the developing world which talked about delinking, and a great belief that by doing a bit of delinking and sort of developing autonomously for a while, you were actually in a better position to relink at some point in the future. I don't think anybody seriously holds this view today. So the issue of having an alternative is simply not there. I mean, most are saying, 'Well, we have to globalize because we have to deal with a globalized world.' But that's not the same thing as saying that everybody believes that everybody will be better off. I mean, there are lots of doubts whether countries in certain kinds of situations will be able to benefit from globalization. I think the difference is that India is quite convinced, and so far as the professional thinking classes are concerned, India is quite convinced that we are one of the countries that could benefit from globalization if we do things right that we have to do ourselves. A lot of this increased self-confidence is not based on any analytical belief that we have comparative advantage that others don't have or any such thing, but just the knowledge that as we have liberalized in the last ten years or so, we have, in fact, been one of the better performing countries. I mean, the fact is that in the last two decades, India is one of the twelve fastest growing developing countries in the world. It hasn't been as fast growing, clearly as China. It hasn't been as fast growing as some of the very fast growing East Asian countries, though for some of those countries the very dramatic slowing down in 1997-8 kind of lowers the average growth rate certainly in the 1990s, but still all things taken together, Indian growth rates have accelerated in the last two decades and India is one of the faster growing countries among the developing countries. This is very different from the experience of the many other developing countries who have found that their growth rates during the period of globalization had been lower than that used to be in the 1960s and 1970s. India has done better in the 1980s and 1990s than she did in the 1960s and 1970s. So, this is an important factor that conditions India's approach to globalization.

More recently, you know in some of the areas that are being greatly emphasized as important in the context of globalization—i.e. Information Technology, the experience that we have is very small and limited but it is also very good. This seems to be an area where our companies and firms have grown very rapidly. They're still a rather small part of the global picture but, for the first time, the assessment both internally and externally, is that this is an Indian sector that actually could grow very rapidly. I mean, the numbers that have been talked about—we had virtually no exports of software 4-5 years ago. Probably the export level this year is 3.5 billion Dollars, which is not very much, but many people, including McKinsey, project that there are no effective constraints on India being able to export 50 billion Dollars in IT enabled services, not just software but software plus IT enabled services, say by the year 2008. Now 50 billion Dollars becomes a much more significant number, though I realize that by the year 2008, it will be much less significant that it looks today, since world trade will also grow. But even taking that into account, it's clearly an area where India perceives that if things go right, 80 per cent of that really means that we have to do a lot of things by ourselves, particularly in areas like telecommunications and so on that there are huge win-win possibilities from our point of view. Now having said that, I think there is a lot of concern whether the international environment or the international institution bases to support globalization is being put in place. Both the speakers have spoken about the WTO. I think that's a very crucial thing. I would like to make just one comment. You know our perception of Seattle is that domestically, the government and, in fact, the intellectual opinion in this country had gone through quite a major change of attitudes to go to WTO to the Seattle meeting in a much more positive frame of mind than we used to do in the past. I mean, India did not go to Seattle with the kind of negative approach that critics often said India and other countries had in the past. And it's been a great pity that what we have seen after changing our mind, frankly from our point of view, looks like a completely blatant victory for protectionism. And I see the point that's being made and I see the concern about labour. It's not just a protectionist concern, that's true. But the point is that if people are concerned about labour, there are forums where we can discuss it. There's a real issue whether it makes sense to link labour to trade. I am not saying that if the belief is that linking labour with trade is necessary, then we will insulate the trade regimes, from what maybe perfectly legitimate concerns about other things, and I don't know whether developing countries will be willing to put teeth into ILO, but one can readily concede the importance of who lay the standards, and simply say, 'Yes, let's take it up in the appropriate form'. The second issue is the underpinning of the international financial system. For many years, developing countries used to go on about the flow of official assistance. I think one of the structural facts about the world is that official flows have declined dramatically as compared to private flows. The argument whether there should be more official flows or not will no doubt continue, but as far as India is concerned, I think we are quite prepared to adjust to that change. I think India can attract private capital and the potential for attracting private capital is very large. I think that's true for all developing countries. The notion that private capital will solve all the development and financing problems is not valid, because 90 per cent of the private capital is going to approximately 15-16 countries. India happens to be in that group. So as far we are concerned, we recognize that there is a change in the world and that we can benefit from that change. While this may be true, I think the East Asian crisis has raised real questions about how stable the international financial system is. If countries are going to open up and integrate fully, in order to benefit from the flow of capital, I think there is legitimate concern that potential instability in the system is high. The potential instability is due to deficiencies in the recipient countries and this relates to the whole agenda on the financial system. I think the good thing is that, in the last two or three years, there has been virtually no intellectual disagreement in the developing world that the financial system has to be made much stronger and unless that doesn't happen, developing countries will get exposed to all kinds of liquidity risks and instabilities, which could lead to very serious problems. So, most developing countries have recognized that most developing countries are going through a very intensive process of financial restructuring, improving the norms and improving the prudential standards and so on. This is a process that will take a very long time. We know that banking system have been fragile even in industrialized countries, and until very recently, nobody would have said, until five years ago, that the Japanese banking system is an utter mess. Today, it is difficult to think of a rude remark about banking which is not freely applied to the Japanese banking system. Now we are not so arrogant to think that if the Japanese couldn't get it right and they have been subscribing to international norms. It's not that the Japanese did not subscribe to the bars of norms. I think developing countries have to recognize that even having accepted the right standards, it's going to take several years before a high-quality, supervised system can be put in place which can make sure that the banks are actually strong. Japan is not the only example. You have France also, where banks have run into serious trouble. So we expect that with the best will in the world, fragility in the banking system will remain, and this raises the question that if internal action cannot be a guarantee against financial turbulence, then whether the international financial community is willing to put in place some kind of a protective mechanism, some sort of a lender of last resort type institution. Now, here there has been a very extensive debate on whether the IMF can be made into a sufficiently strong lender of last resort. Michel Camdessus, just before he gave up office, in a very interesting speech in Georgetown University, spoke about the kind of IMF we need. He quite clearly took the view that the IMF needs to be much larger, better endowed, and needs more access to resources in order to be able to step in when there is a crisis situation. But I don't think that this is a universally accepted position. There is the other view which is possibly more powerful, that frankly, a large IMF only encourages an impudent behaviour—the problem of moral hazard. This is actually unresolved. My own feeling is that on the globalization front, as far as financial architecture is concerned, there is a lot of consensus on what we have to do to prevent crises, improvements in financial systems, etc. But I don't think that there is adequate consensus on what we have to do to resolve crises. The crises resolution, the post-crises phase, that issue that of whether more money needs to be made available to the International Monetary Fund when times get difficult, or whether it's better to have a much smaller, a more selective operation and let countries that if you run into trouble, you will just have to suffer. That's morally good for you and will actually discourage you from misbehaving. This issue remains somewhat unresolved. I think, in all this, one issue that needs to be looked at is, we are getting integrated. I think of the East Asian crises, how it spread from East Asia to Russia and how it affected the long-term capital, the market fiasco in Wall Street. The same crisis emerging in Brazil, lots of uncertainty emerging in Latin America. I mean, things haven't gone as bad as people feared in 1998. East Asia is recovering quite well, Brazil was controlled easier than we thought. But, one of the issues that comes up is: Do we have an international framework that is sufficiently consultative in which the developing countries have a sufficient voice? Or, are all these decisions actually being taken by the G7? Or, actually, by the G1 if actually one is being quite frank about it! And my suspicion is that we don't have a good enough consultative forum. The interim committee is one forum, but when the East Asian crisis happened, the United States or any other country didn't find it useful to look at the interim committee, because it had too many representations from too many small countries, including developing as well as European countries. They set up an ad hoc group called the G22, which included many developing countries that don't actually find a representation in the interim committee and had a separate set of discussions. More recently, the G7 has set up a new group called the G20, in which many developing countries, including India, are involved and this is an informal forum for discussion but it's outside the actual fora that deals with the Bretton Woods institution. So, one can't help feeling that in the whole area of governance, we don't have a sufficiently participative credible forum where these kinds of issues are actually discussed. The very fact that we are setting up something like the G20 means that the interim committee is not good enough. There have been many proposals on how we should deal with this issue, and I think that it is an area that we need to focus on. As I said, India is a member of the G20, as are Brazil and Mexico, but these are informal groupings at present, they are not part of the former international structure. Well, I think I will stop with that, maybe when issues come up we can take that up.

Economic Globalization and Multipolarity: Problems, Prospects and Proposals

ZAKI LAÏDI

The transformation that has occurred in the status of globalization in these last three years is the major characteristic. In the eighties, globalization implied an intensification of economic and commercial intercourse. Today, we note its wider comprehensiveness, which operates in two ways.

The first arises out of the fact that globalization is not restricted to traditional tradable goods alone, but extends now to the entire range of human activity. What Seattle has revealed is the competition now arising between social systems and value systems. One of the wagers before us will be to see if we can regulate this competition of value systems through the mechanisms available to us on the commercial level, or if it will become necessary for us to consider some other way of managing these contradictions in the framework of platforms, which are more political in nature.

The issue of the status of globalization presents itself in another way. It has become the model for social change both in the countries of the North as in those of the South. Globalization has become the theory par excellence of social change.

This is a basic shift as it can naturally lead to everything being explained away by globalization. By way of example, the fact of the polarization of a debate over whether economic liberalization increases inequalities or stimulates growth, is absolutely simplistic as it comes down to considering that the dynamics of a country is capable of being encompassed within the sole parameter of liberalization/constriction. The polarization of this debate is fuelled as much by neo-liberals as by the Marxist or post-Marxist opponents of globalization. We have to break free of this polarization, as we are, indeed, aware of the fact that other elements need to be taken account of, such as sequencing or the coalition of interests capable of promoting change. The notion of liberalization is moreover, a very relative one. There are closed economies which are also market economies.

The fact that globalization is in the process of becoming the theory of social change in the world is, however, not a simple ideological illusion. Since the last ten years, globalization has intensified quantitatively as also qualitatively. The following are the five events of note on the subject of globalization:

- The information revolution (finance)
- Chernobyl (environment)
- The fall of the Berlin Wall (ideology)
- The Internet phenomenon (new economy/participative world democracy)
- Seattle (social takeover of globalization)

The fundamental question that globalization throws up is that of the future of politics, of its very survival, in the face of four not negligible developments, namely:

- The erosion of the national framework as a backdrop for evolving social compromise
- The growing commercialization of social and cultural activities
- The declining purchasing power of democracy
- The growing individualization of preferences

It is striking to note that in Seattle, for instance, even the States seemed increasingly to defend very specific interests rather than the general interest.

The social and cultural basis of globalization is an overriding factor today. It is impossible to politically reflect on globalization if one restricts oneself to comparing figures and statistics, for globalization is a portrayal and pertains also to the imagination. To say that problems are appearing because globalization has not made enough advances is as absurd as to claim the contrary. This is, moreover, a subject being debated in Europe. However, the fact that globalization is giving rise to so much apprehension at a time when the economic situation in the world is improving, is a real problem. It results from the fact that the economic, social, and cultural stability of the European middle class, which constitutes the pillar of democratic coalitions, is potentially threatened. The mobility of capital, in contrast to the relative immobility of labour, works against the middle class, particularly in the matter of taxation.

In the present set-up, fears of globalization are expressed both in the North as well as in the South. This shared anxiety shows, however, that we have stepped into the phase of a takeover of globalization by society. In some ways, this social takeover is the expression of a refusal to permit the commercial mould to dominate the entire social field. However, in other ways, it is obvious that it signals the advent of conflicts between ethical preferences.

To decide whether globalization will be beneficial or disadvantageous to the countries of the South is now an outdated matter. At Seattle, most of these countries expressed their desire to be integrated on condition that their inclusion be effected on an equitable basis—Equitable between nations as also within nations. Having said this, the matter of the pace of liberalization and its bearing notably on the definition of the rules of internal competition has still to be settled (Russia versus China).

There are some genuine conflicts of interests between the countries of the North and the South, particularly, between the countries of Europe and those of the South. It is difficult to deny this. Our economic interests are sometimes divergent and our ethical preferences are not always systematically compatible. It must be also acknowledged that numerous countries of the South—India being one of them—have not fully benefited from the Uruguay Round while they are already undergoing the constraints imposed by the WTO (pharmaceutical products). In some ways, the social takeover of globalization by NGOs makes it more difficult to arrive at a compromise.

Having said this, there do exist some means to reduce this antagonism, based on an agenda in the form of the democratization of globalization. How is this to be done? By adhering, firstly, to what I call the principle of coherence. It is not possible to talk of social rights without a prior ratification of the ILO conventions on the matter. Europe has ratified them; the United States has not done so. Let us, therefore, decide as a matter of principle that these conventions must be ratified and let us then ponder over the means to ensure their application.

Europe and the countries of the South can come to an agreement over reforms to be conducted in multilateral institutions, such as the

WTO and the IMF. It is not acceptable that the role of the latter be altered without a real prior discussion, particularly if it is sought to put an end to its action in its fight against poverty.

It is possible to revive the idea of an Economic Security and Development Council whose function, on the basis of a consensus, would consist in defining the legitimate agenda of the international community in the matter of international economic relation every year. This is the crucial point on which Europeans and Indians can find a meeting ground. However, for the countries of the South, there is an important political counterpart. It lies in the necessity of thinking on a regional basis, of uniting rather than becoming divided. Without regionalization, there will be no economic multipolarity.

It is not impossible that the need will arise to redefine the methodology of the liberalization of commercial intercourse. It is increasingly acknowledged that while protectionism is no remedy, liberalization is devoid of meaning, unless accompanied by internal reforms, in the matter of competition, for example, or of the setting up of stable financial institutions. The Asian crisis has brought out the limits of a policy of liberalization not based on internal institutional reforms.

There is, perhaps, a way to work out this matter of internal reforms which would make it possible for the countries of the South to avoid the pitfalls of a liberalization of commercial intercourse without internal institutional reforms. To begin with, this structure could be attempted within a regional framework.

DISCUSSION 3

Participant: I have been concerned that the subject for discussion was 'Economic Multipolarity and Globalization'. Now it has been interpreted by all three speakers as simply globalization and it has been assumed that the only polarities here are bipolar, the developing world and the developed world—the G77 and the G7. I would have thought that we could have spent some time in analysing the actual distribution of economic power and interest in the world, which is not as simple as these speakers describe. For instance, the groups, the regional groups are important and their interests are not the same, even within the G7. As Montek pointed out, G1 and G7 are not always of the same views. So the division of the problems of economic decision-making into simply this one framework seems to be against what we were supposed to discuss here. I will give one example—that one of the things that is developing is the rise of Euro zone and the Euro as a reserve currency. So, potentially, we may be moving into an area where there will be now three reserve currencies, the Dollar, the Euro and the Yen, this means a certain number of new outlooks and choices for the rest of the world. I would have liked to have seen perhaps some recognition of the differences in polarities, not just developed countries versus developing countries. In the same vein, the extent of convergence of interests between the G77 and the G7 has been somewhat exaggerated by Montek that these differences still exist and spill over into problems about the structure of the financial institutions, the distribution of power within the financial institutions, the question of the speed of integration and so on, which one could I think, have been discussed with some benefit.

Participant: May I be perfectly frank? I felt somewhat disappointed that there was absence of any concrete steps being recommended for reform of the system and for keeping globalization in check. There were a number of vague generalizations and, of course, Montek was good enough to mention about the role of the IMF, the increased role of the IMF but he ultimately kept the issue open and did not come out frankly with exactly what he would like IMF to do. So perhaps, he may like to clarify what his views on this matter are.

Also, it is not clear what exactly will be the effect of globalization on the poor and vulnerable. After all, if you want to take advantage of globalization, you must have the necessary infrastructure, heavy investments in computers and adequate power supply and so on. There, I think, the poor sections of the community and the poor countries are at a disadvantage. So could it be argued that globalization is likely to widen differences as between nations? Probably it is the more developed and advanced countries that would benefit from globalization, while those who are lagging behind will be a case of devil take the hindmost. Is this a true apprehension or is it not? And also, does it mean that there would be even greater differences than exist at present between the comparatively wealthy people and the comparatively poor people who cannot afford a computer and cannot enter into e-commerce? Now there was another thing that I felt I should bring up. Does it mean that globalization might result in the import of inflation from outside? Does it mean that any changes in interest rates or in stock market prices in Wall Street or in industrial countries is likely to have an effect on us through no fault of our own? Does it also mean that there is likely to be erosion of control of monitory policy and financial policy by the Reserve Bank and by the Ministry of Finance because of these external influences coming from outside?

Participant: I wonder if the problem of labour standards isn't much more difficult than has been suggested. It is true in a sense the logic of 'why not discuss this where labour standards are discussed is there' but there, is a further point that it is such a difficult issue in the sense that it can't be discussed in isolation. Second question: The environmental effects of globalization and a very rapid growth of the hole in the ozone layer in many parts of the world. No one seems to have discussed that. Again, it seems to me as another very large issue which is difficult to leave out of any larger picture of this.

Participant: I want to intervene but I am tempted by the observation just now made about labour standards. Now frankly, Mr Laïdi, you said you spoke like a scholar but you actually spoke like the advisor to Pascal Lamy. I don't think that debate can be addressed in terms of the ethical issues you have raised. It is not an ethical debate. If it is ethics that is defining the issue of labour standards and trade, then there are so many other ethical issues in the area of economic policy, trade policy, the functioning of IMF, the functioning of the World

Bank, patterns of aid flows, patterns of trade flows, etc. Once you bring ethics into all these things it becomes far more complicated. So, if you are suggesting that we should address the problem that you have raised, not because it is protectionist but because there are ethical issues involved, I am afraid you are opening up a Pandora's box. There are so many ethical issues in international relations which cannot be addressed by organizations like the WTO or by trade regimes, which is the point that Dr Ahluwalia made. There are serious ethical issues involved in linking environment to trade but OECD has done a study which shows that 300 years ago, China and India together accounted for a little less than 50 per cent of world national income and in the last 300 years our share has come down from about 48 per cent to 10 per cent together. All projections into the next ten years suggest that these two shares are going to increase. When we talk about multipolarity and globalization in the context of multipolarity, I think the central issue which we are addressing is: How does the world cope with the growth process of China and India? As China and India claw back this share of world income and as their industries grow and as their people find new work, how are Europe and America—whose share increased over the last 300 years going to deal with that situation? If you are going to say, protect our standard of living, our quality of living, that every American worker will have a car and every European home will have a certain minimum level of income and that touching this is ethical attack on our quality of life, then how do we, in the developing world, cope with it?

Participant: I think we are not in deep disagreement. That is precisely the reason why I said that we have and we need to enlarge the debate and give to the south the possibilities for expressing its own ethical preferences. I have personally written many times that it is unacceptable that ethical preferences are always defined by the north. So I want to have all ethical preferences discussed and debated in a new institutions concerning the core labour standards. What I said was simply the fact that we cannot just say that the question is raised for protectionist reasons. I said that a certain number of groups, economic groups are using this argument in order to defend their own interests but you cannot limit the issue to this protectionist dimension. That is what I said concerning the necessity of having much more balanced institutions. I mean, which is the crux of the matter? I agree 100 per cent with you.

Participant: But the intensity of this very interesting debate impelled me to say a word or two. What is being missed out in all this is, whether it is based on ethical issues or whether it is based on other interests. Gradualness is being missed out in the whole thing, if one-tenth of Indian labour force or one-twentieth of the Indian labour force, which means millions, is child labour. Is anybody saying in the policy-making circles in India or in the other circles that this should continue? No, it is all clear that the idea is for our own good of our soul and our good, our own good. The idea is to slowly move away from this, but can we get rid of millions of workers overnight? We can, if phasing out has to be done and are the people who are criticizing Indian child labour—as they ought to—reconciled to the idea of policies being made, implementations being expedited and gradually the child labour force eliminated. That is one of the reasons why the conference failed and did not come to grips with this issue successfully. It was the via media of gradual social change which United States went through, which England went through, which Europe went through. Look at the history of the eighteenth and the nineteenth centuries. I teach that subject in universities and so on. And then, through democratic processes, through gradualness, through social influences, these things were slowly eliminated. That will happen in India. It is happening everyday but nobody is opposed to that, the government has not said we are going to stand by child labour. The same with Human Rights and many other things, the same with environmental improvements, which do come into conflict in the short run interests. But India is not saying and there are many countries in the developing world are not saying that we will continue to persist in environmental degradation. That is not the point.

Participant: I have the feeling that Indians at this stage have more faith in Adam Smith than China at the beginning of the reform and of Chinese economy. The model is the so-called East Asian model and now, only now, slowly the transition was made into the Smith's kind of thinking of free trade. The measures taken in East Asia are very important in China. Certainly other East Asian countries are creating a large area of so-called spatial or special economic zones, meaning you still have protection for the necessary minimized risk, at the same time attracting public capital. And I don't know if India ever thought about it or is thinking into it or it simply doesn't apply to the Indian economy.

Participant: I don't want to get into an argument with the scholar, as he called himself. Are we going to discuss matters which are not directly related to exports? In which case what are the matters that I am going to take up? Why not ideological issues? If the advanced countries do not have any objections to import goods from countries where there is no democracy, we can also raise that question. And so far as child labour is concerned. I think there is a very wrong impression about India. I can speak only about India. India, perhaps, is one of the first countries to appoint a commission on child labour. In our constitution, child labour has been abolished but it has not been fully implemented and there are certain cracks in our country—for instance carpet. The art does not come from training in colleges or schools. It is a traditional art, it comes down from fathers to sons or daughters. And, therefore, this matter should be treated as a very serious matter. I can understand that you object on the ground of quality or competitiveness. That is different. Therefore, I think the present attitude in WTO as a whole and the advanced countries has to change.

Participant: One is that we have gradually, in fact, very easily from the beginning, slipped from multipolarity to globalization and the whole discussion has been on globalization. It is a very good discussion, no doubt. Congratulations to the participants and I think we have taken notes from this. Multipolarity also has to be addressed and I have only one point to make here. If you have only bipolarity in the minds of many people as the dominant feature that creates monopoly and monopoly, it has always been regarded even in the United States as a very bad thing, unproductive, less productive and so on. Far better to move on from dualism or duality to multipolarity and that is the main thrust or should be the main thrust of this discussion. The larger the points of trade, commerce, sale, production, exchange, the larger the number of points, the better it would be for the world. That is how a direction has to be towards multipolarity. Oligopolies and monopolies, dependence on one country by a developing country or—shall we say—dependence on a few countries creating monopolies and oligopolies, is not good enough. We have to move out of that. National policies also have to move away from monopoly, oligopoly and I am very glad that my own country in the whole of this decade, has been moving away from the controlled economy, the monopoly in government and the monopoly in the corporate sector. It has been moving away from that, liberalizing and our liberalization basically—as you know—has been delicensing industries. Go ahead and expand your capacity. Move away from the position where, in India, for forty years, what to produce, how much to produce, where to produce, when to produce, with what capacity to produce, with what technology to produce, was being determined by monopolistic, oligopolistic governmental organizations. Bad enough and that is why our growth has been slower than what it could be. Now these new policies that move away to competitiveness, liberalization and then to globalization and so on in the same direction. I end up by saying that there are secular trends in the world. Nobody will be able to stop globalization whether you think of this or that, whether your view is this or your view is that, whether your view is obstructive or not, globalization will come. Every age has certain master tendencies against which it is as difficult to oppose. So that will come. The question is: With what efficiency? With what efficiency of transition can globalization come? But coming it is and I think it will come. I will end with only one assertion and that is that those countries that believe in multipolarity and globalization should notice that there will be obstructions to globalization in many areas of the world. When the playing fields are not level and some have marched away for 150 years of industrial revolution and commercial revolution and others are lagging behind, it is silly to talk about equality of treatment and globalization as though all have to. The playing fields are not level. Those who want globalization ought not only to globalize themselves but think of the globalization of others as well. That can happen only if aid, assistance, technical change, transfer of technology or whatever methods, through these methods, those who have lagged behind have to be assisted. Why? Because if they grow through these assistances and the markets widen, it will be good for the developed countries to have this kind of treatment of uplifting those who have lagged behind in the process of globalization. It is not just sympathy but a technical necessity for the first world. They will soon notice it. Recessions have also occurred. Now we are not talking of the recession because this is a phase of prosperity, particularly in the United States and elsewhere in Europe too and now the East is also coming out of that but the phenomenon could occur again quite easily so the fourth or fifth major recession in the world, in the Western world in particular, and heaven forbid that it should not happen. But should it happen, some of the things mentioned even by Mr Laïdi about managing the financial matters better, managing recessions better and helping each other out for the sake of expansion of the markets, in the short run, to get out of the recession and expansion secularly so that those countries of the world, the developed countries that are reaching some level of secular stagnation will be able to overcome that through the expansion of trading in other countries which are at the moment, poor. In India, we are trying to uplift the poor, reduce the level of adversity and reduce the level of poverty. What for? Not for social good, not for ethical reasons alone, although ethical reasons are very important. But we want to improve the opportunities for those who have, but cannot go further until those who have not develop further and give opportunities for further expansion to those who are reaching near stagnation.

Concluding Session

SPEECH BY HUBERT VÉDRINE

This Franco-Indian Seminar which has just been held, constitutes an additional milestone in a relationship which is developing and growing stronger, as recent events show:

- the State visit by President Chirac to India in January 1998,
- the four meetings of the Franco-Indian Initiative Forum, the latest of which ended just yesterday,
- the two visits to India by Claude Allègre, Minister of Education, Research and Technology,
- the four sessions of the strategic dialogue between our two countries, the most recent of which took place last week in Paris,
- the visit by the Indian Prime Minister to France in September 1998,
- the visit by my colleague Jaswant Singh to Paris in May 1999,
- the visit by the Indian Minister of Defence, Mr Fernandes, in January 1999 as a prelude to the State visit by President Narayanan in April 2000.

Not to mention the many high-level economic contacts which confirm a new and mutual interest on the part of businesses and investors. You can see that, if we had to catch up, we have to a large extent done so and we're in the process of building something new.

It was high time that our two countries, both of which are committed to making their own assessments of world realities and autonomous decision-making with regard to the major issues affecting the planet, take the time for an in-depth dialogue. A start has been made. The benefits are obvious. We must continue.

For nearly ten years now, international relations have no longer been dominated by bipolar confrontation. It is regrettable that we were unable to move straight from the bipolar world order—which although intellectually convenient was, in reality, a source of instability and conflict, particularly in the Third World countries, and which ignored freedoms—to a more equitable international system more in line with the new demographic, economic and geopolitical realities. However, although history may sometimes proceed in leaps and bounds, miracles do not exist. The task of building this equitable world remains to be performed. It lies before us.

The current world is characterized by a virtual unipolarity. A single State, the United States, is in a position of supremacy on the world scene in every area. To describe this situation I have used, as you know, the term 'hyperpower'. I believe that the term 'superpower' is no longer adequate to describe the United States, because it refers, above all, to the cold war and to military power. In the United States, I have sometimes been criticized for doing this. And yet American specialists in political science have themselves employed the term, while others have used the word 'omnipower'. Whatever the term, it is intended as a statement of fact, not criticism.

The United States has today, as no country before it, concentrated all forms of power and influence, from the most conventional, 'hard' forms, such as military power, to the Dollar and advanced technology and now to the most recent, 'softest' forms of influence—culture, communications and media. American versions of the words and images circulating in the world constitute 70 per cent. Perhaps this is less noticeable in India, thanks to the strength and vitality of Indian culture. This allows the US to shape a perception of the world, and if one adds to that the global dissemination of standardized products of mass consumption, including cultural products, there is a risk of ultimate cultural uniformity.

Is proof needed? At the time of the announcement of the 183 billion Dollar merger between AOL—America on Line—and Time Warner, the *Washington Post*, in its 11 January 2000 issue, reported the following comment by an American futurologist, Bruce Sterling: 'It's a great day for American cultural imperialism. Demand has never been greater. America has never been more culturally dominant.' And the newspaper added: 'Resistance is pointless'. The natural slope of this combination of 'hard power' and 'soft power' is in the direction of hegemony. We admire the creative vitality of America, but we think that all cultures and all languages have the right to live and flourish and interact with each other.

The current state of the world is not satisfactory.

In an address in Paris on 7 February 2000, the Special Adviser to the Indian Prime Minister, Mr Brajesh Mishra, put forward a concept which I found striking, that of global lateralism, to describe the relationship between the United States and the rest of the world.

It is true that in many areas the US engages in unilateral practices, be it in the desire to bypass international institutions, in strategic decision-making, or in failing to meet commitments expected by the world community. But at the same time, we have to be honest. This approach is due far more to Congress than to the administration, which in very many instances, seeks dialogue and partnership.

But there is no point in complaining. After all, the United States has achieved this enormous power and this exceptional position because many powers in the world failed and many others turned to the United States for assistance and relied on it for their security. The United States has no hidden agenda; this has occurred as the result of the historical cycle of events, due largely to the huge failures of the European powers at the beginning of the twentieth century.

The United States, furthermore, remains a central and major factor in international stability. Nevertheless, this unipolar system is excessive, questionable and has negative implications, including for the United States. There's a debate going on in the US itself on the counterproductive aspects of this superpower. This is why we are determined to work for a multipolar world which exists potentially.

This concept goes back a long way in time. In 1962, a distinguished French thinker, Raymond Aaron, was already challenging the 'universal monarchy' and calling for a 'plurality of protagonists'. The term would be nothing more than a slogan if it referred only to an inescapable development. However, there are no foregone conclusions. It's for us to build this future.

This seminar has quite rightly highlighted the need for us to rethink the way in which the international system is organized. This will be a lengthy process and its terms must be clarified.

What conditions must be met for the multipolar world to emerge and signal progress? Let me, here, try to answer that question.

First of all, for us, the French, there can be no multipolar world without a strong Europe as one of its poles. This is why France is working to make Europe a power based on a dynamic internal market, a single currency which will be the world's second reserve currency and which we hope our British friends will soon join, a common approach to defence and defence capability—both of which have been considerably strengthened over the last year—as well as a European foreign policy able to assume responsibility, particularly with regard to establishing lasting peace in the crisis zones on Europe's periphery and establishing strategic partnerships with all

Europe's major partners. We will ensure that the enlargement of the European Union does not lead to a dilution of what has already been achieved or paralyse Europe's ability to act.

I would add that in my view, Europe is particularly predisposed to be a pole of cooperation in the multipolar world by virtue of its over four decades of experience, its organization, its internal coordination procedures and its ability to produce compromise among the old nation states which make it up and to overcome the divisions which battered it far too long. If the great States of Europe had remained unilateralist, the European Union would never have been born.

For me, the second prerequisite, which flows from what I have just said, is that the poles which emerge should not oppose each other individually or in groups, but rather, maintain mutual relations based on cooperation. Multipolarity will have to be, to the greatest extent possible, cooperative.

A plurality of poles won't be enough to guarantee stability. We saw this in the past with the 'balance of powers' which turned into the 'imbalance of powers'. Those who enjoy thinking up scenarios could describe situations in which the major poles confront or threaten each other or at least refuse cooperation. What sort of progress would we have made if at the end of the day, new blocks were set up, lending themselves to alliances and counter-alliances among the poles, in a situation fraught with long-term instability?

It is with this quest for controlled and constructive multipolarity in mind that France has embarked on an advance dialogue with all the other potential poles: an ongoing and wide-ranging dialogue with the United States, which is our friend and ally but with which we are not aligned, development of our relations with Russia to establish a long-term strategic Euro Russian partnership—regardless of the gravity and scale of the problems that country is facing today. It is in Europe's interest to have as its neighbour a stable Russia which solves its problems peacefully—a global partnership with China, an increasingly substantive strategic dialogue with India, of course—I have already stressed its growing depth—a stronger dialogue with Japan, and development of our dialogue with Brazil and the whole of Mercosur, South Africa and other states which will contribute to the structuring of tomorrow's world.

Another prerequisite of a multipolar world is that India be a full participant. If a multipolar system is built, I am convinced that India will be, and must be, one of its poles. This country-civilization as old as history, has many assets of which one of the main ones is to be the world's greatest democracy and a strong one.

In the eighteenth century, as you know, one of the French thinkers of the Enlightenment, Jean-Jacques Rousseau, believed that democracy could function more easily in a small country. India has, happily, proved him wrong. An open society, enlightened by a free press, is a lasting guarantee of domestic stability and international influence.

Furthermore, in this part of the world, the vast Asia, where many things are in a state of flux, where many tensions and uncertainties remain, it is important that large states contribute to stability and that the emerging groupings of states—I am thinking here of ASEAN consolidate, including in the area of security.

If these prerequisites were met—there would be others, but I don't want to speak for too long—stability would be guaranteed not, as the conventional theory of international relations had it, by the balance of power alone (though that common sense idea should not be thrown out of the window), but also by shared common rules accepted by all and, better still, whenever possible, by common values.

This is why a multipolar world must be combined with an improved version of multilateralism.

All states or groups of states which are or intend to become poles have the responsibility to promote and practice a multilateralism which respects all the other members of the international community, as expressed by the United Nations Organization, which today has 188 members.

France is committed to the establishment of and compliance with international rules. Both President Chirac and the Prime Minister regularly press this point. 'The world needs rules', the French Prime Minister declared when addressing the United Nations General Assembly in September 1999. It needs them now more than ever. This applies especially to conflict resolution through negotiation between the parties and to compliance with multilateral dispute settlement procedures. Negotiated conflict resolution is one of the responsibilities of the powers of today and the poles of tomorrow. I will not here go into the need for rules in economic affairs, but it is as obvious as in the strategic area.

The quest for a multipolar world is not at odds with the role of the Security Council, to which France, as you know, is very committed.

The Council's authority must be strengthened by means of reform to make it more representative of today's realities and enable it to provide a link between the multipolar world and the multilateral system.

A strong Council is especially needed at a time when the United Nations Organization risks finding its effectiveness weakened by the proliferation of micro-states, or even pseudo-states with no viability, whose sovereignty exists only on paper and which often fall prey to organized crime, the Mafia; the proliferation of such artificial sovereignties contributes to instability in the world. Contrary to an idea widely held by public opinion in the West, the states of today's world are not too strong but often too weak. In any case, in this Security Council, enlarged, reformed, and relegitimized through this reform, India obviously has its full place. That is our position.

Your seminar also examined the relationship between democracy and security. In an ideal world, stability would arise out of shared, common political values. This is a fantasy. We haven't got to that point and we aren't living in a world without dangers. Every state has the duty of ensuring the security of its citizens without threatening that of others, but paying due regard to the rules I recalled just now.

Today the great political values of democracy and respect for human rights are tending to become universal and this is a huge step forward. But the way in which the Western countries sometimes impose them through threats, or use them for their own purposes, can lead to suspicion and rejection, because in them, we can detect neocolonialist ideas or efforts indirectly to exercise power. Nevertheless, universal values do exist. So we must transcend these apparent inconsistencies.

How can we ensure that men and women the world over recognize these universal values as their own, embrace them and benefit from them? As I see it, democratization is not like a conversion, an ideological or religious revelation, but is rather a historical, sociological and economic one. Therefore, all things considered, a political process which has to move forward, should be consolidated in states. This process of transformation is driven by a constant dialectic between development, modernization and democratization. But we must not allow the legitimate incremental approach to political transformation to be used by autocrats as a pretext for freezing the status quo and justifying domestic repression of the forces of democratic change.

India is exemplary from every point of view because it has been able democratically to take up all the challenges it has faced.

There is a similar debate with respect to the dialectic between state sovereignty, on the one hand, and intervention to protect peoples, on the other—what in France we call the issue of interference—which Kofi Annan so clearly described in September 1999. How can these two needs be reconciled, especially when massive human rights violations occur? Recognition of and respect for equal sovereignty of states is the foundation of the international system; but we can no longer accept that leaders who perpetrate massacres and atrocities should, in the name of sovereignty, be able to oppose international intervention to protect peoples, provided this has been decided legitimately. We must together devise rules which organize and provide a legal framework for sovereignty. Sovereignty must be preserved, since where it is being eroded, it's the jungle that is spreading, but, at the same time we must establish limits to the excesses of certain states and enable the necessary humanitarian interventions to be decided on under less difficult conditions than those provided by the United Nations Charter. That is the exercise today assigned to the international community and especially to the permanent members of the Security Council and not just them, but also those destined to join them.

This brings me to my conclusion.

The establishment of the multipolar world, which we want, requires an overall approach, vision of the future and unremitting effort. This seminar is a useful contribution to this necessary endeavour because it has broadened the remit to include security, economics and international institutions. It demonstrates how productive the Franco-Indian relationship is at the intellectual and geopolitical levels. India and France—and through it, Europe, whose presidency France will be assuming in the second half of this year—are well placed to work together to design this cooperative multipolarity, which is our common goal.

INTERVENTION DE HUBERT VÉDRINE

1. Ce séminaire franco-indien qui vient de se tenir, est une étape supplémentaire dans une relation en train de se développer et de se renforcer. J'en rappellerai les étapes les plus récentes:

- la visite d'Etat du Président de la République en Inde en janvier 1998,
- les quatre réunions du Forum d'initiative franco-indien, la dernière venant de s'achever hier,
- les deux visites en Inde de Claude Allègre, ministre de l'éducation, de la recherche et de la technologie,
- les quatre sessions du dialogue stratégique entre nos deux pays, dont la plus récente a eu lieu la semaine dernière à Paris,
- la visite du Premier Ministre indien en France en septembre 1998,
- la visite de mon collègue Jaswant Singh à Paris en mai 1999,
- la visite du Ministre indien de la Défense, M. Fernandes en janvier 1999, en attendant la visite d'Etat du Président Narayanan en avril 2000;

sans compter les très nombreuses visite à caractère économique au meilleur niveau, qui confirment un intérêt nouveau, et mutuel, des entreprises et des investisseurs. Vous voyez que si nous avions un retard à rattraper, nous l'avons largement fait et nous sommes en train de construire quelque chose de neuf.

Il était temps que nos deux pays, attachés tous les deux à avoir leur propre analyse des réalités du monde et à leur autonomie de décision face aux grands enjeux planétaires, prennent le temps d'un dialogue approfondi. L'impulsion a été donnée. L'intérêt est évident. Il faut poursuivre.

2. Depuis bientôt dix ans, les relations internationales ne sont plus dominées par l'affrontement bipolaire. On peut regretter que l'on n'ait pas été en mesure de passer directement de cet ordre bipolaire – sans doute commode pour l'esprit mais qui fut en réalité instable et conflictuel, notamment dans les pays du Tiers Monde; et qui faisait l'impasse sur les libertés – à un système international plus équitable et plus conforme aux réalités démographiques, économiques et

géopolitiques que nous observons désormais. Mais si l'histoire procède parfois par bonds, les miracles y sont inexistants. La tâche de bâtir ce monde équitable reste à accomplir ; elle est devant nous.

Le monde actuel est caractérisé par une quasi unipolarité. Un seul Etat, les Etats-Unis, se trouve en position de suprématie sur la scène mondiale sur tous les plans. Pour décrire cette situation, j'ai employé à quelques reprises, vous le savez peut-être, le terme nouveau **d'hyperpuissance**. J'estime en effet que le terme de « superpuissance » ne suffit plus pour décrire les Etats-Unis, car il se réfère surtout à la guère froide et à la dimension de la puissance militaire. Ceci m'a été parfois reproché, aux Etats-Unis. Ce terme a pourtant été employé par des analystes américains de science politique, d'autres experts américains parlent d'ailleurs « **d'omnipuissance** ». Quel que soit le terme, ce sont des **constats**, et pas des critiques, le point de départ de toute analyse étant la clarté.

Le Etats-Unis réunissent en effet aujourd'hui, comme aucun pays avant eux, toutes les formes de la puissance et de l'influence: des formes les plus classiques ou les plus « hard », comme la puissance militaire, aux formes les plus nouvelles, les plus « soft » de l'influence – culture, communications, média – en passant par le dollar et les hautes technologies. Je rappellerai que 70% des mots et des images qui circulent dans le monde sont d'origine américaine, peut être que cela s'aperçoit moins en Inde parce que la force et la vitalité de votre culture vous permettent de modeler une vision du monde, et si on ajoute la diffusion planétaire de produits de consommation de masse standardisés, y compris culturels, le risque apparaît de l'uniformisation culturelle.

En veut-on une preuve ? Lors de l'annonce de la fusion entre AOL – America on Line – et Time Warner, pour un montant de 183 milliards de dollars, le *Washington Post* du 11 janvier rapportait le commentaire suivant d'un futurologue américain, Bruce Sterling : *« It's a great day for American cultural imperialism », c'est un grand jour pour l'impérialisme culturel américain. « Jamais la demande n'a été aussi forte. L'Amérique n'a jamais été plus dominante au plan culturel »*. Et le journal d'ajouter : *« toute résistance est futile »*. La pente naturelle de cette combinaison de « hard power » et de « soft power » c'est l'hégémonie. Or, si nous admirons la vitalité créatrice de l'Amérique, nous pensons aussi que toutes les cultures, et que toutes les langues ont le droit de vivre de se développer et de dialoguer entre elles.

3. L'état actuel du monde n'est pas satisfaisant.

Lors de sa conférence le 7 février dernier à Paris, le conseiller spécial du Premier Ministre indian, M. Brajesh Mishra, a avancé une notion qui a retenu notre attention, celle d'**unilatéralisme global**, pour désigner la relation des Etats Unis au monde.

Il est exact que sur bien des plans, les Etats Unis ont des pratiques unilatérales, que ce soit dans la tentation de contournement des institutions internationales, dans des décisions stratégiques, dans le fait de se soustraire à des engagements attendus de la communauté mondiale. Mais il faut être honnête en même temps, cette attitude est beaucoup plus le fait du Congrès que de l'administration qui recherche, elle, le dialogue et le partenariat dans bien des cas.

Mais se plaindre ne sert à rien. Après tout, si les Etats Unis ont conquis cette énorme puissance et cette position exceptionnelle, c'est parce que beaucoup de puissances dans le monde ont échoué et que beaucoup d'autres se sont tournées vers les Etats-Unis pour obtenir leur aide et s'en remettent à eux pour leur sécurité. Les Etats-Unis n'ont pas de plan secret, c'est l'action de l'histoire, due en grande partie à l'immense ratage des puissances européennes au début du XXème siècle.

Les Etats-Unis sont et restent d'ailleurs un facteur central et majeur de stabilité internationale. Il n'empêche que ce système trop unipolaire est excessif, contestable et comporte des aspects néfastes, y compris pour les Etats-Unis. Un débat a lieu aux Etats-Unis même sur ce sujet, sur les aspects contreproductifs de cette superpuissance. D'où notre volonté d'œuvrer à un monde multipolaire qui existe potentiellement.

4. Ce concept est d'ailleurs de conception ancienne : un penseur français éminent, Raymond Aron, en 1962 contestait déjà la *« monarchie universelle »* et appelait de ses vœux la *« pluralité des acteurs »*. Mais ce terme ne serait qu 'un slogan s'il était présenté comme une évolution automatique. Or, rien n'est écrit d'avance. C'est à nous de construire cet avenir.

Votre séminaire a mis en évidence, à juste titre, la nécessité d'un effort de réflexion sur les modalités concrètes de l'organisation du système international. Il s'agit d'un processus de longue haleine, dont les termes doivent être clarifiés.

5. Ce monde multipolaire, à quelles conditions peut-il émerger et marquer un progrès ? Je voudrais, devant vous, essayer de répondre à cette question.

– D'abord, pour nous Français, le monde multipolaire ne serait un progrès que si une Europe forte était un de ses pôles. C'est pourquoi la France s'emploie à ce que l'Europe devienne une puissance, assise sur un marché intérieur dynamique, une monnaie unique qui sera la deuxième monnaie de réserve du monde et à laquelle nous espérons que nos amis britanniques se joindront bientôt, une volonté et une capacité de défense commune qui se sont beaucoup renforcés depuis un an, une politique étrangère européenne capable de prendre ses responsabilités, notamment pour pacifier durablement les foyers de crises à la périphérie de l'Europe et établir des partenariats stratégiques avec tous les grands partenaires de l'Europe. Nous veillerons à ce que l'élargissement de l'Union européenne ne se traduise pas par une dilution de ses acquis et une paralysie de ses capacités d'action.

J'ajoute que, à mes yeux, l'Europe est particulièrement prédisposée à être un pôle coopératif dans le monde d'orientation multipolaire, en raison même de son expérience depuis plus de quatre décennies, de son organisation, de ses procédures de concertation interne, de sa capacité à produire des compromis entre les vieux Etats-nations qui la composent, du dépassement des clivages qui l'ont si cruellement meurtrie. Si les grands Etats de l'Europe étaient restés unilatéralistes, l'Union européenne n'existerait pas.

– Pour moi, la deuxième condition, qui découle de ce que je viens de dire, est que les pôles qui émergent ne s'opposent pas en pôles, ou alliances de pôles, antagonistes, mais entretiennent entre eux des relations fondées sur la coopération. La multipolarité devra être, dans toute la mesure du possible, coopérative.

La pluralité des pôles ne suffira pas à garantir la stabilité. (...). Les amateurs de scénarios pourraient décrire des situations dans lesquelles des pôles majeurs s'affronteraient ou se menaceraient, ou au moins refuseraient toute coopération. Où serait alors le progrès si en fin de compte des blocs se reconstituaient, propices à un jeu d'alliances et de contre-alliances de pôles contre pôles, porteur d'instabilité durable ?

C'est dans cet esprit de recherche d'une multipolarité maîtrisée et constructive que la France a engagé un **dialogue précurseur** avec tous les autres pôles potentiels: dialogue permanent et multiforme avec les Etats Unis, qui sont nos amis et nos alliés, mais par rapport auxquels nous ne sommes pas alignés; développement de nos relations avec la Russie pour établir un partenariat stratégique euro-russe à long terme quelles que soient la gravité et l'ampleur des difficultés que ce pays rencontre aujourd'hui (c'est l'intérêt de l'Europe d'avoir pour voisin une Russie stable qui règle ses problèmes pacifiquement) partenariat global avec la Chine; dialogue stratégique de plus en plus nourri avec l'Inde naturellement,–j'en ai déjà souligné la densité croissante, approfondissement de notre relation avec le Japon, développement de notre dialogue avec le Brésil et le Mercosur tout entier, l'Afrique du sud, et avec d'autres Etats qui pourront être appelés à structurer le monde de demain.

– Une autre condition d'un monde multipolaire est que l'Inde en fasse pleinement partie. Si un système multipolaire se construit, ma conviction est que l'Inde en sera et en doit être l'un des pôles. Ce pays-continent, ce pays-civilisation ancien comme l'Histoire, a des atouts multiples, dont l'un des principaux est d'être la plus grande démocratie du monde et une démocratie vigoureuse.

Vous savez sans doute que l'un des penseurs français de la période des Lumières, au XVIII ème siècle, Jean-Jacques Rousseau, considérait que la fonctionnement de la démocratie était plus facile dans les pays de petite taille. L'Inde a apporté depuis lors un heureux démenti à cette appréciation. Disposer d'une société ouverte, éclairée par une presse ouverte, est un gage durable de stabilité intérieure et de rayonnement.

D'ailleurs, dans cette partie du monde, la vaste Asie, où beaucoup de choses bougent, où beaucoup de tensions et d'incertitudes persistent, il importe que de grands Etats soient des contributeurs de stabilité et que les groupements en devenir – je pense à l'ASEAN – se consolident, y compris au plan de la sécurité.

6. Si ces conditions étaient réunies, il y en aurait d'autres amis je ne voudrais pas être trop long, ce ne serait plus l'équilibre des forces qui serait le seul garant de la stabilité, comme le voulait la théorie classique des relations internationales, encore qu'il ne faille pas jeter aux orties cette notion de bon sens, mais aussi le partage de règles communes acceptées par tous et mieux encore chaque fois que c'est possible, de valeurs communes.

C'est pourquoi le monde multipolaire doit être combiné à un multilatéralisme perfectionné.

Tous les Etats, ou groupes d'Etats, qui sont ou qui entendent devenir des pôles ont la responsabilité de promouvoir et de pratiquer un multilatéralisme respectueux de tous les autres membres de la communauté internationale, telle qu'elle est exprimée par l'organisation des Nations Unies qui compte aujourd'hui 188 membres.

La France est attachée à l'établissement et au respect de règles internationales. Le Président de la République comme le Premier Ministre insistent régulièrement sur ce point. « Le monde a besoin de règles », déclarait le Premier Ministre français à l'Assemblée générale des Nations Unies, en septembre 1999. Il en a besoin plus que jamais. Ceci vaut particulièrement pour le règlement des conflits par la négociation entre les parties et le respect de procédures multilatérales de règlement des différends. Le règlement négocié des conflits fait partie des responsabilités des puissances d'aujourd'hui et des pôles de demain. Je ne développerai pas ici le besoin de règles en matière économique mais il est aussi évident que dans le domaine stratégique.

La recherche d'un monde multipolaire ne contredit pas le rôle du Conseil de sécurité auquel la France, vous le savez, est très attachée. L'autorité du Conseil doit être renforcée par une réforme qui le rendra plus représentatif des réalités d'aujourd'hui et lui permettra d'être une charnière entre le monde multipolaire et les dispositifs multilatéraux.

Un conseil fort est d'autant plus indispensable que l'Organisation des Nations Unies risque de voir son efficacité affaiblie par la multiplication de micro-Etats, voire par des pseudo-Etats, sans viabilité, qui n'ont qu'une souveraineté formelle et qui sont malheureusement parfois la proie d'organisations criminelles, mafieuses; la prolifération des souverainetés factices contribue à l'instabilité du monde. Contrairement à une idée répandue dans les opinions en Occident, les Etats dans le monde d'aujourd'hui ne sont pas trop forts, ils sont souvent trop faibles. En tout cas, dans ce Conseil de sécurité élargi, réformé, relégitimé par cette réforme, l'Inde a évidemment toute sa place. C'est notre position.

7. Votre séminaire s'est également interrogé sur la relation entre démocratie et sécurité. Dans un monde idéal, la stabilité résulterait du partage de valeurs politiques communes. Ne rêvons pas. Nous n'en sommes pas là et nous ne sommes pas dans un monde sans menaces. Tout Etat y a le devoir d'assurer la sécurité de ses ressortissants sans se menacer celle des autres, mais dans le respect des règles rappelées à l'instant.

Les grandes valeurs politiques de démocratie et de respect des droits de l'homme tendent aujourd'hui à devenir universelles et c'est un immense progrès. Mais la manière dont parfois des pays occidentaux les imposent sous la menace, ou les instrumentalisent en les orientant, peut susciter méfiance ou rejet, car on peut quelquefois y déceler des conceptions néocolonialistes ou des jeux indirects de puissance. Et pourtant, il y a bien des valeurs universelles. Il faut donc dépasser ces apparentes contradictions.

Comment procéder pour que les hommes et les femmes du monde entier s'y reconnaissent, les fassent leurs et en bénéficient ? Selon moi, la démocratisation n 'est pas assimilable à une conversion, à une révélation de nature idéologique ou religieuse, mais relève d'un processus historique, sociologique, économique, et donc au total politique, qui doit avancer par consolidations successives. Ce processus de transformation se nourrit d'une dialectique combinée et constante entre le développement, la modernisation et la démocratisation. Nous devons refuser que la prise en compte légitime d'étapes dans ce processus qui peut prendre des siècles comme cela a été le cas pour nous en Europe, soit utilisée comme un prétexte par des autocrates pour verrouiller le statu quo et justifier la répression intérieure contre des forces de changement démocratique.

A cet égard, l'Inde est exemplaire à tous points de vue car elle a su relever démocratiquement tous les défis qu'elle a rencontrés.

On retrouve un débat similaire à propos de la dialectique entre souveraineté des Etats d'une part, et interventions nécessaires à la protection des peuples d'autre part, - ce qu'en France nous appelons la question de l'ingérence – et que Kofi Anan a lucidement décrite en septembre dernier: comment concilier ces deux exigences, notamment lors de violations massives des droits de l'homme? La reconnaissance et le respect de la souveraineté égale des Etats est le fondement du système international ; mais on ne peut plus accepter qu'au nom de la souveraineté, des dirigeants qui commettent massacres et exactions puissent s'opposer à des interventions internationales pour protéger les peuples dès lors qu'elles sont légitimement décidées. Nous devons concevoir, ensemble, des règles qui organisent et encadrent la souveraineté. La souveraineté doit être préservée, car là où elle recule, c'est la jungle qui progresse. Mais il faut, en même temps, fixer des limites aux abus de certains Etats et permettre aux indispensables interventions humanitaires d'être décidées dans des conditions moins difficiles que celles prévues par la Charte des Nations Unies. Moins difficiles, mais tout aussi légitimes. Voici l 'exercice proposé aujourd'hui à la communauté internationale et surtout aux membres permanents du Conseil de sécurité mais aussi à ceux qui ont vocation à le devenir.

J'en viens à ma conclusion.

La mise en place du monde d'orientation multipolaire que nous voulons exige une approche globale, une vision d'avenir et un effort de tous les instants. Ce séminaire est une utile contribution à cette nécessaire réflexion, car il en a élargi le champ à la sécurité, l'économie, les institutions internationales. Il témoigne de la fécondité de la relation franco-indienne sur le plan intellectuel et géopolitique. L'Inde et la France – et à travers elle, l'Europe, dont elle assumera la présidence au second semestre – sont bien placées pour concevoir ensemble cette multipolarité coopérative qui est notre objectif commun.

SPEECH BY JASWANT SINGH

Mr Chairman Sir
Your Excellency Mr Minister
Excellencies
Ladies and Gentlemen

After your Excellencies' very wise intervention filled with statesmanship and far-sightedness, it's difficult for me to add anything original or novel.

France and India share a very interesting and, to my mind, a very unique quality—that of intellectual enquiry—what is known in India as the Shastra. And finding this similarity between these two, I address myself to the theme of this Seminar which is 'India, France and the Multipolar World'. In addressing this issue, we are simultaneously trying to examine what a unipolar or multipolar world is; whether we are moving towards polycentricism or whether the qualified unipolarity we witness today will continue. And if we are talking of multipolarity or unipolarity, are we only talking in political and military terms? Or is it really the totality a nation state comprises—political, economical, military as also cultural. It is in this respect and context that I reflect on the journey that India started on 50 years back and the journey that the European Union has just commenced. India has, in the past 50 years, demonstrated the effectiveness of a uniquely Indian brand of multipolarity. What you, in Europe, are attempting today is to bring together many nation states in the form of a working federation. I am struck by the enormity of the experiment that Europe has embarked on so that out of those many peoples, one centre comes into being. This attempt is being made in the absence of a historical experience of federalism—just as India, having set out on the course on the great adventure of democracy 50 years back, set upon that path in the absence of a historical memory of democracy. And that is why, this Seminar seems not only topical, but interesting.

Let me, therefore, make some preliminary observations. We seem paradoxically to have come a full circle. Doctrinaire Marxism always asserted its centrality and aspirations to global pre-eminence on the grounds that in that creed alone lay the answer, hence all human kind must follow it.

Your Excellency, you mentioned Jean Jacques Rousseau—I wonder sometimes whether the seeds of dialectical materialism were not sown in the eightienth century by Rousseau's assertion that there is only one right way for all human beings to follow—to me, personally, this is an expression of fundamentalism. Such advocacy denies the reality of human diversity, of different ideas, concepts, social norms, of ways of life. Does it not, therefore, I wonder, strike at the very roots of liberty, equality and fraternity—that ringing and inspiring call of your great revolution as it has echoed down through centuries along the corridors of time.

Your Excellency, when we consider unipolarity, the challenge of finding an order in the seeming anomie that seizes the world today, we must reflect on the future of nation states and the aspects of sovereignty. The experiment that you have set upon in Europe is, therefore, particularly relevant. We are today entering an era of diffused sovereignty. If, as I believe, nation states are to continue to have relevance, and if sovereignty and nation states are the fountain springs of inspiration for human kind, then how are we to find a harmony with the assertion of unipolarity? Unipolarity, to my mind, amounts to the assertion of political unreality. For whereas unipolarity asserts, at least ideologically, freedom from bias, yet paradoxically, it denotes the very same intoxication of ideology—an intoxication that is born of precisely such an assertion of the relevance and centrality of the nation state and the sovereign interests of the one versus the many.

If there is anything that history teaches us, it is that any movement, order or system that is based upon an arrogance or certainty is undoubtedly going to create challenges and resistance. When we judge events, we judge them through time. Do we measure time in a linear fashion? Is time the only determinant to inform us of what is the right answer for today? Self-evidently times moves—and must move—but not always in the evolution of concepts. That is why understanding and judgement can come only through an informed study of history. History informs us that different approaches have been adopted to sustain the equilibrium of power in the past centuries. Human ingenuity in meeting the challenges of seeking order and stability, arrived upon equilibrium through either homogenous stability, through a balance of power between nations or their groups, and most recently, the bipolar structure built around military alliances and the terror of destruction. After the World War II, we did attempt in the UN Charter the hope of a collective security order. Fifty years down the line, this is yet to be achieved.

With the demise of the cold war, about a decade ago, the general expectation was that the bipolar world, which had dominated thinking during the earlier five decades, would evolve into a multipolar world. This expectation was based on the logic of increasing democratization, as well as the technological imperatives of globalization. Now, ten years later, it is evident that these expectations were premature or unrealistic, or both. Today, even the transition to a multipolar world flounders in the turbulence of what is described as the post cold war environment. Thus, the twenty-first century is qualitatively different. Today we have to search for a new idiom and that simply cannot be unipolarity. I would, in an attempt to get away from the notions associated with poles, offer an earlier term—polycentrism. In many ways, this is more descriptive in today's structures, dominated as they are by overlapping networks, a worldwide web of information and interaction. Even as we explore this idiom, we have to take into account the basic principle that has characterized mankind's search for stability. At its core lies the challenge of reconciliation of power with legitimacy, which legitimacy is the moral quotient of power. Let us also, therefore, recognize that peace is a product of justice. It is not simply an absence of violence. And this moral quotient of legitimacy is not, and cannot be, conferred by any supra-national authority. It is the consequence of the process of normative convergence. Only such a process can confer legitimacy to any global equilibrium.

At this point I find it necessary to indulge in what I can only call a subjective assessment of the objective reality of the post-cold war period. It is a fact that about a decade back, the US had emerged as the pre-eminent global power in terms of its economic strength, military might, advancement in science and technology and leadership in regional and global institutions. Yet, it has become equally clear that the US alone cannot find solutions to most of the major international issues facing us, whether in the area of security or economics or in the area of institution-building. We have seen time and again that the US too has worked towards creating and relying on coalitions. I do not think this is the right occasion for citing examples of the coalitions that the US has created in the last 10-15 years. However, the dilemma is that while the US has successfully demonstrated its ability to build such coalitions, it is also able to and does have a veto on the emergence of all such coalitions that it perceives as a constraint upon its own freedom of action. There is a perception—also perhaps a reality—that the US action is often driven by its own domestic agenda and interests. In consequence, the US approach tends to be perceived by other countries as an attempt at imposition of US values and standards—whether on human rights, nuclear and missile proliferation, multilateral trade issues, intellectual property rights, etc. The setback at Seattle, which can be seen as an example of system overload, the reluctance to appreciate the regional and global implications of pursuing a national missile defence, the use of sanctions, expansion of NATO, NATO's actions in Kosovo—all these are recent examples which indicate the validity of this perception.

It is also clear that many countries, notably France and India, as well as Russia and China, have expressed reservations about at least some of these developments. If all these countries continue to enjoy important bilateral relationships with the United States of America, this is how it ought to be. That is, after all, an engagement that all these countries value. Secondly, bilateral relations amongst these countries have, in consequence, shown signs of movement and improvement. Is this an indicator for the future or is it a re-assertion of the ancient verity that attempts at unipolarity create their own resistance? I share with you, Your Excellency, a certainty that in this transition or movement towards polycentric world, the essence lies not in confrontation, but in cooperation. Thus within Europe too, the four-decade-old tradition of regional cooperation reflected most recently in the launching of Euro and the institutionalising of the common foreign and security policy.

If, however, we step back from our preoccupation and immersion purely with the political, it is clear that multipolarity or polycentrism has to be the alternative trend. The aspiration of a people is never limited to just the political. Globalization ought, among other things, to be a celebration of the global cultural diversity. In fact, I would strongly assert that the logic of globalization leading to uniformity and, thus, to a kind of unipolarity is a sterile pursuit. Globalization ought to be its obverse, a development that delights in the many cultural hues of the globe, indeed promotes them. The world would be poorer if globalization became the synonym for deculturization or the imposition of one dimension alone.

The earlier bipolar structure conditioned us into thinking in terms of symmetric threat perceptions. Today, not only do we have new challenges, we also have asymmetries which demand a coalition of interest amongst equals, rather than alliances built around a hegemony, however well intentioned. It is evident that such a polycentric order in the twenty-first century will involve countries from Asia, Europe and Americas, even though the precise shape will depend on the processes currently underway. Reform in Russia, economic and concomitant political changes in China, economic liberalization and growth in India, unification on the Korean peninsula, the growing influence of Japan, European integration, revitalized and reformed United Nations—these are some of the currently unfolding processes that will define the contours of the new order.

It is in this movement towards the new order that I believe that India and France are uniquely placed to contribute. Both countries are inheritors of a rich civilizational past. Both societies pride themselves on a tradition of independent thought and action in foreign policy. Leaders in both countries have consistently chosen the broader and universal over the narrow or parochial. It is this approach reflecting a sense of shared values that brings France and India together in a quest for a multipolar world.

A plural order based on a cooperative approach supported by an overlapping network of institutions among governments and civilian societies, strengthened by democracy, openness and transparency should constitute the new framework that will enable us to move from the flux of the post-cold war to 'A Concert of Open Societies'. And it is in these open societies, that France at the heart of Europe and India as a stabilizing factor in Asia are uniquely placed to work together. It is my belief that it is our duty towards the future generations of our two countries that we must so work.

I propose, as an Indo-French initiative, the early convening, Your Excellency, by our two countries of a global 'Congress of Cultures'. Just as you and Europe represent a great continuity and a great culture, we do believe that amongst the many strengths that India has is the strength of its culture and its continuity—a strength that unipolarity can never extinguish. It is my belief that if France and India take this initiative and convene such a global Congress, we will be attempting to move towards finding a multipolar world that is, I think, the answer for tomorrow. And that, I believe, is also and will remain, a lasting tribute by India and France to the polycentrism to the globe, towards the aspiration for and the reality of it.

Mr Chairman Sir, I am grateful to you for the honour that you do me by asking me here. I am very grateful to my distinguished colleague, His Excellency, the Foreign Minister of France for gracing this occasion and to all of you ladies and gentlemen for giving me this opportunity to share some views. Thank you very much.

DISCOURS DE JASWANT SINGH

M. le Président
M. le Ministre
Excellences
Mesdames et Messieurs

Après les interventions fort judicieuses de vos Excellences, aussi fines que clairvoyantes, il m'est difficile d'ajouter quoi que ce soit d'original ou de novateur.

La France et l'Inde partagent une qualité très intéressante et ont en commun une tradition de questionnement intellectuel connue en Inde sous le nom de *Shastra*. C'est cette similarité entre les deux pays qui me ramène à ce séminaire, traitant de «l'Inde, la France et le monde multipolaire». En nous attachant à ce sujet, nous essayons simultanément d'analyser ce que sont les mondes unipolaire et multipolaire et de savoir si nous nous dirigeons vers le polycentrisme ou si l'unipolarité mitigée, dont nous sommes les témoins aujourd'hui, va continuer. Et si nous parlons de multipolarité ou d'unipolarité, parlons-nous seulement en termes politiques et militaires ? Ou cela recouvre t-il l'ensemble de ce qui fait un Etat-nation, dans ses dimensions politiques, économiques, militaires et culturelles ? C'est dans cette perspective et ce contexte, que je me réfère toute à la fois au parcours que l'Inde a entamé il y a cinquante ans et à celui que l'Union Européenne a juste débuté. L'Inde a démontré, dans les cinquante dernières années, l'efficacité d'une multipolarité opérant seulement à l'échelle indienne. Ce que vous tentez aujourd'hui en Europe, est de rassembler plusieurs Etats-nations sous la forme d'une fédération en action. Je suis frappé de l'ampleur de la tâche dans laquelle l'Europe s'est engagée, pour que de ces différents peuples émerge un centre unique. Cette tentative s'est faite sans expérience historique d'un système fédéral, tout juste comme l'Inde, ayant mis le cap sur la grande aventure de la démocratie, il y a cinquante ans, s'est attaquée à ce parcours en l'absence d'une mémoire historique de la démocratie. Et c'est pourquoi ce séminaire me semble non seulement d'actualité mais intéressant.

Laissez-moi donc faire quelques remarques préliminaires. Il semble, paradoxalement, que la boucle soit bouclée. Le marxisme doctrinaire a toujours affirmé le caractère central de la prééminence du global, fondé sur le fait que cette croyance est la seule réponse possible ; l'humanité entière se doit donc de la suivre.

Monsieur le Ministre, vous avez mentionné Jean-Jacques Rousseau - Je me demande parfois si les germes du matérialisme dialectique n'ont pas été semés au XVIIIe siècle par l'affirmation de Rousseau selon laquelle les êtres humains ne peuvent suivre qu'un seul chemin - c'est selon moi une expression fondamentaliste. Un tel plaidoyer nie la réalité de la diversité humaine, faite d'idées, de concepts, de normes sociales, de modes de vie différents. Et ne va-t-il pas à l'encontre des fondements même de cet appel résonnant 'Liberté, Egalité et Fraternité', source d'inspiration de votre grande Révolution, dont les échos nous parviennent à travers les siècles, le long des corridors du temps.

Monsieur le Ministre, quand on considère l'unipolarité, le défi de trouver un ordre dans l'apparente anomie qui s'est emparée du monde aujourd'hui, on doit réfléchir ainsi au futur des Etats-nations et aux aspects de la souveraineté. L'expérience que vous vivez en Europe est alors particulièrement pertinente. Nous entrons aujourd'hui dans une ère de souveraineté diffuse, de souveraineté diluée, de souveraineté transférée. Si, comme je le crois, les Etats-nations doivent continuer à avoir une pertinence, et si la souveraineté et les Etats-nations sont les sources d'inspiration pour l'humanité, alors comment pouvons-nous rester en harmonie avec l'affirmation d'unipolarité ? L'unipolarité, à mon avis, équivaut à l'affirmation d'une irréalité politique. Car, alors que l'unipolarité affirme, au moins idéologiquement, un détachement des partis pris, elle fait cependant preuve, paradoxalement, d'exactement la même intoxication idéologique - une intoxication née précisément de l'affirmation de la pertinence et de la centralité de l'Etat-nation et des intérêts souverains d'un seul par opposition à la multitude.

Or ce que l'histoire nous enseigne, c'est que tout mouvement, ordre ou système qui se fonde sur l'arrogance ou la certitude, entraîne invariablement défis et résistance. Les événements se jugent à l'aune du temps. Est-ce-que l'on mesure le temps de manière linéaire ? Le temps est-il le seul déterminant à même de nous informer de ce qui est la bonne solution pour aujourd'hui ? A l'évidence, le temps est en mouvement et doit être en mouvement, mais pas toujours en phase avec l'évolution des concepts. C'est pourquoi la compréhension et le jugement ne peuvent se faire qu'à travers une étude documentée de l'histoire. L'alliance nous renseigne sur le fait que différentes approches ont été adoptées, pour maintenir un équilibre des pouvoirs, à travers des siècles. L'ingéniosité humaine à affronter les défis de la quête de l'ordre et de la stabilité a abouti à un équilibre, par le biais, soit du contrôle hégémonique, soit d'un équilibre du pouvoir entre les nations ou leurs groupes, soit, exemple le plus récent, par la structure bipolaire fondée sur les alliances militaires et sur la terreur. Après la seconde guerre mondiale, nous avons bien tendu, avec la Charte des Nations Unies, vers l'espoir d'un ordre de sécurité collective. Cinquante ans plus tard, cela reste encore à accomplir.

Avec la fin de la Guerre Froide, il y a près de dix ans, on s'attendait à ce que le monde bipolaire, qui avait dominé la pensée des cinq décennies précédentes, évoluât vers un monde multipolaire. Cette attente reposait sur la logique d'une démocratisation grandissante de même que sur celle des impératifs technologiques de la globalisation. Dix ans plus tard, il est évident que ces attentes étaient prématurées ou irréalistes, voire les deux. Aujourd'hui, même la transition vers un monde multipolaire est embourbée dans les turbulences du contexte de l'après-Guerre Froide. Le XXIe siècle se distingue ainsi qualitativement. Nous avons aujourd'hui à chercher un nouveau credo et ça ne peut vraiment pas être l'unipolarité. Je proposerais de nous déprendre des notions associées aux pôles, et d'utiliser un terme déjà existant, le polycentrisme. A de nombreux égards, ce terme rend mieux compte des structures d'aujourd'hui, dominées comme elles le sont par des réseaux qui se chevauchent ou par une toile d'informations et d'interactions à l'échelle mondiale. En étudiant ce credo, nous devons aussi prendre en considération le principe de base que constitue la recherche de stabilité par l'humanité. En son sein repose le défi de la réconciliation entre pouvoir et légitimité. Cette légitimité est le quotient moral du pouvoir. Reconnaissons alors aussi que la paix est le produit de la justice. Ce n'est pas simplement une absence de violence. Et ce quotient moral de légitimité n'est et ne peut être conféré par aucune autorité supranationale. Il résulte d'un processus de convergence normative. Seul un tel processus peut conférer la légitimité, dans le cadre de tout équilibre global.

A ce stade, je trouve nécessaire de me laisser aller à ce que je ne peux qu'appeler une évaluation subjective de la réalité objective de l'après-Guerre Froide. Il est indéniable qu'il y a de près dix ans, les Etats-Unis avaient émergé comme puissance globale prééminente au regard de leur pouvoir économique, de leurs forces militaires, de leur avancée scientifique et technologique et de leur position dominante dans les institutions régionales et internationales. Il est indéniable cependant que les Etats-Unis ne peuvent seuls trouver de solution à la plupart des principaux problèmes internationaux auxquels nous sommes confrontés, que ce soit dans le domaine de la sécurité ou de l'économie, ou celui de la construction institutionnelle. Nous avons vu avec le temps, les Etats-Unis travailler encore au soutien et à la création de coalitions. Je ne pense pas qu'il soit opportun de citer des exemples des coalitions que les Etats-Unis ont créés dans les dix quinze dernières années. Cependant, le dilemme est que, alors que les Etats-Unis ont démontré avec succès leur capacité à construire de telles coalitions, ils peuvent et ont également un droit de veto sur l'émergence de n'importe quelle autres de ces coalitions s'ils la perçoivent comme une limite à leur propre liberté d'action. Certains pensent, peut-être à raison, que l'action des Etats-Unis est souvent dictée par leurs propres intérêts et agendas nationaux. Par conséquent, l'approche des Etats-Unis a tendance à être perçue par d'autres pays comme une tentative d'imposition des valeurs et références américaines - que ce soit en matière de droits de l'homme, de prolifération nucléaire ou de missiles, d'enjeux commerciaux multilatéraux, de droits de la propriété intellectuelle, etc. Le revers de Seattle peut être pris comme un exemple de la répugnance à mesurer les retombées régionales et internationales de la poursuite d'une défense nationale axée sur les missiles, l'usage de sanctions, l'expansion de l'OTAN, les actions de l'OTAN au Kosovo - sont autant des exemples récents qui vont en ce sens.

Il est clair que de nombreux pays, notamment la France et l'Inde, de même que la Russie et la Chine, ont exprimé leurs doutes quant à certains de ces développements. Si tous ces pays bénéficient de relations bilatérales importantes avec les Etats-Unis d'Amérique, c'est ainsi que cela devrait être. C'est après tout un engagement que tous ces pays apprécient.

Deuxièmement, les relations bilatérales de ces pays ont montré des signes de mouvement et d'amélioration. Est-ce une indication pour l'avenir ou la réaffirmation d'une ancienne vérité selon laquelle les tentatives en faveur de l'unipolarité créent leur propre résistance.

Je partage avec vous, Monsieur le Ministre, la certitude que dans cette transition, dans ce mouvement vers un monde multipolaire, l'essence n'est pas dans la confrontation, mais dans la coopération. L'ordre polycentrique qui naît de l'unipolarité doit être un ordre basé sur la co-opération et le travail en commun. Ainsi, en Europe également, la coopération régionale traditionnelle des quarante dernières années s'est exprimée tout récemment dans le lancement de l'Euro et l'institutionnalisation de la politique étrangère et de sécurité commune.

Si cependant, nous nous écartons de notre préoccupation centrée simplement sur le politique, il est clair que la multipolarité ou le polycentrisme doit être l'alternative. Les aspirations d'un peuple ne sont jamais limitées au politique. La globalisation devrait, entre autres choses, être la célébration de la diversité culturelle globale. En fait, j'insisterais sur le fait que la logique de globalisation menant à l'uniformité, et donc à une sorte d'unipolarité, est une recherche stérile. La globalisation devrait être son contraire, le développement enchanteur des différentes nuances culturelles du globe, travaillant en fait à leur promotion. Le monde perdrait de sa richesse si la globalisation devenait synonyme d'une « déculturation » ou de l'imposition d'une dimension unique.

La structure bipolaire précédente nous a conditionné à penser en termes de perception de menaces symétriques. Aujourd'hui, non seulement nous avons de nouveaux défis, mais aussi des asymétries qui nécessitent une coalition d'intérêts entre égaux, plutôt que des alliances construites autour d'une hégémonie, bien que bien intentionnée. Il est évident qu'un tel ordre polycentrique au XXIe siècle inclura des pays d'Asie, d'Europe et des Amériques, même si la forme précise dépendra des processus aujourd'hui en cours. Les réformes en Russie, les changements économiques et politiques concomitants en Chine, la libéralisation économique et la croissance en Inde, l'unification dans la péninsule coréenne, l'influence grandissante du Japon, l'intégration européenne, des Nations Unies revitalisées et réformées - ce ne sont que quelques-uns des processus qui se manifestent actuellement et qui définissent les contours du nouvel ordre.

C'est dans ce mouvement vers le nouvel ordre, je crois, que l'Inde et la France sont dans une position unique pour contribuer à ce processus. Nos deux pays sont les héritiers d'une riche civilisation passée. Nos deux sociétés se targuent d'une tradition d'indépendance de pensée et d'action dans le domaine de la politique étrangère. Les

dirigeants dans les deux pays ont constamment opté pour un esprit universel, le plus large possible, face à un esprit de clocher, réducteur. C'est cette approche reflétant un sens de valeurs partagées qui unit la France et l'Inde dans la recherche d'un monde multipolaire.

Un ordre pluriel fondé sur une approche de coopération, soutenue par un réseau d'institutions à cheval sur les gouvernements et des sociétés civiles, renforcé par la démocratie, l'ouverture et la transparence devraient constituer le nouveau cadre susceptible de nous diriger du flux de l'après-Guerre Froide vers « Un Concert de Sociétés Ouvertes ». Et c'est dans ces sociétés ouvertes, que la France, au cœur de l'Europe et l'Inde en tant que facteur de stabilité en Asie, sont dans une position unique pour travailler ensemble. Je suis convaincu qu'il est de notre devoir, pour les générations futures de nos deux pays, de travailler ensemble dans cette direction.

Je propose comme initiative indo-française, la convocation rapide, Monsieur le Ministre, par nos deux pays, d'un « Congrès des Cultures » à l'échelle globale. De la même façon que vous et l'Europe représentent une grande continuité et une grande culture, nous avons la certitude que parmi les forces que l'Inde possède, réside celle de sa culture et de sa continuité - une force qu'aucune unipolarité ne peut anéantir. Je crois fermement que si la France et l'Inde prennent cette initiative et convoquent un tel Congrès global, nous allons tendre vers ce monde multipolaire qui est, je pense, la réponse pour demain. Et je crois que cela est et restera un hommage durable de la part de l'Inde et de la France au polycentrisme, dans le monde entier, pour les aspirations et la réalité d'un tel projet.

Monsieur le Président, Monsieur, je vous suis reconnaissant de l'honneur que vous m'avez fait de m'inviter ici. Je suis très reconnaissant à mon distingué collègue, Monsieur le Ministre des Affaires Etrangères de la France d'avoir honoré cette occasion de sa présence et à vous tous, Mesdames et Messieurs, de m'avoir donné la chance de partager quelques points de vue.

Je vous remercie infiniment.